# 1–800–WORLDS

# 1–800–WORLDS

## THE MAKING OF THE INDIAN CALL CENTRE ECONOMY

MATHANGI KRISHNAMURTHY

OXFORD
UNIVERSITY PRESS

# OXFORD
UNIVERSITY PRESS

Oxford University Press is a department of the University of Oxford.
It furthers the University's objective of excellence in research, scholarship,
and education by publishing worldwide. Oxford is a registered trademark of
Oxford University Press in the UK and in certain other countries.

Published in India by
Oxford University Press
2/11 Ground Floor, Ansari Road, Daryaganj, New Delhi 110 002, India

ISBN-13: 978-0-19-947605-3
ISBN-10: 0-19-947605-5

Typeset in Typeset in Berling LT Std 10/13.5
by Tranistics Data Technologies, Kolkata 700 091
Printed in India by Replika Press Pvt. Ltd

For Uma and Krishnamurthy

# CONTENTS

# FIGURES

# ACKNOWLEDGEMENTS

It takes a village. And in this case, many villages across many continents. Emblematic of the concerns of this book, are the set of transnational relationships, engagements, and friendships that have sustained its possibility. As I pontificated upon time-space compression, globalization, and work—those in my immediate vicinity reminded me about located-ness, body, and everyday life. The life of this book is also my life across the United States of America and India, and those that I owe gratitude to, run the breadth of these nations, and then some.

At The University of Texas at Austin, where I conceptualized the doctoral study that is at the heart of this book, I owe gratitude above all to John Hartigan, who believed in the possibilities of this project and generously steered it through uncertain waters with characteristic candor and tremendously skillful care. I also thank James Brow, Kamala Visweswaran, Katie Stewart, and Itty Abraham for their unstinting and ever pertinent critique, provocation, and support. Never prodding me in any official capacity, but always available with their vast intellect and generous resources were Kaushik Ghosh, Kamran Ali, and Martha Selby who I thank for their warmth and friendship. I would also like to thank Sharmila Rudrappa, who, in suggesting that I focus on Pune as a particular site for call centre work, helped provide the scaffolding for this book.

I am terribly fortunate in my fellow travellers who are now scattered across the world but who have, at various times, generously given their time, attention, and love and made available home and hearth as and when I showed up. Among them, I thank Mubbashir Rizvi, Alia Hasan Khan, Azfar Moin, Faiza Moin, Brenda Sendejo, Elizabeth LeFlore, Shaka McGlotten, Nick Copeland, Diya Mehra, Reena Patel, Raja Swamy, Can Aciksoz, Zeynep Korkman, Susy Chavez Herrera, Ken MacLeish, Maryam Kashani, Halide Velioglu, Ruken Sengul, Siyar Ozsoy, Mohan Ambikapaiker, Keely Wolf, and Nathan Tabor. I also thank Harmony Siganporia, Mridula Rani, Peggy Brunache, Jahnavi Phalkey, Roland Wittje, Billy O'Leary, Adriana Dingman, Alisa Perkins, Sharika Thiranagama, Vivian Newdick, Teresa Velasquez, Amanda Morrison, Amporn Jirratikorn, Gardner Harris, Kora Maldonado Goti, Christine Labuski, Heather Teague, Christine Karwoski, Anand Taneja, Srinath Perur, Raghu Karnad, Vellachi Ramanathan, Gaurav Mehta, Vidhya Sankarnarayan, Meghana Rao, Preethi Sanjeevi, Aniruddhan Vasudevan, and Mark Westmoreland for friendship and presence.

This project was birthed in Pune, long before I had any inkling of an academic future. In this city, I thank Stephen de Souza, Veena Yadav, Kunal Khosla, Suzanne Fernandes, Senthil Kumaran, Shrikanth Aithala, Yashoda Joshi, Nikhil Phadke, Jui Tawade, Khushru Irani, and Awanti Seth-Rabenhoej for being inspirational, intellectual, material, and affective companions. Special thanks to Gouri Dange for not only providing a roof over my head when I first arrived on fieldwork but also generously donning various hats—editor, mentor, and friend—through this process.

At The University of Wisconsin, Madison, I was fortunate to be housed at The Institute for Research in the Humanities as well as the Department of Anthropology, for the duration of an Andrew W. Mellon Postdoctoral Fellowship. I am particularly grateful to Ken George for being a generous, kind, and inspiring mentor as also to my fellow world citizens, Lee Friederich and John Nimis, for their engaged presence and vibrant intellect. I also thank Kirin Narayan, Susan Friedman, Claire Wendland, Tejumola Olaniyan, Aliko Songolo, Henry Drewal, Mary Rader, and Rob Nixon for their interest, engagement, and support. My gratitude, also, to my dear friends and housemates, Sonya Newenhouse, Christina Carlson, and Marta-Laura Suska, for being exemplars of the good life worth living. And lastly, life in Madison would have been terribly bleak without the homes and company of Sana Aiyar and Daniel Ussishkin, themselves stellar academics, but more importantly, friends-in-arms.

This project was made possible by funding from various grants, including an Andrew W. Mellon Postdoctoral Fellowship at The University of Wisconsin, Madison; a Liberal Arts Graduate Research Fellowship, and a Meyerson Research Grant from The University of Texas at Austin; travel grants from the South Asia Institute at The University of Texas at Austin; a National Science Foundation Doctoral Dissertation Grant, and an American Association of University Women International Dissertation Fellowship. For their generous support, I am greatly thankful.

The support and vital interlocution provided by many, has nudged along this manuscript at key moments. I am thankful to Rita Kothari, who invited me to present an early version of the project's understanding of language usage at a conference on Hinglish in 2009, which was subsequently published as part of an edited volume titled *Chutnefying English: The Cultural Politics of Hinglish*;[1] this paper has been revisited for Chapter 4, 'Eliza Doolittle'. I am additionally fortunate to have had invitations to present at various conferences and workshops, comments and questions from which helped hone my concerns for this book: The South Asia Institute at The University of Texas at Austin; Centre for South Asian Studies at the University of Edinburgh; Annual Meetings of the American Anthropological Association; The Association for Asian Studies and International Convention for Asia Scholars Joint Conference; Third Workshop of Young Scholars from the Global South at the Graduate Institute of International Studies, Geneva; The Institute for Research in the Humanities and The Center for South Asia Studies, both at the University of Wisconsin-Madison; The CSL Colloquium at the Palo Alto Research Center; The Urban Research

---

[1] 'Furtive Tongues: Language Politics in the Indian Call Center'. In *Chutnefying English: The Cultural Politics of Hinglish*, Rupert Snell and Rita Kothari (eds), pp. 82–97. India: Penguin.

and Policy Programme at The National Institute of Advanced Studies, and The R&D Lecture Series at IIT Madras.

The writing of this manuscript came unstuck, as these things do, multiple times, and was brought back on track by the brilliance of my cohorts at various writing workshops and retreats. I am thankful for the writing seminars offered by Kamala Visweswaran and Katie Stewart at The University of Texas at Austin, and Dinty W. Moore and Maggie Messitt at 'The Kenyon Review Workshop for Literary Non-Fiction'. I additionally thank Wendy Singer for her generous invitation to be a part of the 'Kenyon Review Workshops'. Ara Wilson chaired and helmed a workshop and offered comments on an early chapter draft at The University of Wisconsin-Madison; I thank her for her generous endorsement of the book. I also thank Jacob Copeman and Matthew Wolf-Meyer for their kind comments and support. An invitation from the editors and curators at 3quarksdaily helped mitigate some of my many writing blocks; I am thankful for the space they provide and the work they invite. I also thank the two anonymous reviewers at Oxford University Press, India, who offered productive and detailed comments on the manuscript. I am also terribly thankful to the editorial team at Oxford University Press, India, for their patience and support. And finally, I am so very grateful to my friend Radha Rathi for her generous gift of the cover design for *1–800–Worlds*.

I am deeply obliged to my colleagues and students at the Department of Humanities and Social Sciences, Indian Institute of Technology Madras, for their presence and support. Many of them I owe thanks to, for always showing up; Arvind Sivaramakrishnan generously read and offered comments on the introductory chapter at a particularly crucial point; Yashasvini Rajseshwar, Shilpa Menon, and Krupa Varghese proofread key chapters at very short notice with great care; Divya Vijaykumar made do with my limited photography skills to help produce the images for this book; Veena Mani, Suraj Nair, Sneha Annavarapu, and Pranathi Diwaker provided interlocution without their ever knowing it. IIT Madras and my department also provided a sabbatical to help get me through the last stretch; for this I am thankful.

I am tremendously fortunate in my family and friends, who have been vital to life as I know it. I am beyond grateful to count among my people, Madhuvanthi Anantharajan, Arvind Srinivasan, Karthik Kumar, Lotte Hoek, Anjana Raghavan, and Anandamoy Roychowdhury, who, besides being thoughtful and engaged interlocutors, also sustain my sanity, vitality, and probity. Among my family, I thank K.T. Ravichandran, Vidya Ravikumar, K.V. Thyagarajan, Anand Kalambur, and K.N. Nagarajan who I can always depend upon, to care. This project, its fears, these concerns, all joys, come from my parents, Uma and Krishnamurthy. This book is dedicated to them.

# 1

## A CALL CENTRE STORY

*Now the phenomenon of the social body is the effect not of a consensus but of the materiality of power operating on the very bodies of individuals.*

—Michel Foucault
(Foucault and Gordon 1980: 55)

### Story-Telling

This is the story of flexibility and knotted-ness, of movement and stoppage. Of becoming new. Evermore. Always. It is the story of a flexible subject. Sort of.

And of the constraints to flexibility, in the face of its desirability.

We like names, places, animals, and things that are flexible. The guest who comes home and sleeps on the couch; windshield shades that flex into small palm-size pieces of matter that can then be tucked under the seat, out of sight, only to come out, magically expand, and shield the insides of the car from searing sunlight; people who travel to our countries and pick up fragments of the languages we speak; bodies on airplanes that shrink and pull their elbows inward; hotels that give in to our needs and find us the right phone charger; gymnasts. And we try and do the same for others.

Flexibility is embedded in the economy of our everyday lives. Things brush past us; we curl inward or push outward; we change clothes to suit people and places; we adapt to new tongues and faces. If we were not flexible/adaptable/adjusting/accommodating/ understanding/negotiating/compromising/changing, we would cease to be able to live in the world. This is a truism. And yet, it is flexibility that I choose as my vantage point.

This is also the story of in-between-ness, of the forever failing to catch up, and of the chronic inconsistencies of being, learning, knowing, and doing. This is the story of identity, its breakdown, its hauntings, its exclusions, and its desires. Of subjects that invest in knowing themselves, but nevertheless modify their habits, tuck in their egos, and forge, abandon, and reinvent tenuous half-remembered links to their pasts, as they march resolutely into the future. This is the story of call centre workers.

## Origin Myths

This story began as a curiosity. It began as an exploration into a new Indian service economy heralded by call centre work. A few simple questions underlined two years of investigation. What does it feel like to stay up at night? Can one 'affect' an accent all the time? Who are you when you work? Is it fun?

Since 1998, when the first call centre was set up in India, corporations in the US and UK have been subcontracting large amounts of customer service work to the transnational Indian out-sourcing industry. The process, known variously as business process outsourcing (BPO), offshoring, and Information-Technology enabled Service (ITeS), is responsible for the dramatic increase in call centre work across a number of Indian cities and semi-urban or mofussil areas. Multinational corporations hired call centre workers to interact with American and British audience, by training them to mask their spatial and temporal location in India. Such jobs required young workers, most of them between the ages of 18 and 25, to assume a different name, location, cultural and language markers, and work through the night to service the 9 to 5 workday of the American customer. Similar working conditions were adopted to serve the UK and the Australian markets, thus giving rise to a burgeoning industry.

I have been tracking the Indian call centre industry since 2004. By 2006–7 when I conducted the bulk of the fieldwork that this book builds upon, the Indian ITeS/BPO industry had yielded an export revenue of US $8.4 billion at an annual growth rate of 33.5 per cent and supported an employment base of nearly half a million (NASSCOM 2008). Member organizations provided customer support and maintenance, and handled myriad business processes ranging from insurance and credit card help-lines, to gas and electricity billing account enquiries, as well as back-office support operations such as insurance underwriting and other kinds of documentation functions. Their roles were characterized as either inbound or outbound, meaning that the work could consist of receiving customer service queries in case of the former, or making sales and promotional calls or follow-up enquiries in case of the latter.

My research has focused on the transnational outsourcing of inbound, voice-based customer services to Indian call centres. These call centres were either company-owned operations wherein a US or UK-based organization entered into a joint venture or spun off an entire corporation in India to provide voice-based customer services to their existing body of customers, or Third Party Service Providers (TPSPs) wherein an organization in India provided contract services within a single office, for multiple clients based abroad. So, for example, at large TPSPs, different floors of a single office building catered to different kinds of industries, such as insurance or airlines. The same outsourcing vendor in India was even likely to serve operations for rival airlines. Each operation housed in a large TPSP was called a process. Customer service operators within each process were called agents or customer service executives, and were most often entry-level workers.

A call centre owned directly by a US- or UK-based organization would be considered a corporate member of the parent company. Hence, the workers were expected to perform and internalize the company's corporate culture, no matter the location. Third Party Service Providers, in contrast, did not require their employees to acclimatize themselves to a single parent culture, as business contracts varied across time. The hierarchy within both kinds of organizations was fairly uniform with the lowest rung occupied by customer service associates or agents, who were in turn supervised by team leaders (TLs), group heads, quality heads, and operations managers. A separate function of the call centre was served by trainers, who were hired to perform two different sets of tasks. Voice and accent, and/or culture trainers were concerned with the formalization of language, tone, voice, and fluency and also provided training modules towards awareness of lifestyles and cultural knowledge specific to the US or the UK. Operations trainers were concerned with the technical training, specifically in relation to the software interface that agents utilized in order to make or receive calls. Full-time shifts of call centre work averaged eight hours in length with an additional set of breaks for an hour and a half, and a large number of shifts functioned through the night in order to serve the US workday.

On the one hand, stakeholders in business and government viewed this transnational call centre industry as an advanced economic solution for corporations as well as literate populace in newly liberalized economies. It was, after all, a clever way to leverage new communication technologies, thanks to which, not only manufacturing but also service costs could be optimized by outsourcing them to bidders offering lower rates than the norm in North America and Europe. Indian and international media, on the other hand, criticized this emerging service sector as surreptitiously replacing labour forces in the West, with maltreated and culturally alienated Indian workers. Indian public debates also increasingly deplored the rampant consumerism, and promiscuous and hedonistic lifestyles that this industry seemed to foster.[1] Around

---

[1] Advertisers also identified call centre employee as the ideal customer for new affluent west-inspired lifestyles. An article from 2006 identifies the new customer for the Indian edition of a men's magazine, *Maxim*, as 'Apparently, a call centre employee who is earning more in his mid-20s than his father was being paid in his mid-40s; a young man with small-town roots but big-city ambitions. A social climber keen to sample the best food, wine, clothes, movies and machines; an image-conscious trend-follower with enough disposable income to afford the latest gizmos and gadgets; a guy with his finger closely on the pulse and the latest mobile phone in his palm.' (Bryant 2006).

2003–04, call centre workers began to be recognized as an important driving force behind the Indian consumerist wave, with an average salary equaling two and a half times the salaries in other job openings at the same skill level. A consumer and retail study from 2004, for example, classified Indian youth between the age 20–25 years as 'Impatient Aspirers' whose population would surge to 16 million over the next ten years. This study predicted that 'BPOs and retail will not only be the new income avenues ...' but also that 'their top five spend areas will be eating out, books and music, consumer durables, apparel, movies and theaters' (Mookerji 2004).

The details of such lives seemed to hint at larger changes in urban India. The call centre though a singular site, seemed to signify a shorthand, a network, and an assemblage of a larger set of practices, habits, and spatial and temporal changes. At the same time, the production of the call centre worker also coincided with a new kind of Indian modernity waking up to the aftermath of the events of 1991, wherein the Indian economy was liberalized and opened out to foreign investment and globalization. David Harvey and others have called this phenomenon 'flexible accumulation' (1990b). In *The Condition of Postmodernity: An Enquiry into the Origins of Cultural Change*, Harvey (1990b: 147) characterizes such a regime of accumulation thus:

> Flexible accumulation, as I shall tentatively call it, is marked by a direct confrontation with the rigidities of Fordism. It rests on flexibility with respect to labour processes, labour markets, products, and patterns of consumption. It is characterized by the emergence of entirely new sectors of production, new ways of providing financial services, new markets, and above all, greatly intensified rates of commercial, technological, and organizational innovation.

One of the imperatives of a regime such as this, or any other for that matter, is 'to bring the behaviours of all kinds of individuals—capitalists, workers, state employees, financiers, and all manner of other political-economic agents—into some kind of configuration that will keep the regime of accumulation functioning' (Harvey 1990b: 121). Harvey argues that this is achieved through 'labour control' which he understands to be brought about through 'some mix of repression, habituation, co-optation and co-operation, all of which have to be organized not only within the workplace but throughout society at large' (Harvey 1990b: 123). In other words, Harvey argues that regimes of flexible accumulation are totalizing ones, which can be read through their varied and flexible forms of control. In order to understand the locations, compulsions, and subjects of call centre work in relation to forms of flexible accumulation, this book engages with three main bodies of theory—flexibility and power, gender and labour, and ethnography of and in the corporation.

### Flexibility and Power

*In the end, we are judged, condemned, classified, determined in our undertakings, destined to a certain mode of living or dying, as a function of the true discourses which are the bearers of the specific effects of power.*

—Michel Foucault
(Foucault and Gordon 1980: 94)

David Harvey understands time and space as modes of social power in their ability to be radically compressed in late capitalism, and of flexibility as the latter's chosen mode of operation (Harvey 1990b). Aihwa Ong critiques this formulation as missing 'human agency and its production and negotiation of cultural meanings within the normative milieus of late capitalism' (Ong 1999: 3). This project expands on Harvey's formulation by recasting the flexibility commanded of call centre workers, in order to navigate time and space, as a mode of power that operates through their bodies (Foucault and Gordon 1980). It also addresses Ong's understanding of agency by staging the various ways in which workers were asked to be flexible, against those modes of flexibility that they 'failed' to attain, and exploring the resultant changes in the socio-political milieu of the call centre. I further argue that discourses that demand flexibility are differentially positioned across bodies, and this lack of equivalence is elided by talking about how everybody needs to change. But the changes required of some are far more than those required of others. In keeping with feminist intersectional theories of subjectivity that ask that lived reality and subjectivity be recognized as positioned along the intersection of a variety of social and bodily identities such as race, class, and gender I posit flexibility on a differential continuum. Even as the ability to be flexible continues to be valorized, questions in regard to who is asked to be repeatedly and intensely flexible, and who fails remain unanswered. We do not meet each other halfway. Flexibility is the new individuality.

According to Aihwa Ong, flexible citizenship refers to 'the cultural logics of capital accumulation, travel, and displacement that induce subjects to respond fluidly and opportunistically to changing political economic conditions' (Ong 1999: 6). This book understands the possibility of flexibility on a slightly different note. While I am in fundamental agreement with the ways in which Ong chronicles the compulsions of such cultural logic, I argue that flexibility not only requires an orientation towards opportunity in the long run, but also an attachment to creating and re-creating normality in daily life. This project therefore takes inspiration from Stewart's poesis of everyday feeling, and 'ordinary affects' (Stewart 2007). Through the question of flexibility, I explore the intensities, thoughts, and feelings that fuelled and made possible, call centre work and the call centre world. Flexibility, I argue, can also be seen in the push towards combating change and an attachment to an imaginary, yet powerfully desired normality in the face of the various demands of call centre work. Perhaps it consisted of the few moments of sleep possible even when jolted by bright sunlight. Perhaps it involved a tongue caught midway in perfect accent, without a thought towards the effort that brought it about. Perhaps it was brought to fruition in the ability to leave the call centre.

Call centre workers were trained to cultivate signifiers of everyday Western culture (accents, slang, sports, news, weather, and so on) and don a governed and culturally inflected or neutralized identity to mask their national, cultural, and geographical location from American consumers. In this sense, they strove to be the ideal 'flexible citizens' (Ong 1999) of transnational discourse. The already problematic isomorphism of place and culture was further compounded when these workers attempted to simultaneously inhabit different times and places, and transcend through technology and self-management, the cultural gaps between home and away, us and them.

This book is therefore particularly interested in the ways in which call centre workers actively partook of new forms of speech, bodily and circadian rhythms, comportment, and orientation to the world in order to make possible the act of customer service in the call centre. In the process, I read the call centre as a symptom of the condition we call flexibility, and argue therefore that regimes of flexibility consciously, deliberately, and relentlessly produced the call centre. I use the term flexibility, not in a way that will reify it as a property of the global economies of late or post-Fordist capitalism (Harvey 1990b; Sennett 1998), but as an ongoing set of cultural discourses and bodily practices that makes such economies possible, desirable, and tenable. I also use it to signify a property of late capitalism that despite its claims of having already come to fruition, needs particular forms of work in order to produce a set of historically situated, labouring, and desiring bodies. My work therefore speaks of flexible economies in relation to subjects who come to flexibility. Aihwa Ong suggests and argues that individuals as well as governments in globalization 'develop a flexible notion of citizenship and sovereignty as strategies to accumulate capital and power' (Ong 1999: 6). In her understanding, such 'flexible citizenship' demands that subjects emphasize a 'flexibility, mobility, and repositioning in relation to markets, governments, and cultural regimes' (Ong 1999: 6). While, my ethnography works within this understanding of flexibility and is concerned with the flexible subjects of the call centre economy, it also understands flexibility as an effort.

In chronicling the machinations of a subject who seeks to become ever more flexible, it exposes flexibility as tyranny, and as a violent demand couched in the language of opportunity, new orders, change, and growth. I further argue that what is produced—a never-enough flexibility—is a contested terrain that must grapple with other logics of state, gender, class, and everyday life, all of which exert force in mutual tension to produce a range of differentially flexible subjects. Flexibility in this project is a mode of power. It is also a condition of the new Indian service economy. In this, it bears continuity with other ethnographers interested in flexibility and flexible subjects, such as, Karen Ho and Daromir Rudnyckyj who chronicle the ways in which locally situated discourses of flexibility seek to produce relentlessly energetic subjects who partake of new worlds in an ongoing and anxious pursuit of a future (Ho 2009; Rudnyckyj 2011).

The call centre is my ethnographic anchor, even as this organization is not my term for a generic industry in homogenous time. Through examples culled from various call centres in a particular city at a particular time, I examine the ways in which flexibility came to be produced in this economy. By working from the assumption that flexibility is a property of late capitalism that is both desired and rewarded, I then elucidate the specific conditions under which the subject becomes flexible and the history, conditions, and results of the failure to be such. I also ask as to the limits of flexibility, and what such a terrain, now appearing and now disappearing, may look like.

The body and its centrality to voice-based 'disembodied' work are essential to this analysis of call centre work and workers' daily lives. In this, I follow Foucault's notion of the body as socially produced through regimes of knowledge and power. I understand 'flexible' bodies as deeply interlocked with systems of flexible accumulation (Martin 1994).[2] Such 'loose coupling' (Martin 1994: 144), I argue, indexes one of the primary modalities of late capitalism—its ability to condition bodies that work on themselves as projects to be continually changed—while also subjecting self to the disciplinary forces that direct the nature of change. Toby Miller chronicles life in the United States as a project, and a national one at that. The flipside to this national obsession with reinvention, he argues, is 'the grand national paradox', 'a duality of free choice and disciplinary governance' (Miller 2008: 20). Similarly, I seek to understand the functioning of flexibility as power in creating productive call centre bodies, as well as the ways in such calls to flexibility then make themselves invisible by dissipating across sites other than the

---

[2] See Chapter 7 of Martin (1994) for a tightly argued discussion on flexibility in human resource discourse in the modern corporation. While on one hand, the use of the term indicates the company's need for 'nimble' workers, on the other it indexes the company's ability to be similarly flexible by hiring and firing workers at will.

call centre, thereby rendering themselves benign and commonsensical (Certeau 1984: 48). In this project, flexibility functions as power in that it increasingly structures modes of life, and is consequently repressive as well as productive. To this extent, I do not consider the 'labyrinthine and unanswerable question' of the bearer of power (Foucault and Gordon 1980: 97). In flexibility and its effects, I see the possibility of studying power at its 'external visage, at the point where it is in direct and immediate relationship with that which we can provisionally call its object, its target, its field of application, there—that is to say—where it installs itself and produces its real effects' (Foucault and Gordon 1980: 97).

Further, I argue that such flexibility does not stay within the call centre, but travels and circulates as a chain. The calls for becoming ever more flexible did not emanate solely from the call centre nor did they stay within its precincts. Accordingly, 'not only do individuals circulate between its threads; they are always in the position of simultaneously undergoing and exercising this power', they are also 'the elements of its articulation' (Foucault and Gordon 1980: 98). Call centre workers, I argue, were groomed to be vehicles of flexibility.

This route to flexibility is no doubt prescribed by the will to experiment with oneself, in order that one can surpass and transgress historical conditions of subjectivity. If individuals effect 'by their own means or with the help of others a certain number of operations on their own bodies and souls, thoughts, conduct, and way of being so as to transform themselves in order to attain a certain state of happiness, purity, wisdom, perfection, or immortality' (Foucault 1988: 18), then power and its changing modalities are perpetuated through these desires for self-transformation and becoming (Venn and Terranova 2009).

### Gender and Labour

The awareness of gender and gendering were always already present in talk about call centres. Since the late 1990s when the industry gained traction, some of its earliest interrogations were posed around questions of women workers, nightly labour, and rupture, both in terms of respectability and tradition. Questions of gender and gendering are therefore important to all the chapters in the book, and show up when investigating nightly work, language training, and affective labour. My concerns are however, not only about women workers, even as there exist able ethnographic interventions that pay particular attention to the inculcation and experiences of women in the Indian call centre economy (Basi 2009; Mirchandani 2004; Patel 2010; Singh and Pandey 2004). These studies demonstrate how call centre work made a palpable and constitutive difference to women's lives even as they question the narratives of mobility and seeming liberation that accompanied the rise of female worker populations in the call centre economy. They also locate the changes in call centre and service work opportunities for women within the gendered landscapes of urban India. My book is similarly attentive to these insights, and in being well aware of work as a differently felt set of consequences and effects on male and female bodies, focuses on rendering aloud voices that clarify such difference. Through these voices, *1–800–Worlds* seeks to engage with the ways in which gender works on this site as an axis of differentiation, be it in the calls to particular kinds of voice and care, hierarchical and gendered relationships between male and female managers and trainers, and male and female workers, or in the strident adherence to a belief in gender neutrality as a requirement mandated of corporate subjects in both stated and assumed fashion. A brief discussion might help clarify these questions.

A large portion of the work on gender and labour in globalization has focused on the feminization of workforces in free–trade zones (FTZs) and other newly industrialized sites in the developing world (Fernandez-Kelly 1983; Freeman 2000; Ong 1991; Safa 1995; Wolf 1992). In these accounts, migrants, both men and women, 'represent a pool of vulnerable, feminized labour in the lowest wage sectors of the world's wealthiest economies' (Mills 2003: 45). Other recent accounts have looked at women in developing and non-Western countries as entrepreneurial subjects (Freeman 2014) as well as economic agents, interpellated by regimes of debt and finance capital (K. Kalpana 2017; Karim 2011). *1–800–Worlds* adds to this latter set of debates in looking at how gendered subjectivities, while often neutralized and disregarded, are also at other times co-opted into a matrix wherein such difference functions as capital.

Recent work has also paid attention to how masculinity features as an important dynamic in understanding the gendered effects of trans-national and global work. Many remind us that 'gendered struggles in the global economy are not only contests about norms and practices of femininity; they are also about meanings and experiences of mas-culinity' (Mills 2003: 52). Most of this work is located in the literature on transnational migration (Osella and Osella 2000) and is involved with questions of attaining masculine and class privilege through work (Nonini 1997), or the failure to achieve class mobility and its resultant effects on masculinity (George 2000; Goldring 2001).

Gender in this book, is therefore, not only about the effects of call centre work for women, but also an examination of the circulation of gender discourses among and within working bodies. I examine masculine authority, gender hierarchy, the feminization of work, and the shifting relationships between men and women as signifiers of ideological tensions between old and new orders of modernity. Even as gender discourses are conduits for the reproduction of existing structures of power, in many instances these complex iterations also prove to be remarkably dynamic in their ability to disturb these very accounts of power. Even as these suddenly de-territorialized enunciations may quickly re-territorialize, they nevertheless pro-duce confusion, possibility, and hope. For example, as Mary Beth Mills reminds us, 'new demands for feminine "caring" in corporate cultures exist in uneasy relationships with longstanding metaphors of "cowboy" competition and related models of masculine aggression in global business practice' (Mills 2003: 54). *1–800–Worlds* is there-fore, interested in all the ways in which male and female workers in the call centre both felt themselves implicated within steady and shifting structures of gender differentiation, as well as contributed to the maintenance or rupture of gender as an axis of difference.

### Ethnography in and of the Corporation

The third crucial site of investigation for this project is the cor-poration. In the introduction to a special supplement of *Current*

*Anthropology* on corporate forms, Marina Welker, Damani J. Partridge, and Rebecca Hardin argue for extending to the corporation 'the same critical weight or significance accorded the nation-state' (2011: S5), and insist that transcending the applied/ academic divide might be necessary for the study of corporations. They show how even as there have been multiple anthropological conversations situated in and around the corporation (Welker, et al. 2011: S4), little has been produced by way of a sustained engagement, 'a coherent set of research questions', or 'competing schools of thought' in the anthropology of corporations. They make a powerful case for a range of objectives such as, among others, 'an anthropological effort to pluralize, relativize, and contextualize corporate forms geographically and historically' (Welker, et al. 2011: S6), an 'interdisciplinary analytical framework that is actively engaged with the body of substantive empirical work on corporations carried out in other fields' (Welker, et al. 2011: S6) and 'and an understanding of the formation of subjects in and through corporations' (Welker, et al. 2011: S6). In recent years, we have seen a partial response to this call, as anthropologists of the non-applied school have begun to situate corporations as community formations in their own right, and study corporate forms as 'institutions that pervade the social and material fabric of everyday life' (Welker, et al. 2011: S4).

Greg Urban and Kyung-Nan Koh (2013) consider the curious fact of an anthropology of corporations having burgeoned since the 1980s along with the increase in the number of anthropologists working in corporations, and use this to argue that the effects that corporations have as powerful agents in the world need to be brought into dialogue with their inner workings as distinct societal formations. Such a call has been particularly important in relation to the corporations of late capitalism, which function increasingly as providers of service and affects. I expand on this in Chapter 5, but want to specifically focus on service work in the corporation as a location rife with possibility for ethnographic research and anthropological analysis.

I was once a consummate corporate subject. I began my corporate career in the year 2001 with a fancy title and a fat paycheck.

As a newly minted marketing degree holder, I came to Pune armed with the ability to rent an apartment, pay my bills, and dazzle with my zeal and expertise the small entrepreneurial corporation that had offered me a coveted position. The corporation signalled a tentative entry into adulthood, since it was a legitimate way to channel my time and my sense of self. Of course, not all corporations are the same, and as a category display high internal variation. Distinguished by size, profit margins, form of organization, geographical location, work style, and final product or service, no two corporations are the same. And yet, one can walk from one corporation to another and assume a similar mantle of seriousness, productivity, and possibility. While my interest in studying the corporate space of the call centre was to be able to better understand the place where my respondents spent their waking and working lives, I also walked in with my own history of corporate work and competence. Further, my acquaintance with the corporation came with an intimate understanding of its capacity to order time and imagination. The call centre, while peculiar, was nevertheless, in my memory of corporate work, a similar, profit-making organization. As studies of corporations across the spectrum have demonstrated, work makes possible certain kinds of lives. George Marcus astutely states that thinking about corporate culture allows us to ask integral questions about the kinds of 'predicament(s) embedded in capitalism, and its current state ...' (Marcus 1998: 9). This book is therefore also about the social order of the call centre. I study the corporation not as my primary object of ethnographic analysis but as the physical and affective site where my respondents and collaborators spent many hours of their days and nights. My analysis then is geared toward describing the space of the corporation as a lived space that also exerted its own modes of social control. However, I do not wish to claim that the social realm is beholden to economic constraints, but rather that the economic discourse of the call centre structured, brought forth, and formed a dialectic with the social orders of its worker population. As Harvey asserts, in order to critique globalization as a universal, one must focus on the institutions that mediate between specificity and universality (Harvey 2000: 242). I analyse the call centre as one such mediating body.

The peculiarity of the Indian call centre also lay in its being the consummate communicative corporation. As theorists of labour have posited, new forms of work focus not on industrial factory labour, but on communicative, cooperative, and affective labour (Hardt 1999). I use 'communicative corporation' to embody both the site of work, as well as those processes of work meant to smooth relations between worker populations and their clients. The clients in this instance were two-fold, the first being client organizations in the US or UK that subcontracted to Indian call centres, and the second being consumers at the other end of the telephone line.

It is perhaps easier to understand such communicative labour in relation to the idea of the network. As a metaphor that characterized both the IT industry and the routes through which workers related to the corporation and to other workers, the network was constantly at work. The wires of the network were technological, but its nodes human. The network therefore needed to be animated by subjects who could speak, listen, and communicate with one another. The scale of the network varied and in order to successfully populate and activate its channels, one needed to constantly communicate. Hence, I suggest the use of the term, 'communicative corporation'. Here, I follow Manuel Castells' suggestion that the corporation has to imagine itself as a network in order to be able to leverage the benefits of flexibility (Castells 1996). By this I mean the acts of imagination and daily/nightly work that must be carried out by the corporation in a professional, ordered, and interpretive fashion in order that time and space continue to be flexible. These acts included managing work processes in the night while serving customers' day time, impressing upon workers the need for accent modifications and the language of customer care, and producing an easily absorbed version of 'American' or 'British' culture. The function of the communicative corporation primarily revolved around creating and maintaining a culture that could manage difference and foster flexibility.

In time-honoured anthropological commitment to participant observation, I had to myself become a cultural and acculturated worker. After a number of pilot studies in Bangalore, Pune, Delhi, and Chennai, I chose Pune as a field-site because of both, its particularly interesting history as an educational destination for young college students, as also my own familiarity with the city. I additionally chose to locate myself in the transnational world that the call centre sought to manage and streamline. This book is based on twenty-one months of research in Pune. These include a short study over the summers of 2004 and 2005 and a longer stint of fieldwork from July 2006 to December 2007. During this period I recorded in-depth interviews with sixty call centre agents, five voice and accent trainers, two operations trainers, three consultants, five human resource managers, and five operations managers. The workers I interviewed were all mainly between the ages of 18 and 25, with equal numbers of female and male respondents.[3]

While I conducted extensive and repeated interviews and focus group discussions with call centre workers, a crucial part of field-work also involved four months of work in a transnational call centre. My reasons for this were manifold. For the first five months of fieldwork, I interviewed respondents, built networks, and hung out with workers during weekends or on their days off from work. While this was neither difficult nor unproductive, it nevertheless proved inadequate in that it did not give me any access to their nightly relationship with work; a relationship that structured most of their weeks. Our interviews would be interrupted by errands, sleep, alcohol, or phone calls. Over a few months, the content of the

---

[3] All interviews were conducted at residences, coffee shops, and malls in Pune. Additionally, I was also granted permission by an outsourcing organization, focusing on business sales to the US, to interview its employees at the company premises, as many of them had formerly been employed at call centres.

|              | No. | Women | Men | 18–25 | 25–30 | 30–35 |
|--------------|-----|-------|-----|-------|-------|-------|
| Agents       | 60  | 30    | 30  | 55    | 5     | 0     |
| V&A trainers | 5   | 3     | 2   | 0     | 4     | 1     |
| Ops. trainers| 2   | 1     | 1   | 0     | 2     | 0     |
| Consultants  | 3   | 0     | 3   | 0     | 0     | 3     |
| HR managers  | 5   | 3     | 2   | 0     | 0     | 5     |
| Ops. managers| 5   | 2     | 3   | 0     | 4     | 1     |

interviews began to be repetitive and lacking in new insights. Many workers would answer questions by saying that my questions were difficult to answer since I had never been to a call centre, or worked there. Access to call centres was nearly impossible, because of high security and paranoia around information leakage. While I could wrangle a few visits, these were official and I was not given access to the 'floor' where workers answered calls.

Hesitant to be intrepid, I began to tentatively apply to various call centres to find work as an agent, or an entry-level worker. I volunteered all information possible, including that I was conducting research, and that this was part of my doctoral work. While I managed to successfully clear all the interviews, the question of my research remained a stumbling block and I was refused employment at two large call centres. At two others, I was considered overqualified and being in my late twenties, too old to last as an agent for long. Some of the human resource personnel I interviewed with, advised that I apply instead to work as a trainer. Given that I had spent a few years living in the US, they surmised that I would be considered a cultural expert. At this point, I took their advice, and leveraged a prior master's degree in business communication, my experience of living in the US, and the fact that I had already conducted research on call centres for my master's thesis in anthropology, to apply for the position of a voice and accent, or cultural trainer. In these interviews, I made it clear that I did not intend interviewing workers for research while on the job. On successfully clearing the interviews, I suspended fieldwork. My motive at this point was to enter into gainful employment at the call centre and let this play out for me as a worker, while giving neither the corporation nor myself any sense of how long I would last.

During the four months that I was at this call centre, I conducted no interviews and only recorded field notes around events and conversations wherein I was physically present. I did not record or write what could have been considered as sensitive information including financial data, employment figures, and specific client information. I did not set myself any goal as far as the number of months I would spend working were concerned, and lived the life that call centre trainers lived. I made friends, hosted parties, ran amok across town, and worked through exhaustion, sleeplessness, excitement, and joy. I inhabited the corporation productively, did my job diligently, and even doubted my future when I was confronted with the end of my call centre tenure. The conclusions to this book bring together my thoughts about leaving the call centre. I refer to this organization as Systematix Ltd. It was one of the top ten BPO outfits in India and housed multiple processes at its Pune office. As a result, I was able to work alongside agents servicing various businesses across the US and the UK including credit card services, airlines, and computer help desks, and train customer service personnel performing outsourced work for utility services such as electricity, telephone connections, and gas services.

I argue that this model of corporate ethnography gave me subjective access to not only a space and time, but also its force. Participant observation is a sacrosanct anthropological norm, as are the ethics of participation. I suspended fieldwork as a way of engaging fully with the job that held up my research. In irony, surprise, and surreal stupefaction, I went to work and trained workers to speak in an American accent. I also brought in new business, spoke to clients, made presentations extolling the benefits of outsourcing, and participated in workshops towards developing better training models. I made very little money for very long hours of work, and found myself riveted. I performed the functions of my role, but also used my position to support workers through first-time professional experiences, harsh training demands, and disorientation. During this process I discovered that unlike the Weberian bureaucratic office and its stable rules, the call centre was a moving target. It was a 'heterogenous culture, rife with diversity and conflict, and possessed of domains of thought and action not represented in the boardroom' (Newfield 1998: 30). After this experience, I was also able to focus on talking to workers about matters beyond daily work life and processes. I was able to relate to the ways in which they sought to be good workers, and to their fears, hopes, and desires, as well as their notion of the call centre as a transformational space. It was in many ways, the defining encounter of fieldwork. To this extent, this project does not provide 'knowledge about others' (Marcus and Cushman 1982: 25) and I am not 'an anonymous presence' (Marcus and Cushman 1982: 32). I am imbricated in the web of call centre relations that I detail. This is also, my story.

I turn next to the story of the nation-state, globalization, and the call centre economy.

## The Political Economy of the Call Centre

The call centre boom in India began around the late 1990s when multinational companies (MNCs) took note of India's stable political conditions, English-speaking population, and technologically advanced telecommunications environment, as well as the favourable time zone difference of 8–12 hours between the US and India, in order to set up night shift based telephonic customer support services to Western economies. This was in part catalyzed by the Indian government's New Telecom Policy of 1994, which allowed privatization of the telecom sector. Soon, the New Telecom Policy of 1999 privatized Internet Protocol (IP) telephony and ended the state monopoly on international calling facilities, bringing into existence several of the infrastructural requirements for the call centre industry. The other important link in the call centre puzzle was the existence of computer-literate populations that could be easily trained to provide transnational customer service work. The ready existence of such a specifically skilled labour pool can be traced to the demand for Indian knowledge workers and their software coding skills during what was popularly understood as the Year 2000 (Y2K) technology crisis (van der Veer 2005: 282). The Y2K crisis called for the employment of a large number of software workers possessing the necessary technological skills to reconfigure and update programs with pre-millennial date and time mechanisms that were predicted to fail in the year 2000. As a result, both state and private players promoted investments in computer education and infrastructure. Western countries began to recognize India as a repository for cheap software development. These demand conditions stand as direct precursors to the rise of the 'Information and Communication Technology' (ICT) sector in India.

The origin myth, of course, can be located in the economic liberalization of India in 1991. Multiple literatures trace shifts in the Indian economy from an initial post-Independence policy of import-substitution industrialization (ISI) 1947 onwards, to liberalization and export-oriented industrialization (EOI) in 1991, with a concurrent impetus to foreign investment in key industrial and service sectors (Bajaj 2001; Byres 1998). What they also showcase are the contested ways in which this change was positioned in order to confer on it the status of a moral economy in post-Independence and post-socialist India. I use morality here in the sense of what Foucault calls a 'moral code'—'a set of values and rules of action that are recommended to individuals through the intermediary of various prescriptive agencies' (Foucault 1985: 25). This positioning, as is the fate of all discursive constructions was nevertheless incomplete, and liberalization has concurrently been the subject of multiple critiques and debates. These discussions expose the contested history as well as contentious decision-making processes that ushered in the New Economic Policy of 1990–1, as also the ways in which it has benefited a rising middle and upper middle class sector while dispossessing a majority of the Indian population (Chandrasekhar and Ghosh 2002; Corbridge and Harriss 2000; Harriss-White 2003). Economic liberalization and this valorization of the middle class and its cultural capital were thus, strong catalysts for the outsourcing industry.

The Indian call centre economy is also entrenched within a fragmented trajectory of state-led technological development and educational policy in India (Chakravartty 2004; Pitroda 1993), and I argue, a manifestation of what Ashis Nandy has called the post-Independence predilection to 'spectacular technology' (Nandy 1988). Nandy cites nuclear policy as the specific instance of such scientific progress. Other scholars have also analyzed India's nuclear policy and the development of nuclear technology as simultaneously a sign of national pride and indigenous intellect, as well as the chosen route towards visibility and significance in global geopolitics (Abraham 1998; Bidwai and Vanaik 2000; Chengappa 2000). This commitment bears relation to the ways in which science, while clearly an instrument of empire, also symbolized liberty, progress, and universal reason for nationalists wedded to the idea of a modern Indian nation (Prakash 1999).

These pre- and post-1947 yearnings and attempts to actualize the project of Indian modernity can be traced across many other initiatives, most notably in the disinvestment decisions made by the Indian government in a piecemeal fashion between 1984 and 1989, and then in the more dramatic liberalization processes of 1991. Since the late 1990s, this has further translated into large transnational investments in call centres, with the availability of both, telecommunications infrastructure, and skilled English-speaking workers. The language skills that also catalyzed the rise of this industry were the result of pre- and post-Independence language education policies that privileged English as a medium for school and college education, especially among the middle class (King 1997; Pennycook 1998; Sonntag 2000). Given such specific histories that made possible the rise of the call centre industry in India, this project works on the assumption that globalization processes have historically passed through the Indian state. The state, I therefore argue, is not just historical, nostalgic memory, or a detriment to transnational conversations with global capital, but an active participant in the meanderings of global corporate investment (Gill 2000; Hansen and Stepputat 2005; Sassen 1996). This project understands call centre work as partly contingent upon historically circumscribed and state-supported policies intended to form progressive, modern, and productive subjects.

Narratives of historically teleological contemporaneity or of globalization, and more specifically global modernity and the free market economy as the necessary and unidirectional endpoint of history (Fukuyama 2002), ignore the contingent and variously configured conditions of local possibility and powerful state practices that precede and permeate such events (Tsing 2005). The conditions for the rise of the call centre industry were an amalgamation of factors bearing as much continuity with pre- and post-Independence modernity (Chakrabarty 2002) as with neoliberal reform. The trajectory of the call centre and IT industry therefore necessarily stretches back in time and cannot be solely located in the newly liberalized regimes of the 1990s.

The industry was also facilitated by the other widely discussed determinants of this transnational equation—global or multinational corporations. In their attempt to find leaner and cheaper possibilities of 'wage arbitrage', multinational corporations, have increasingly foraged developing and former third-world economies for large unemployed or 'underemployed' labour pools.[4] 'Wage arbitrage' simply means that efforts to find cheaper labour across a worldwide population will lead to larger differences between the lowest-paid and highest-paid members of the spectrum. This, the proponents of outsourcing argue, will result in pressure on the higher ends to lower costs and simultaneous fear on the part of the lower ends to maintain the cost advantage, thereby benefiting the corporation and leading to larger profits. The labour market in this scenario becomes a demand driven monopoly where suppliers are chosen as per their ability to provide services at the lowest cost, thus also driving down the market price of labour.

Multinational corporations have been on a worldwide lookout for a wider range of accessible labour pools. Outsourcing helps such a forage by breaking up business activities into interlocking yet discrete blocks or activities, each of which can be performed, created and delivered by geographically disparate units as per a centrally defined logic or set of rules. This is often promoted as a functional, instrumental Lego-model, made possible by regimes of late capitalism. It is not only an important financial and business phenomenon but also a politically disempowering and divisive practice. Keith Hart identifies the factors propelling American imperialism since the 1990s as a confluence of new technologies and Internet usage, financial instruments and restructured industry processes predicated on large global networks facilitated by local downsizing and international outsourcing (Hart 2000). Aihwa Ong also writes about varied flexible economic systems that have subcontracted blue-collar work like sewing to sweatshops in Asia and Central

---

[4] In economic parlance, 'underemployment' can mean (*a*) employment of high-skilled workers in low-skill jobs, (*b*) underutilization of economic or productive capacity due to lack of work opportunities, or (*c*) disguised unemployment where employers hire more workers than are required. I use underemployment in the sense of underutilization of productive workforces due to lack of work opportunities.

America since the early 1970s (Ong 1991: 279). Jay Mandle, in his discussion on the student anti-sweatshop movement in the United States, traces the loss of 850,000 jobs in the clothing industry in the US, and relates it to the concurrent employment growth in the clothing industries of Bangladesh, Indonesia, Thailand, and Philippines (2000: 93). The global search for inexpensive labour thereby runs the spectrum from sweatshops, subcontracting, off-shoring, and BPO, to the phenomenon called knowledge process outsourcing (KPO).[5]

The foundational works of economic anthropology (Douglas 1963; Mauss 1990; Malinowski 1961) were incumbent upon the inseparability of the cultural from the economic realm. From the 1960s to the 1980s, the move towards Marxist analyses of modes of production and critiques of structural-functionalism led to the marginalization of culture as explanation and analytic. Exchange began to be seen as peripheral to production, and culture was cast as super-structural ideology (Althusser and Balibar 1977). From the late 1980s onwards and through the 1990s, culture began to be re-centred in the analysis of themes such as power, process, and history (Dirks et al. 1994). Located squarely within this legacy of culture as an important facet of current studies of the political economy, my project seeks to look at the transnational outsourcing economy and its call centres as a system of signs and cues. Zizek argues that capitalism 'overdetermines all alternative formations, as well as non-economic strata of social life' (Zizek 2004: 294). Globalization, to call centre workers, was not only an economic relationship but also a discourse that had material effects on their desires and world-views. In particular, their willingness to perform accent, language, and demeanor in order to reap the benefits of transnational capital movement, had profound impact on their

---

[5] Organizations that are part of the KPO industry claimed expertise in more advanced services, and separated themselves from the monotonous, low-skilled offerings of the BPO economy. New processes under this industry included medical diagnostics, technical writing, science and mathematics tutorials, development of advanced analytic software tools, valuation, research, patent filing, and legal and insurance claim analysis.

social identities even outside of the workplace setting (Du Gay 1996; Hall 1996). Even as MNCs have increasingly sought cheaper services across borders, the countries soliciting such business have experienced exponential rates of urban growth, rapid change in local cultures, and an almost hegemonic turn to conspicuous consumption in the wake of increasing foreign investment. The question that this book explores is, how do these new modes of production and employment affect experiences of life and labour in developing economies? Is there an increasing tendency to despotic labour practices on unsuspecting populations or do these give rise to new opportunities, world-views, and cosmopolitan lifestyles for hitherto sheltered populations? Between these two extremes, how is it that people make sense of these new mobilities of people, goods, knowledge, and capital? If the phenomenon called globalization ' ... emerge(s) in and through the everyday practices of individuals and communities in various parts of the world' (Benessaieh 2003: 120), then how is it that they themselves understand, term, and signify their actions?

Aihwa Ong chronicles how international outsourcing has given rise to 'unexpected conjunctures of labour relations and cultural systems, high-tech operations and indigenous values' (Ong 1991: 280). Similarly, this project argues for an understanding of the processes whereby urban India and its workforce re-oriented themselves towards new economic opportunities. The notion of call centre work while not new, but another rendition of late capitalism or flexible accumulation, bore continuities as well as discontinuities with these other forms of outsourcing and subcontracting. While similarly made viable by formations of technology, and national and international restructuring, it diverged from sweatshop economies in the nature of its workforce. The largest number of workers employed by the call centre industry were telephone agents, who were mainly young middle- and lower-middle-class men and women between the ages of 18 and 25. They practised what was considered a white-collar job oriented towards a global market, thereby socially, culturally, and economically giving rise to a new and burgeoning Indian middle class.

## Tracking the Indian Middle Class

The Indian middle class is a peculiar entity. Ambiguously defined through modes of consumption, levels of education, and economic and cultural mobility, its nature is far more elite and its numerical composition far lesser in the larger scheme of the Indian class demographic, than the name would suggest. Ranging anywhere between 30 to 300 million, this class numbers less than 30 per cent of the Indian population.

Debates on the middle class in India have revolved around the centrality of national identity to its experience of modernity. In other words, the middle class has borne the discursive mantle of representing an India that is capable of self-governance as a modern entity, even as it retains a core identity of Indian-ness. This enunciation aside, some literatures have emphasized middle class seclusion from questions of national and political agency (Kothari 1991; Varma 1998), while other discussions have foregrounded the nation within both political and consumerist narratives of middle class identity (Fernandes 2006; Mankekar 1999; Rajagopal 2001). Recent work has also focused on the relationship of this class to practices of consumption, both of goods and services, as well as media images of globalization (Dwyer 2000; Lukose 2009; Mazzarella 2003; Rajagopal 1999; van Wessel 2004). However, class, as Sanjay Srivastava points out (Srivastava 2007), is increasingly a site of contest rather than an easily definable social (or economic) category. Consumption as a phenomenon and practice therefore, becomes a key strategy for not only consolidating existing class identities but also attending to aspirations of upward mobility. Middle-classness is, to him and others (Mankekar 1999), a phenomenon that lies in the nature of claims, aspirations, and negotiations rather than settled fact and self-assured pronouncement.

Leela Fernandes' analysis (2000) of the relationship between nation, media images, cultural politics, and the middle class straddles these diverse strands of analysis, and takes as its organizing principle, the nation as both an artifact and a process. As opposed to narratives of the enduring or the failed nation-state, Fernandes is interested in examining how a global world is produced through

the middle class nationalist imagination. Challenging views on globalization as a de-territorialized phenomenon that transcends and
overwrites the nation-state, her analysis is rooted in the cultural
politics of the nationalist narrative of globalization, with the middle
class as its main imaginative protagonist.

Satish Deshpande's discussion of the middle class in India is in
a similar vein, in that he considers its import mainly in terms of its
political ability to articulate the hegemony of the ruling bloc. In a
collection of essays titled *Contemporary India* (2003), Deshpande
surmises that the middle class is more of a symbolic than factual
description, given how internally differentiated it is by large differences of income and social status, and on account of the mismatch
between its claimed and actual strength. Its importance lies therefore in the values it articulates. This class, in his argument, is most
dependent on cultural capital and the mechanisms of reproduction
of such capital. Lastly, he argues, that as an increasingly differentiated class, its elite section specializes in the production and dissemination of ideologies, and its mass faction, in the consumption
of the same. This formulation makes clear the comparatively limited numerical import of this class, its relatively elite status, and the
various paradoxes of its discursive merit.

Arguably, there has always been a crisis element to being
middle class in India, part of its constitutive and divisive force. As
Mazzarella eloquently argues, the spectres of illiberality, hypocrisy,
and incivility that constantly haunt the actual practices of the urban
middle-class elite, are projected onto 'politically "immature" or
"regressive" fractions—the mofussil middle classes, the vernacular
middle classes, "new" middle classes of whatever rambunctious
stripe' (Mazzarella 2005: 13). The middle class population that has
been absorbed, and fostered by the call centre economy in India,
is perhaps best described as one consisting of this new set, a rising breed that forms an essential foil, and successor to an 'older,
relatively coherent understanding of what "middle class" con-
noted—classically, a Nehruvian civil service oriented salariat, short
on money but long on institutional perks' (Mazzarella 2005: 13).
This new breed was brash, young, consumerist, and unsteady while
also simultaneously more voluminous than the older middle class,

given that its borders were far more elastic. As Satish Deshpande argues, the older middle classes were 'gripped by the idea that a credible claim to national identity necessarily involved explicit and visible loyalty to the national economy, even at the cost of inconvenience to oneself' (Deshpande 2003: 58), whereas 'the new middle classes—those qualified to participate in the global economy—were now encouraged to strive for individual material affluence' (Deshpande 2003: 73).

Ultimately, the notion of the Indian middle class is a dizzying misnomer. A minority population that is considered the closest thing in India to a national class, the Indian middle classes are more divided by language, religion, and social position than any other in the world (Beteille 2001). It is only as an aspirational and discursive force that the Indian middle class makes most sense. In this book, middle-classness retains contestations, and is brought into being by virtue of two inter-related frameworks: (*a*) A Weberian understanding of class in its relation to market conditions, and (*b*) Bourdieu's understanding of class identities as related to the accumulation of social and cultural capital (1984). Class in such a formulation is defined, not only by relations of production, but also by virtue of 'cultural traits, values, skills, expertise, taste, manners, and other embodied attributes that reproduce difference and with it hierarchical relationships in every sphere of life' (Donner and Neve 2011: 6).

The call centre, I argue, captures the various crises of the Indian middle class in the twentieth century, and the discursive and material gaps between its elite and mass factions. Even as theorizations of these new Indian middle classes remain tentative, call centres function as astute sites to locate their formation. Here, I am concerned with the labour practices, life-worlds, and media atmospheres of Indian call centre workers, and locate the call centre economy within the socio-political context of the new Indian middle classes. Through a thick description of the nightly routines of transnational Indian call centre workers, and their lives in both the call centre, and in the university town of Pune, India, I show how the call centre world is neither insular nor singular but a set of symptoms that can help read changing forms of urban Indian middle-classness. I argue that the young Indian middle class population was simultaneously the site as well as the product of the transnational call centre corporation between 2004 and 2008.

This book explores the ways in which young middle-class workers located themselves within practices, contentious representations, and material outcomes of the transnational Indian outsourcing economy. I focus on workers' nocturnal routines, in order to imagine globalization, and the workings of late capitalism more specifically, through their impact on body, ritual, space, and identity. Working through questions of cultural and physical malleability, and the material dimensions of the corporate campus, the cityscape, and virtual networks, I examine how middle-classness was mandated through bodily practices and cultural change as well as the material and formal restructuring of space and time. By examining the ways in which young men and women between the ages of 18 and 25 were moulded into workers, I locate changes in the discourse and composition of the Indian middle class in tension with the demands of a burgeoning urban service economy.

A critical paradox animates this book's central thesis: the anxieties of the middle class in relation to its expanding membership, even as the economically advantageous service work that allowed for such expansion secured its rising presence and voice in Indian public space and its globalizing economy. I chart two simultaneous processes: the separation of the markers of middle-classness from their historical constituency, and their relocation through commodification onto the aspirational middle classes that populated the Indian call centre. Thus, I demonstrate how the tenability of call centre work lies not in its financial rewards but more specifically in its powerful and continually unstable promise of middle-classness.

While the desired product of the corporation was the flexible worker, s/he was simultaneously also a producing and consuming middle class subject in the making. The call centre then was not just a space of productivity, but also one of discipline; a space meant to make a particular kind of self, as much as to produce a good or a service. Therefore, the call centre, I argue was also an incubator meant to create future workers of the Indian service economy. Such an organization can be understood to form a vital institutional member of what Gilles Deleuze has called a 'society of control', with 'the corporation, the educational system, the armed services being metastable states coexisting in one and the same modulation, like a universal system of deformation' (Deleuze 1992: 5). One forms attachments to the idea of becoming the ideal subject capable of inhabiting and thriving in such institutions, and becomes flexible in order to become the ideal pan-institutional subject.

## Training the New Indian Middle Classes

The 2008 demographic profile of India's population lists the largest section of the population to be located between the ages of 18 and 64. The primary working population of the call centre in Pune was drawn from men and women between the ages of 18 and 25. Bodies walking into the call centre were nearly always young men and women workers, eyes aglow, and the notion of growing up writ large on eighteen-year-old faces. As Douglas Foley reminds us, 'Experts who write about generation gaps and adolescents as distinct, rebellious counter-cultures sometimes forget how much teenagers long to be adults' (Foley 1990: 65). Work appealed not just because of the money, or the excitement, or the atmosphere, but also because it was an early initiation into a space of professionalism and by corollary, a 'grown-up' world.

This notion of growing up, was no doubt, gendered and classed, but the success of the call centre lay in its ability to be exactly what it claimed to be, a space of work. The corporation and its brick and mortar structure seek to radiate an atmosphere of professionalism, urgency, and adulthood. So it was with the call centre industry. Chrome and glass were ubiquitous as were security networks, surveillance infrastructure, and prominent and swanky signage. The buildings were tall, and the spaces inside were contained and ordered. The corridors were wide, as were the staircases. Everyone walked around with an identity card flopping off various body parts on a lanyard or a clip. The call centre proclaimed by various means its identity as a place of serious business, while at the same time, also functioning as a place to train workers in the practices of an ideal adulthood. I argue that it is important to ask as to why and how the call centre successfully recruited young students from between the ages of 18 and 25.

While I discuss recruitment strategies in the next chapter, my understanding of call centres as sites for reproducing workers also takes inspiration from Doug Foley's thesis in *Learning Capitalist Culture* (1990). While for Foley, schools stage inequality in and through their cultural practices, call centres in this analysis are a site for reproducing the flexibility required of workers across institutions in the service economy. I see the call centre functioning as an institution of learning in distinct ways. Workers were young, and often prioritized work over education in the hopes of achieving three distinct goals: (*a*) financial independence, (*b*) professionalism, and (*c*) respect. These goals found consonance with the call centre economy's need for cheap and ample labour. Such need for 'nimble' workers has an illustrious lineage, and as I mention earlier, can be found emphasized across literatures on the gendering of work, especially in SEZs and manufacturing zones employing third-world women and children (Massey 1984).[6] Workers' aspirations thus 'provide a conceptual link between structure and agency in that they are rooted firmly in individual proclivity (agency) but also are acutely sensitive to perceived social constraints (structure)' (MacLeod 1995: 139).

I propose the following argument: through the gendered logics of flexible capital, it was the young that were seen as the most malleable and the most affordable. However, the class background of workers complicated the ability of transnational outsourcing outfits to draw them in with easy promises of money. Only by utilizing the language of opportunity, personal growth, and globalization could call centres recruit young, middle-class workers. In the wake

---

[6] During the 1980s, feminist geographers began to explore how in both advanced and newly industrialized nations (NICs), women were a reserve for cheap labour, thus attracting flexible capital investments. This discourse also included the stereotyping of young, female labour in developing nations as young, dexterous and obedient such as when industrial discourses refer to the female worker in terms of a set of bodily competencies; as eyes and fingers adapted for assembly work.

of these calls, factors such as time, body, and self became reconfigured as valuable sources of worth that could speak to workers' own
desires to participate in a brave new world. As E.P. Thomson notes
in his seminal essay on time-work-discipline, 'Time is now currency:
it isn't passed but spent' (Thompson 1967: 61).

John and Jean Comaroff rightly critique the tendency in Western
public discourse to consider youth as a 'transhistorical, transcultural
category' (Comaroff and Comaroff 2006: 267). The employment
of youth in Indian call centres is thus not a pan-historical phenomenon, but one specific to India in the twenty-first century. Reading
Bourdieu, Jay MacLeod speaks about how 'people absorb from
their social universe values and beliefs that guide their actions'
(MacLeod 1995: 139). Middle class youth in Pune in the early
2000s similarly absorbed messages that promised a particular kind
of life. Even when they left the call centre, one can imagine that
they carried with them this promise and sense of a palpable potentiality—in themselves and in the world. Flexibility in this analysis
is thus not just the 'extensive tendency to temporary contractual
labour and the high level of fluidity in the job market' (Upadhya
and Vasavi 2006: i). Flexibility in this account is the work that the
workers performed every night or day, even as days and nights turn
into weeks, months, and sometimes years in the will to perfect the
ability to be flexible.

## Anthropologists in Call Centres

Research on call centre populations has been on the rise, as has
ethnographic work on this sector. I classify existing work as falling into one or more of the following categories: language usage
in call centres, and specifically the deployment of accents to mask
location (Cowie 2007); socio-political changes and the conditions
of work influencing the participation of women call centre workers (Aneesh 2006; Patel 2010); everyday work practices, discipline
and resistance, (Mirchandani 2004; Poster 2007a); globalization
and the IT economy (Aneesh 2006; Poster 2007a); and mimicry,
imitation, performance, authenticity, and its relationship to identity
(Aneesh 2015; Mirchandani 2012; Nadeem 2011; Poster 2007b).

There have also been a number of books published on a related set of concerns, such as the Indian middle class and its relationship to globalization and work (Fernandes 2006; Xiang 2007; Jeffrey 2010; Radhakrishnan 2011). Radhakrishnan (2011) for example, provides a detailed analysis of the politics, or lack thereof, of middle-class workers in India's IT economy by focusing on the gendered and classed cultural work that Indian middle-class women workers in the IT economy perform, in order to navigate conflictual and contrary positions.

This book builds on the legacy of these studies and their understanding of the Indian middle class and its changing, contrary, and charged socio-cultural milieu. I take particular inspiration from Leela Fernandes' *India's New Middle-Class* (2006), Craig Jeffrey's *Timepass* (2010), Smita Radhakrishnan's *Appropriately Indian* (2011), and Biao Xiang's *Global Body-Shopping* (2007). I read them as components of a bibliography, focusing on different aspects of class and identity as formed in relation to new forms of work or lack thereof, as they chart the desires of middle-classness and its strategies of redress in relation to structures of loss and longing.

In my account, a certain morbid hope animates the every-night processes of call centres, even as it solidifies into normality and ennui. Such a hope and its enduring promise of middle-classness continues to animate the ritual invocations, and indeed, economic success of call centre work. My work is also a deeply located analysis, in that it is based on my own participation in corporate call centre work and its nightly functions as a paid, rostered worker. In some ways, the stake that I have in this project, is illustrated by my ability to have seamlessly become a call centre worker. In spite of the ways in which I differed in position and need from other workers, I inhabited the call centre like one. As I proceed to demonstrate in the rest of this book, the things I shared with other workers were as important as those that I did not. One could read this as a plea to transcend 'self' and 'other', a suggestion that we are all inextricably bound in projects of desire and intention. My efforts, however, are far less humanist, and much less ambitious. All I can offer is the confession, that part of my own subject formation is lodged in the histories that have contributed to the material and discursive formation of the call centre worker. I am, for all purposes, a middle-class subject, and share the paradoxes of this position, its desires, and its aspirations with my interlocutors. This project is an attempt at mitigating the fear of the realization that the conditions I describe are my own. In this fear is also the possibility of side-stepping the 'failed' project of a feminist ethnography (Visweswaran 1994), of inhabiting a partial 'sameness' as a way of compensating for the inability to speak for. In tentative compromise, I heed Trinh T. Minh-ha and seek instead to 'speak nearby' (Chen and Minh-ha 1992). While reflexivity has been a condition of ethnographic research in anthropology ever since the cultural turn, in conducting this research, I am forced to confront and also acknowledge my own position as native and bi-cultural (Abu-Lughod 2000, 1993; Kondo 1990; Narayan 1993), a set of terms which valiantly tries, but stops short of chronicling the disturbances of 'hybridity' and 'positionality' as immensely difficult but direly needed ethical propositions.

I am native to this ethnography in two ways. In the first instance, I conducted fieldwork in the country of my birth and the city of my youth. I had lived in Pune for six years from 1996 to 1999 while pursuing an undergraduate education, and then again, from 2001 to 2003 for my first job. Initially, Pune formed only one of the many cities that I imagined I would conduct research in, as part of an ambitious multi-sited ethnography. Over many months of summer research, I realized how a large amount of my time was occupied in shadowing Pune's youth, and how little I had covered. Much of the city looked the way I remembered. I rode a scooter as I had done before, but the roads were worse. I haunted the same places as I used to, but the young men and women I encountered were shrill and spent too much money on too little. I attempted to speak their language, but they spoke faster and I found the slang unfamiliar. So many of them worked in call centres. By the time I returned to the city for fieldwork in 2006, I was in my late twenties, and I wondered as to why eighteen-year-old men and women went to work. Why did students who should have been lounging in parking lots, or riding motorbikes on the streets, or snoozing at the back of class go to work? Why did people stay up late in order to go work at night?

What cruel forms of just-around-the-corner desires animated this relentless movement and the will to slay sleep?

A large part of this research was therefore fuelled by my own nostalgia. Or perhaps even melancholia. I bore nostalgia for a different order than what I saw, for a city of students who cruise past with loud voices and no money, for young men and women who lurk at the tables of hole-in-the-wall dives and restaurants, and spend their last change on a cup of tea shared by six.

To the extent that I retain embodiment and memory of my middle-class urban Indian upbringing, my own formations of self will have to necessarily respond to other Indian 'selves' whose stories I do not share. The return to home then is also a return away from home; an understanding of why one leaves in the first place, an unlearning of privilege, a comprehension of loss, and an effort to know differently (Visweswaran 1994: 105). In conducting a 'proxemic of home' (Visweswaran 1994: 94), I am, no doubt, heeding some long-forgotten parental figure exhorting the disciplined and authority-cognizant performance of 'homework', but this return to home is also underwritten by the knowledge that I will, in unlearning, arrive where I started and know the place for the first time.

## On Nostalgic Research Design

When I began investigating call centres, my interests were mainly fuelled by a furtive curiosity about this strange world that a few middle-class citizens like myself seemed to inhabit. I had the same questions as everybody else who knew that I had begun researching this phenomenon—So are call centres good or bad? In bars and restaurants, at colleges and conferences, and among my family, friends, and colleagues, the tenacity of the question was striking. The space of the call centre, while ubiquitous and visible, was also only rarely available, except by way of popular culture and through news stories. Unlike the regular corporation, which was more commonly inhabited and better known, the nightly work of call centres, coupled with negative media attention, rendered them inaccessible to experience. Nevertheless, talk about call centres was always present.

The question of mystery or secrecy, however, did not surface much in the city of Pune. In Pune where I conducted my fieldwork, it was difficult to experience more than two degrees of separation from workers in the call centre industry. Everyone I met was either employed as an agent in a call centre, or knew someone who was working, or had worked in one. It was, as if every young man and woman had passed through the call centre, almost as if it were a rite of passage and a mode of self-discovery meant to provide an answer. In this arbitrary statistic, one can see how call centres and their attendant discourses had either temporarily convinced or even minimally made curious, many of the young men and women in the city.

Pune was furthermore, a very particular site. It displayed simultaneous signs of tradition and modernity, transition and fixity, in a manner that distinguished it from other call centre hubs in India. I have been conducting research in Pune since the 1990s, but from 2002 to 2006 when I began fieldwork for this project, the city had transformed from a manufacturing centre and educational and cultural hub, to a burgeoning site for the IT and software industry, as well as for the call centres. The eighth largest city in India at that time, Pune was home to a population of over 3.5 million (Office of the Registrar General and Census Commissioner, India 2001). Once referred to as the 'Oxford of the East', the city abounded in graduate and post-graduate institutions, with students from all parts of India vying for admission to its many prestigious colleges. The city had also created a network of support structures to accommodate its student population. These included hostels, dormitories, paying guest accommodations, dining halls, coffee shops, shopping complexes, and multiplexes. This student population found increasing opportunities for employment in the new Indian call centre economy. The urban landscape saw concurrent leaps in lifestyle, and increasing capital inputs in other industries like the retail and entertainment sector. This formerly sleepy city, once known as a pensioner's paradise, was transformed with the IT and outsourcing boom into a bustling near-metropolis. The irregular pace of this development, however, had material ramifications, I discovered. There were unfinished seams, unmanned infrastructure, and unplanned growth. The city was at a crossing-point, and in flux, trying to manage an old economy in conflict with the accelerating pace of the new. Call centres were part of this economic and infra-structural in-between-ness.

I located this research in Pune in an effort to add to anthropolog-ical studies of cities that are simultaneously global and traditional (Kondo 1990; Sassen 2001), overwhelmingly affected by trans-local economic forces superimposed over unassailable local phenomena. In keeping with recent anthropological trends, my research takes into account Pune as a 'process geography' (Appadurai 2001) and a work-in-progress. I refer here to Appadurai's reconceptualization of regions within area studies paradigms. I use this to problema-tize the city as a geographical fact and instead, read it as a variable and shifting indicator of transnational cultural processes. Beyond the 'time-honored commitment to the local', this study attends to 'local, cultural and political location' (Gupta and Ferguson 1997: 5) in order to understand 'the nature of locality, as lived experience, in a globalized, deterritorialized world' (Appadurai 1996: 52). Here, I seek to build upon a body of literature that emphasizes urban ethos as a key unit of analysis (Low 1996). Caroline Brettell's formulation of such ethos in terms of how a city represents as well as reinvents its identity (Brettell 2003) is especially useful considering Pune's myriad identities ranging from its embeddedness in the regional and national history of pre-1947 India (Diddee, Gupta, and Bhandare 2000), to its position as a prestigious educational destination, and its investment in a futuristic landscape populated by call centres and the IT industry.[7]

In many ways, Pune became an interesting site to observe the nature of change mainly because of its relatively homogenous call centre worker population as compared to cities like Bangalore or the National Capital Region (NCR). While the city began to increasingly host workers from nearby towns and interior parts of the state of Maharashtra, within which Pune is located, the initial

---

[7] Jaymala Diddee, Samita Gupta, and Sandesh Bhandare's *Pune: Queen of the Deccan* (2000) has a detailed and rich description of the architecture and history of current day neighbourhoods in Pune, and the spatial distri-bution of communities.

impetus to investments in call centres was precisely due to the availability of visible youth populations. The minimum requirement for employment in a call centre was fluency in spoken English. Thus, on the basis of their fluency and communicative ability in English, students barely out of high school could work part-time or full-time jobs. The city boasted 182 outsourcing companies in 2007, each employing anywhere from 100 to 3,000 employees and taking advantage of infrastructure benefits being offered by the local state authorities to IT outfits and BPO concerns. IT and BPO thus became part of daily chatter among young populations in Pune.

On the one hand, apocalyptic theories of global imperialism would have us believe that locality is being de-territorialized and subjects rendered into productive and flexible transnational labour by the onslaught of capitalist modernity. Agentive notions, on the other hand, over-determine the position of the speaking subject and claim the re-territorialization of the local in specific instances of cultural resistance. In this book, I am concerned with neither. Locating the call centre worker squarely in the middle of a dynamic urban Indian locale, in dialogue with the transnational call centre, I am concerned with the ways in which the practices that signify this dialectic between the ostensible 'local' and the 'global' are sought to be normalized.

## A Note on Worlds and Chapters

The 'call centre world' is a term I have heard and used, and yet it does not quite specify what one means by this world. Is it the waking up when it's dark? Is it the American, or British, or unknown accent? Does it encompass the ways in which the manager yells at you if you were to sleep during work? Or is it about the manager who brings you water when you have too many calls? Is it the partying? Is it the language, the special slang, the knowledge of acronyms that you share with your co-workers as you speak of Team Leaders, and Average Handling Times, and the IVR (Interactive Voice Response) that seems to have it in for you everyday? How do these discrete 'things' yield a sense of a collective, complex 'world', simultaneously, the way that the collective complexity we call a world, reveals itself in discrete 'things'? (Wenthe 2007: 121).

Perhaps, it is difficult to pin down, because it is not a thing, but a 'process, motion, struggle' (Wenthe 2007: 128), an agglomeration of several orders of such a world (Wenthe 2007: 130).

Margaret Trawick eloquently and ironically posits the central conceit of the anthropologist. 'One of our most compelling dreams, one that we hold tightest to,' she says, 'is the dream of wholeness, the vision of a world whose meaning is contained within itself, of a life that is complete, of a place where all things touch' (Trawick 1990: xvii). I am also similarly compelled by this desire for wholeness, and hence my notion of a call centre world, a world that is not wholly determined by the call centre, but is certainly influenced, and to some measure, oriented towards it. I do argue however that the desire for such wholeness is not merely mine and that my voice has sought to reproduce this desire for meaningful life in terms of my informants' own articulation of such a world. The one conceit that has propelled this research is that people find ways to make meaning, and the chapters that follow seek to capture a few aspects of this 'whole' world. Each section illustrates an aspect of the call centre life-world that respondents both spoke about and reacted to—in a sense, each chapter illustrates the overriding concerns, practices, compulsions, and logics that structured life for the call centre worker.

'Trespassers will be Recruited' is an introduction to the world of the call centre and the ways in which it created, fostered, and managed a young worker population in the city of Pune. I provide ethnographic descriptions of recruitment drives, interview processes, and worker orientation sessions, in order to explicate what Steven Epstein terms 'recruitmentology' (Epstein 2007). In this chapter, I show how over ten years, the call centre industry created and produced a new set of workers. Through exercises that initially positioned the industry as a quick moneymaking proposition, and later as one imparting professionalism, and the possibility of a future white-collar career, I show how this industry recruited a hitherto unemployed and formerly unemployable class of workers, specifically young college going men and women. 'Nocturne' investigates the question of nocturnal work and simultaneously examines its fetishization in contrast and cohort with its lived experience. This section also engages with the anxieties, compulsions, desires, and attachments that workers bore to the nightly landscape of Pune and the call centre. I show how forms of discipline were configured in order that the body could invert the relationship between day and night. I demonstrate the material ways in which the body was a site of power, and explore the meticulous, calculated ways in which corporate managers sought to bring about flexibility and productivity. Lastly, I explore the tense and gendered nature of workers' relationship to nightly life, and illustrate through a highly publicized case of crime—the figuration of middle-class women workers in the industry.

'Eliza Doolittle' is concerned with English language speech and training as cultural capital among the Indian middle classes, and the ways in which new middle class worker populations sought to harness and access such capital through the call centre. In this chapter, I explore questions of language training in relation to the histories, constraints, and desires of the speaking subjects of the call centre. There are three aspects to the question of language training that I examine. One, how was language co-opted in the service of the call centre? Two, how did this presuppose the emotional labour of a speaking subject that could inject language with certainty, conviction, and care? Lastly, what questions of, both, historical and contemporary subjectivity can one find inherent to this moment of speech and this process of training the worker to speak? 'The Affective Corporation' takes seriously the question of service work and its relationship to the management of an affective service, and asks through ethnographic detail, as to the logic of its distribution. In the process, I also examine the forms of 'immaterial labor' (Hardt 1999) that were constitutive of the call centre economy. The chapters frame discussion around key questions of time, language, and the body, and examine regimes that sought to construct the perfect speaking subject. They illustrate how forms of discipline were configured in order that the body could invert the relationship between day and night. They also investigate the ways in which linguistic ability, voice, tone, and pitch were directed in order to create an appropriately vocal subject. In a Foucauldian sense, the body was treated as the site of power, and I explore the meticulous and calculated ways in which corporate managers sought to bring about flexibility and productivity.

*1–800–Worlds* details everyday life in and around the call centre, and a typical night in the working life of agents, managers, and trainers. Through the experience of male and female workers, I show the ways in which flexibility begins to be inserted and naturalized within the regimes of the call centre. I am concerned here with the processes of normalization that sought to render call centre work into just another job. Collectively, the chapters of this book demonstrate the machinations and workings of flexibility as a technique of management, a technology of self, and a mode of power that sought to form the subjects of the call centre economy. In the conclusion, I bring together the themes of the chapters, and show how middle-classness as a social construct functions as an agglomeration of habits, rituals, and learned daily/nightly life.

# 2

## TRESPASSERS WILL BE RECRUITED

### Finding the Worker

In the winter of 2006, young men and women walking in and out of the campus grounds of the Brihan Maharashtra College of Commerce, The Institute of Management Development and Research, and the Deccan College of Architecture in Pune would have found, parked adjacent to the sidewalk, a bright orange and blue mid-sized Eicher truck, its side and back carved out to form an exhibition booth. They would have been accosted by pictures of young, hip, and urbane men and women—their own aspirational doppelgangers—splashed across the walls of this booth (Figure 2.1). Slogans advertising careers in 'Enterprise Solutions', 'Banking', and 'Information Solutions', would have attempted to capture their attention as they milled back and forth between classes and mid-day snacking at the makeshift food stalls or *tapris* stationed across from the truck. A few listless young men and women, also in bright orange clothing, would have handed them application forms, hoping that some would buy into promises of work, professionalism, and global opportunity.

The truck, the salespeople that accompanied it, and the papers they were handing out were invitations to apply for jobs at the city office of a call centre. Hoping to capture some of the material urban evidence of the call centre or BPO boom, I had fancied myself a *flaneur* and walked by one day, photographing billboards, posters, and flyers on dilapidated walls. As I passed the truck, one

**Figure 2.1**    Recruitment and Publicity Van
*Source*: Author.

of these salesmen approached to ask if I would be interested in working for the BPO industry. He pulled out a few papers from the sheaf draped over his arm, and showed me application forms for entry-level positions at the call centre. I politely refused, but waited around to see if there were others who might be convinced by this pitch. A few young men asked curiously about the truck. Some took away application forms. Much like in the postmodern novel, nothing eventful happened.

The road on which this truck was situated was known as BMCC College Road. Besides abutting BMCC College, it also formed an important and densely populated link to nearby educational institutions such as ILS (Indian Law Society) Law College, Symbiosis College of Arts and Commerce, The Film and Television Institute of India (FTII), and the Gokhale Institute of Economics and was a prime location to attract young college students. Perhaps, their attention spans, in the limited time available before having to head back to the next class on economics, architectural forms, and organizational management might be summarily captured by the prospect of a call centre career offering an escape from unpaid and uncertain student futures.

On my field site, publicity and recruitment campaigns, such as the one I described, were neither singular nor surprising. Through aggressive efforts at information dissemination, the call centre industry made itself increasingly visible and familiar to the city of Pune between 2001 and 2006. Its labour requirements found voice through a complex web of advertisements, publicity, state-supported infrastructural impetus promoting ideas of self-sufficiency, opportunity, fast cash, new consumer goods, and professionalism. Its demand curve staked presence through billboards, signs on walls, radio spots, classified advertisements, and large pennants on building facades. Many of the call centre workers I spoke with, mentioned recruitment drives held in and around their colleges, and boxes that were made available on their campuses for students to drop off résumés and applications. Posters on walls, small advertisements on dingy post boxes, and papers fluttering off trees announced invitations to seemingly innumerable call centre jobs. This awareness was additionally passed on by word-of-mouth and the city had become a gigantic chain of Chinese whispers. Advertisements that I viewed during this period promised 'Earn(ing) while you learn', 'Personality Development', 'Fortune 500 clientele', 'Fun at work', 'New friends', 'International experience', and 'Career Development'. Recruitment thus began even before the worker set foot onto the premises of the call centre (Figure 2.2). In *Shoveling Smoke*, William Mazzarella writes about the advertising business being a 'particularly compelling point of mediation between the local and the global' (Mazzarella 2003: 3). In the wake of the BPO boom, the roads, walls, newspapers, and surfaces of the city of Pune had become such a mediation point—portals between the local and the global. A popular joke in the call centre industry in Pune conjectured, that so relentless was the demand that people accidentally stumbling into call centre premises should beware, because even 'Trespassers will be recruited'.

In 2006 and 2007, as I scoured my networks to find workers who might be willing to share their experiences, I discovered that finding participants was the least of my fieldwork woes. In Pune, it was difficult to experience more than two degrees of separation from workers in the call centre industry. It seemed that anyone who belonged to young, urban, middle-class circles was either employed as an entry-level worker or agent in a call centre, or knew someone who was working or had worked in one. Some kind of urban rite of passage seemed to be playing out on the field. Call centres and their attendant discourses had successfully engaged the attention of young teenagers in and around Pune. The seeming omnipresence of current and former call centre workers indicates in a sense, the ubiquity, power, and persuasiveness of recruitment processes in these call centres.

The desire to work in a call centre was in some cases well thought out, in others impulsive, and in a few accidental. A young worker narrated how he had begun his career as a cell phone salesman. Having been turned away from a prominent call centre many times as the company did not encourage solicitation on its premises, he decided to take the easier way out by interviewing to be an employee in the call centre. Once interviewed, he quit his job to become a call centre agent. Many of the participants in this research

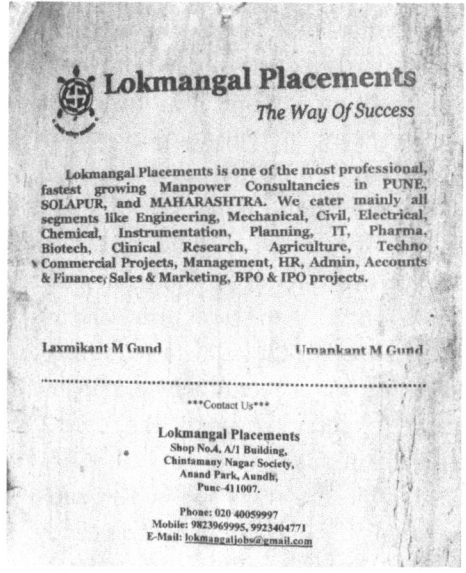

**Figure 2.2** Advertisements and Placement Promises
*Source*: Author.

found themselves wandering into a call centre for their first ever job. They reported gaining access into the industry by walking into a recruitment office without much forethought. Common responses included, 'We thought it would be fun', 'Let's see what happens', 'Might as well try it', and 'My friend told me it would be good'. Like most students in the city, they had entered into full-time employment with what one manager disparagingly referred to as a 'part-time mindset'.

It was, however, this possibility of attracting young students that had led call centres to set up shop in Pune in the first place. The spontaneity of the many workers who responded in this manner is in a way indicative of the relentlessness of the message. The worker who finally wanted to 'try it', was brought to this possibility by the messages sent out by the call centre industry, its existing pool of workers, other stakeholders, and a market and state apparatus serving to culturally, economically, and politically validate new forms of service work. An itinerant worker was only peripatetic between messages. When finally pulled into the web of work, it was because intended and unwitting messages emanating from in and around the call centre had resonated in particular ways.

In this chapter, I trace the recruitment discourse of the call centre and attempt to outline the ways in which the industry attained ubiquity. If the early days are an indicator of how successful and normalized the industry would become, I am interested in the ways in which the call centre industry convinced a largely middle-class audience about the desirability of this kind of work. The business management discourse for the problems faced during the early days of any industry includes the term 'entry barriers'. In some ways, the biggest entry barrier for the call centre industry was the lack of historical precedent towards recruiting workers in an industry both little-known as well as soundly suspect, the reasons for which I will outline further along in this chapter.

I therefore examine the trawl for bodies and voices that was crucial to maintaining the business of the call centre. A close look at daily recruitment activities, I argue, makes clear the ways in which this was a paradigmatic shift in the middle-class understanding of its own capacity to be a working population. This chapter makes a case for the initially uneasy translation and lack of seamlessness between the human resource arms of the call centre corporation, and the working population that both the industry sought to create and recruit. Recruitment, in this chapter, functions as a measure of what I call corporate governmentality, or a set of governing practices that brought in and maintained a call centre worker population. In other words, I ask: How was corporate thought, or the nature of planning towards creating and maintaining labouring bodies manifested, rendered, and questioned or reaffirmed through the daily practices and planning strategies of corporate recruitment? I use corporate governmentality as distinct from corporate discipline by seeking to understand how members of the urban Indian population were considered resources that had to be 'fostered', 'used', and 'optimized' (Dean 1999) towards the end of creating a cache of available workers.

The necessary preconditions for creating such a cache are twofold. The population must be first informed of its capacity to be a potential workforce. Such potentiality must then be evaluated, trained, and put to work. This chapter details the range of processes that sought to attract and invite young men and women, bring them into the space of the corporation, and fashion them into good workers. I analyse recruitment drives, interviews, and orientation sessions in order to trace the ways in which organizations in Pune attempted to identify potential workers and acclimatize them to the workings of the transnational call centre. Alejandro Lugo's critique of transnational corporations in specific relation to *maquiladoras*— manufacturing operations in Mexico's Special Economic Zones— notices how 'multinational corporations manipulated not only vulnerable working-class women, but whoever was accessible and available for production when needed, be they women, men or children, through a process that is locally and historically determined' (Lugo 2008: 81). Similarly, this chapter pays attention to the ways in which the recruitment practices of Pune-based call centre corporations had to render themselves increasingly flexible in identifying suitable labour caches, in order to address both accelerating demand for labour, as well as high attrition rates among their existing middle-class workers.

I read employment trends, growth rates, and predictions of business development in relation to frenzied recruitment into the industry. This was not a continuous frenzy, but rather a pace that had to be frequently accelerated and/or curtailed in response to changes in the volume of work, systemic crises within the corporation, and global competition and adjustments. Frenzy is literally a notion of speed and movement. In this sense, I follow speed and its attendant connotations, to examine what Paul Virilio contends, are its essential ability to dominate the proceedings at hand. In Virilio's understanding, 'the speed of light does not merely transform the world. It becomes the world' (Virilio 2000).

Other scholars of globalization have also paid heed to this exponential mobility of goods, labour, information, and capital (Blim 2000; Ong 1999; Sennett 2006; Sklair 2001). I locate the chapter within this scholarship while also arguing that such staccato and frenzied movement is in itself a requirement mandated by flexible movements of both capital and labour. To this extent, recruitment functions in this chapter, as a symptom of the fault-lines at the heart of the transnational call centre enterprise. I focus on the frenzy of recruitment processes as the energy of a late capitalist regime that attempts to manage the relationship between the dynamics of demand and supply by controlling the extent and registers of labour flexibility.

The nature of recruitment, I argue, should be read not as a measure of the success of the call centre industry, but as a lens through which to examine the implications of flexibility as a mode of power that pervades 'the field' (Bourdieu 1977). This field, I argue, produced subjects beholden to multiple and contrary compulsions. Managers, for example, while ostensibly powerful in relation to workers, were forced to adapt in relation to global business growth that required a continually increasing labour pool, and to workers' economic and social positions that allowed them to quit work at key moments. They learnt to coax and cajole, and adjust and modify hierarchical forms of management, in a bid, to both recruit and retain, capricious and young workers. Young workers, on the other hand, were compelled to learn modes of 'professionalism' and 'service demeanour' in response to globalization, and curb student lives and carefree existence in the service of a promising future. But the ability to absorb these skills quickly and superficially, and the financial freedom allowed by their middle-class position also gave workers the freedom to quit. In other words, the flexibility that compelled workers to enter the call centre also gave them the licence to leave. In response, call centre corporations had to increasingly adopt flexible practices of classification and recruitment in order to broaden the worker pool.

### Counting, Calculating, Speculating

At the beginning of 2007, the National Association of Software and Service Companies (NASSCOM) India,[1] predicted a demand for 1.4 million ITeS-BPO (Information Technology enabled Services-Business Process Outsourcing) professionals by the year 2010. They also estimated that this meant attracting an additional 500,000 workers into the BPO sector. Another NASSCOM-McKinsey report titled *Perspective 2020*[2] estimated that the revenue from the ITeS sector in 2020 would be USD 60 billion, which would be 17 per cent of the gross domestic product of the country. NASSCOM also estimated in 2008 that direct employment in the BPO sector would reach nearly 2.23 million—an addition of 226,000 employees—while indirect job creation was estimated to touch 8 million (NASSCOM 2008). For an industry that employed 45,000 people at the beginning of the Financial Year 2000, this meant a spectacular and steep ten-year compounded annual growth rate of 48 per cent. However, there was a simultaneous worry about the availability of labour to satiate such demand. The Director of NASSCOM's education initiative, Dr Sandhya Chintala, was quoted in her 2006

[1] NASSCOM is a nationwide non-profit association for software and IT services companies in India. According to their website www.nasscom. org, they are 'a premier trade body and the chamber of commerce of the IT-BPO industries in India'. They currently have 1,400 members; these include Indian companies as well as those multinationals that have a presence in India.

[2] Available at http://www.nasscom.in/perspective-2020.

keynote address at the Information Technology enabled Services, Industry-Academia meet:

> But if the present situation continues, we will fall short of 0.5 million candidates. The country has the competitive edge over its potential rivals like China, Philippines and Taiwan, as the country holds 65 per cent of the world IT trade and 45 per cent in the Business Process Outsourcing sector, but human resource development is an inevitable area that has to be addressed. (*The Hindu*, 28 December 2006)

What do these numbers mean? How do we read them? In terms of the industry cycle, the explanation is almost commonplace. In the first stage, an industry enters the market, and provides a unique product or service. In the second stage, it establishes the need for the product or service rendered, and experiences rapid growth. More organizations enter the market at which point the industry consolidates. Weaker competitors leave, while larger ones optimize their services. Individual shares of profits wane, but the market stabilizes as do the prices and value of the product or service rendered. This is the third stage of maturity of the industry. This is followed by rapid decline. While this explanation suffices in terms of understanding the growth of business and the possibility of profit, the story can be told differently from the point of view of workers, especially in the instance of a service industry. Given that call centres produce a service, workers are both, the raw material and the product of the BPO industry. Therefore, at each stage of development, the industry also projects itself into the locale it inhabits—grabbing, coaxing, and inveigling bodies that it then renders suitable to the process of work. Each industry cycle stage therefore corresponds to a concurrent employment trend.

From 2006 to 2008, the period that I was in Pune, the call centre industry was in the middle of a growth cycle. Call centres therefore needed to have workers at hand for any eventuality, be it new business or increasing attrition. At the same time, to serve this frenzied need, the search for employees sought to become more rapid, more efficient and in the words of an HR consultant involved with this aspect of call centre work, 'scientific'. The Indian call centres I surveyed were often partner organizations to IT companies. Their efforts at such streamlining therefore mimicked the trend in body-shopping or low-end outsourced IT work which demands short-term workers at a moment's notice to ensure competitive edge (Xiang 2007). Considering the workers themselves as an integral part of the call centre's offering allows us to consider their numbers in terms of economies of scale. I suggest that in this instance, given the projections that were a part of both NASSCOM and the nation-state's common visions for India's economic future, the stage of call centre work that I discuss sought not to retain workers but to maintain economies of scale with respect to its human resource requirements. 'Economies of scale' are a concept in microeconomics that refers to reductions in unit cost that occur as the size of a facility, or scale of work increases. If one were to tack this concept differently and consider both the efficacy of discourses and recruitment in bringing in bodies, then an economy of scale can be reached if the volume of worker population increases. The unit cost of recruitment, and consequently voice-based outsourced work, lowers with an increase in the worker pool. Therefore, from the point of view of the industry, the larger the number of bodies it allowed as worker populations, the more it could reduce its human resource costs. In this search for suitable bodies, various agencies and acts come into play. In other words, recruitment of call centre workers functioned through a regime of practices (Dean 1999) involving various actors. I am concerned then with such a regime's ways of perceiving and seeing its vocabularies, its actions and interventions, and finally with its 'characteristic ways of forming subjects, selves, persons, actors, or agents' (Dean 1999: 23).

In 2006, business development and employment trends were on an upswing since organizations needed a large number of workers to keep up with the volumes of work flowing into the country. Another factor further complicated this need. Attrition figures have been traditionally high in the call centre industry worldwide. This was particularly so in Indian BPOs. This problem has been variously explained by way of low entry-barriers, itinerant student workers, high-stress work, night routines, repetitive processes, and a pyramidal organization structure with a large number of front and lower-rung workers with little possibility for upward mobility (Babu 2004; Krishnamurthy 2004; Upadhya and Vasavi 2008). Workers moved rapidly, sometime between organizations, and often out of the industry. Work processes such as phone care for lost baggage service handling were particularly stressful, and exhibited very high attrition rates. Organizations therefore calculated attrition figures on a monthly or quarterly basis in order to continually monitor recruitment needs. Recruitment thus served a double function, catering not only to a relentlessly increasing business volume but a matching and even exceeding outflow of workers. As a result, recruitment processes had to be continually flexible to meet both organizational requirements and changes in worker pools.

As much as the work of the call centre was to provide voice-based customer service, an equally significant amount of its administrative energies were utilized in the hiring of new workers. Stress levels were high across the organization, but especially so among human resource (HR) service personnel. Jeet Singh, a manager at a prominent call centre in the city, had begun his HR career with a manufacturing firm before moving to the BPO industry in 2004 because it was 'the latest thing'. He narrated being continually stressed at having to curb attrition. The volume of monthly recruitments in many call centres depended on the size of the organization, the nature of its relationship to the client company, and the industries that the call centre served. For example, one could expect large organizations to have voluminous hiring needs but large captive call centres, or call centres serving a single client tended to have lower attrition or labour turnover, and hence, lower rates of hiring. Similarly, some industries exhibited high attrition rates due to stress factors, therefore needing to hire workers on a regular basis. Recruitment processes thus sought to bring in large numbers of workers into the call centre before parsing them out into areas of insufficiency or accelerated need. Interviews were carried out on a scale of two to five times the required number of entry-level workers in order to successfully hire candidates who were not only qualified, but were likely to stick with the company. The movement of bodies in and out of the call centre was as consistent and constant as its 24/7 service appeal.

### The Cultural Logics of the Lure

Stories I heard from consultants, recruiters, and managers attempting to kick-start the industry in 2000 and 2001, were replete with references to conservative Indian society, reluctant workers, and recruitment drives aimed at demystifying night-time work and safety. The industry was new, its future uncertain, and its work peculiar. Further, the concept of part-time work did not sit well with the families of young, middle-, and upper-middle-class men and women. The middle class were the typical targets for recruitment into call centres since they already possessed conversational skills in English—this being the fundamental requirement for outsourced call centre work. However, until the advent of the industry, the notion of middle-class teenagers soliciting part-time work was hardly entertained. Families were expected to monetarily support teenagers through undergraduate and often graduate education as well. Allowing teenage children to work was tantamount to the middle-class family's admission that they were unable to provide for their own offspring and were mimicking the practices of a lower class in letting their children support themselves and the family. Further, there was also a sense of wariness with respect to the industry and its peculiar requirements of nightly work. The first stage of the industry therefore created a frantic search for suitable bodies among a suspicious and recalcitrant population.

Mani Iyer, a consultant who had helped organizations set up various call centres across the country between 1999 and 2001, described his experience as 'initially *such* an adventure'. He detailed conducting workshops and orientation sessions for workers as well as parents, giving them tours of the company premises, and convincing them that this was indeed respectable and desirable work. He talked about persuading them of the organization's ability to ensure their children's safety and morality, in spite of the odd timings of the work which functioned through the night, and in co-gendered work environments. The work of recruitment during that period was, in his mind, like 'selling a car to a person who cannot drive so he can travel on a road that has not been built'. He added, 'We were selling the future and urging them to be first'.

As a result, the first workers were the young rebels and non-conformists among middle and upper middle class teenagers, who possessed both the skills and the cosmopolitan upbringing to be curious enough about dabbling in a new profession. They were often young students who had travelled to Pune from other cities. They lived in private hostels and paying guest accommodations, and could enter into full-time work without much explanation to their families as to the status of their educational progress. These were the workers who were part of the 'heroic' period—they were the front runners and the risk-takers. These were also the workers who lent call centres the sheen of newness and fun. Workers were, quint-essentially, Bauman's 'sensation-seekers and gatherers' (Bauman 1998), showing a capacity for 'imbibing and digesting ever-greater amounts of stimuli' (Bauman 1998: 23).

Call centre work in this period was reported to me as being not so much a profession as much as an adventure. As with any adventure, this period of recruitment carried its own tales and legends. Former workers and agents who had since risen in corporate hierarchy to be managers looked back with fondness to a period when they were a select few and the rest were trespassers. At that time, they were the workers heralding the country's entry into a new information economy and were thus treated accordingly. Perks were reported to range from private transportation to and from the company, and exclusive access to pubs and discotheques, to salaries and incentives hitherto unavailable to undergraduates and young workers. Client organizations dispatched teams from the US and the UK to person-ally train the first batches of workers. Promotions were often rapid, and employees felt both, beholden and a deep sense of ownership towards this new enterprise. Many workers shared their experiences of feeling like important members of the BPO industry. In parallel, other changes occurred in the socio-political milieu of the call cen-tre. Various Indian states regularized and legalized the employment of women on night-time work, which until then had been prohib-ited by law. Corporations were compelled to provide door-to-door cab services in keeping with the ramifications of concurrent safety caveats, especially for women.

The larger milieu however remained hesitant. Typical news stories from this period express a cautious turn towards the BPO model. One of them dated 2002 and titled 'BPO is new pie-in-sky for India Inc' analyzes IT industry trends in an attempt to predict the future of the IT industry:

> The Indian IT industry, in its evolution over the last one decade, has always seen one trend hogging the limelight on a periodic basis. If it was computer education and training in the early 90s, Y2K was the star during the closing years of the last century. Then as the dot com boom first soared high and then took a steep nosedive, it was the turn of B2B and B2C, followed by the SCM and CRM mantra.
>
> Today, the industry, chastened by the widespread economic slowdown, seems to have found its new pin-up boy (or trend) that goes by the name of BPO or Business Process Outsourcing. The tremendous hype generated over the apparently endless potential of BPO presents a peculiar sensation of déjà vu. The question that now remains to be answered: will BPO too go the way of its over-hyped predecessors, fizzling out without a whimper? (De et al. 2002).

The questions were manifold, and were voiced loudly across popular media and public space. As a result, the worker pool remained restricted to a select few. As the industry established its labour market and experienced growth, the worker population gained both visibility and notoriety. The immediate effects, especially over the first few years of the twenty-first century, were both censure and celebration. In a globalized Indian economy, BPO workers simultaneously became touchstones for discourses on Indian tradition and its concurrent loss in the face of rapid economic liberalization.

As the industry began to consolidate, its practices started to enjoy validity, and word-of-mouth publicity through increasing numbers of workers made this work familiar. Industry, government, and ancillary businesses worked hard at developing a possible pool of workers to satisfy increasing demand in the sector. NASSCOM, for example, held yearly conferences to bring together various industry personnel who could work together to institutionalize and professionalize the business of the outsourcing sector. The Indian central and state governments followed a similar policy of tax incentives to the ITeS sector, effectively giving call centres a ten-year tax holiday through the formation of the Software Technology Parks of India (STPI) where organizations could enjoy infrastructural impetus and technologically advanced work facilities. Training and recruitment departments began collaborating with independent consultants to recruit larger number of workers. Smaller outfits began running training programs in towns surrounding BPO hubs. The necessary precondition to increasing the labour pool was to make call centre work familiar, ubiquitous, and 'normal' and this was what was achieved during the period between 2001 and 2006.

Over nearly a decade, the controversies had thus become less prominent. By 2006, suspicions had been diluted, and BPO work had achieved a modicum of familiarity and a minimal acceptability. The industry continued to display a steadily burgeoning growth rate even as the concept of teenagers gaining financial independence through work had gained ground. As call centre work became a more visible entity, made popular through advertisements, recruitment drives, publicity, and company propaganda, condemnation from kin whittled down especially in the face of teenagers' new-found financial independence. Parents had no alternative but to quietly disapprove since very little argumentation worked in the face of economic logic. As one of my respondents, Sheetal, stated, 'How does it matter as long as I earn my money? I am not asking them for anything, am I?' Recruitment by call centres thus both drew upon and brought into effect varied economic and cultural logics. In this case, I read the continued inflow of workers into the call centre as an instantiation of what might be called the 'cultural economy' of outsourcing. I borrow from Paul du Gay's articulation as regards the effects that economic discourses themselves have in producing the economy that they reference and explain (Du Gay 1997). In other words, lore about call centre work was propagated by the call centre economy; this fostered its own possibility. In a sense, this form of both corporate and state governmentality had successfully instituted ways to see young urban teenagers, both by their employers and by such men and women themselves, as a viable workforce.

Undergraduate education in Pune, while served by a large number of institutions, did not guarantee a career. Many students also felt the need to obtain a master's degree of some sort, as had become the fashion over the 1990s, such as a Masters in Business Administration (MBA). Also, while many middle- and upper-middle-class students were supported by their parents through the course of their undergraduate degrees, their spending was also concurrently controlled by their homes and had to be managed accordingly. Students almost always wanted money, either for their own expenses or future education, and looked for opportunities to make some. Until the late 1990s, while opportunities for part-time work did exist, none were really able to offer either the volumes or the salary values of call centre work. Part-time work before the 1990s also carried with it the negative status connotations of a family that could not support its progeny and hence sent them out to toil in the world of salaried work. The ability to support their children's education was one of the many markers that separated the Indian middle class from the working-class and the poor, who were seen to produce children in order to extract the value of their labour. Moreover, traditional, white-collar work before this time was the bastion of the middle class, and required at the minimum, undergraduate professional education, and in many instances, two years of graduate school. Part-time work therefore seemed to connote the failure of the middle class family to educate its children. Further, it was seen as creating an impediment to education and ultimate employment as a white-collar and upwardly mobile professional.

How did the call centre industry work against these notions? To begin with, call centre work was a natural extension of the ethos of the IT sector. It was therefore in keeping with the upstart nature of the IT bubble and the dotcom boom. In its early days, it was seen as not only a pioneering field, but also an audacious one, meant only for the most forward thinking in society. Part-time work in these places, although nightly and hence controversial, nevertheless attracted bold and young college going students with an English language education, by promising both a steady and high income, as well as a charged, exciting, and 'fun' atmosphere at work. Students in Pune hailed from affluent backgrounds, and were suitably cosmopolitan. Only a very small number of workers were required at that stage, given the tentative nature of the industry. A colleague who had been in the industry for five years talked about how in the early days, interviews would be held in the hundreds, but only a few dozen would make the cut. The focus was on exclusivity, talent, and weeding the English-speaking 'best from the rest'. Naturally, the class composition of this labour pool remained middle and upper middle class bound. As the popularity of the industry increased and more and more organizations began to follow the outsourcing trend, the need for working populations began to exceed the availability of this ostensible *crème de la crème*. The labour pool began to be fragmented, and policing of entry points gave way to accelerated recruitment and training.

## The Everyday Life of Recruitment

In September of 2006, after a few months of fieldwork among workers, I decided to attempt working in a call centre in order to deepen my observations, and perhaps, gain a different set of insights into the industry. I responded to an advertisement in the career supplement of the Pune edition of the *Times of India*, for entry-level positions in a highly ranked outsourcing company.[3] This advertisement touted positions for a company highly ranked in the Indian outsourcing industry. The call centre was located in a prominent suburb called Aundh, located at the northwest end of the city.[4] This was close

---

[3] This supplement was titled *Times Ascent* and published every Wednesday. A large portion of space was taken up by either IT companies or by BPOs.

[4] Aundh included the regions of Aundh, Baner, Pune University, and Khadki. Aundh was known to be a middle class and upper middle class domain. The areas closest to the call centre were some of the highest priced real estate in the city. Aundh was also known for some of the oldest co-operative housing societies—the Sind society and the National Housing Society—that were home to prominent industrialists in the city. Angelina Jolie shot for *A Mighty Heart* at one of the bungalows in the Sind Society.

to ITI Road, so named because it housed the Industrial Training Institute, a government body established under the Directorate of Vocational Education and Training for the state of Maharashtra in 1946. The road on which the call centre was situated led to the Mumbai-Pune highway NH4. The roads were always busy and rickshaws, scooters, cars, and large Volvo buses, plying every hour between Pune and Mumbai, made it difficult to even cross over from the call centre to the McDonald's across the road. The office of the BPO, which I shall call Reservoir Corporation, operated across three floors of a swanky new glass and chrome behemoth, throwing the sun, the dust, and the city landscape off its blindingly shiny surfaces. Behind the complex were new condominiums and housing developments.

I reached the office at around 3 in the afternoon and waited in the lobby with other aspirants. I had been warned by a friend who worked for another BPO to be there early since I would probably have to negotiate long lines of aspiring workers. These long lines however, seemed to be a thing of the past, as I marvelled at the increasing levels of professionalism in the BPO industry. I had to sign in at three separate entrances; one at the main gate to the building, then at the reception for Reservoir, and lastly at the security desk leading into the interiors of the call centre, before being led in to meet people from the Human Resource (HR) department. I was asked to deposit my cell phone, which had an in-built camera at the main desk, and leave my backpack behind. With its sanitized interiors and unimaginative wall colours, the office continued to emanate the aura of a top-secret, security-classified zone. Along with two other men, I walked through a long beige painted corridor into the HR section where ten people worked in four-person cubicles. All of us were ostensibly being considered for the same entry-level customer care position. Above us hung streamers that declared, 'Turn your friends into colleagues'. In other cubicles were soft boards and charts declaring the company's will to reduce attrition by 1 per cent, and increase induction.

We handed in our résumés to a woman in a salwar kameez, and she promptly asked the guy next to me to tell her 'something about yourself'. The guy answered haltingly in English, 'I am coming from Sanghvi[5] and I am wanting opportunity to work with your company'. He was asked to wait in the reception area. When asked to answer the same question, I gave her my name, mentioned my educational background in management, and said something faintly laudatory and aspirational about the outsourcing business. The other candidate, an older man with 12 years of experience in the hotel management industry, was similarly interviewed and then asked to leave. I was told to wait and the woman, who I shall call Ratna, informed me that if selected for this position, I would have to start work the same day. I was taken aback, but attempted to negotiate and told her that I had just moved to Pune and might need time to relocate, and deal with paperwork and the like.

Many of my respondents during the previous months of fieldwork had been experienced workers, and had described to me how call centre HR departments often attempted to arm-twist new and inexperienced workers into getting started at the soonest, since the industry was always short of suitable candidates. However, their warnings had not prepared me for the level of anxiety that such a proposition might generate. I hadn't worked in a corporate office for many years prior to this event, and the thought of any routine, leave alone one that threatened to invert my daily life, caused equal amounts of trepidation and excitement. My position in some ways mirrored that of rookie workers who made their first foray into paid, routinized work through the call centre, even though given that I was in my late twenties at this point, I should have been more experienced than entry-level workers in their teens and early twenties.

I was then asked to wait in order to be interviewed by a voice and accent trainer. I was directed to a conference room and in walked a young trainer, seemingly in his mid-twenties, and dressed in a kurta pajama. He introduced himself as Raj. Looking over my documents, he commented that my background seemed interesting, and asked as to my reasons for being interested in the 'call centre' business. The last part of his question was in an exaggerated American accent with an aspirated emphasis on the 'k' sound, which was dull, soft,

---

[5] A small town in the state located a few hours away from Pune.

almost 'd'-like 't' and a rolled 'r', so it came out as 'khol cender'. I was not sure why he was attempting such speech, unless of course to test if I could understand an American accent or not. I narrated the usual platitudes about growth opportunities in the industry (Gupta 2009).[6] Throughout the process, he maintained a stern demeanor and betrayed neither approval, nor disdain or suspicion. The interview ended and I waited in the HR section for the verdict. While Ratna left the room, another HR manager assured me that I would definitely be hired. One of them asked me if I could start work the same night. I tried to think fast, making quick calculations in my head and wondered if my desperation to be in the call centre should outweigh the pragmatics of the situation. I was still an unsettled fieldworker moving between accommodations and informants. I tried buying some time and told her that I could not start work until the next week. She told me that there might not be an opportunity the next time around and that they had a number of people they needed to hire immediately. She emphasized that I might be missing an important chance. I dithered and muttered excuses. We settled into silence and fifteen minutes passed. Then Ratna called me in to speak to the TL who would be my manager, if I were to be hired. It had taken them a while to locate him as he had been supervising a training session. We went back into the room where my interview had taken place. Ratna called the TL on his cell phone and I spoke to him with her looking on.

TL: So your credentials look very good. But I also had a few specific questions.
MK: Sure.

TL: What is your viewpoint on customer service?
MK: I think customer service is especially difficult when on the phone. I'd like to think that as an agent, I could help the person at the other end of the line, but also know the limitations of this work. So I would work primarily at good communication and establishing a mutual understanding.

[6] Akhil Gupta (2009) discusses the consonance in the usage of 'growth' in national discourse, as well as management and worker circles.

TL: Hmm … and how would you handle irate customers?

MK: I'd stay calm and try and get a clear understanding of the customer's issues.

TL: And abusive customers?

MK: They don't bother me; I'll try and not react. I'd mainly stay calm and try and understand the reason for the customer's anger.

TL: Okay wonderful, this has been great but I would definitely like to meet you before you start work. Face to face is always better if you're going to be on the team.

MK: Sure, I'll stay in touch and Ratna can let me know when we could meet again?

I hung up, confident of being made an offer. This process, which I underwent for the first time, was nevertheless familiar because of interviews I had conducted with call centre workers prior to this incident. Many respondents had detailed similar processes often conducted over a whole day from afternoon until late in the night. One of the HR managers had lamented how shameful it was that the interview process could last up to eight hours. Riya, an agent who had undergone such an endless daylong interview had complained, 'It was so late that I was worried I wouldn't get an auto rickshaw to go home. They didn't even provide transportation'. The company at which Riya had interviewed was situated outside the city and was therefore difficult to access via public transport, which in any case was very inefficient and sparse in Pune. Similarly, I expected that I would be shuttled between managers and departments before being made an offer.

All the information at hand did not prevent the jitters. At every interview, I sat at the edge of my seat, shoulders hunched, legs crossed, back taut, and poised to say the right thing. While talking to the TL, I had been able to sense my voice from the outside, and see this corporate person, who knew how words were to be uttered at the moment of the question (Sennett 1998). This etiquette was one of the skills that distinguished a successful interviewee from an unsuccessful one.[7]

---

[7] Richard Sennett (1998) critiques the ways in which people develop fake personas and know how to say the right things in the new economy.

After the interview, Ratna asked me to wait outside in the cafeteria while the HR department discussed my application. I was assuming that this would be the last stage before being made an offer. I waited and looked at the posters in the cafeteria. One of them listed the benefits available to employees in the company. These included transportation, nutritious meals, some concierge and taxation services, and life and medical insurance. Another explained a project being undertaken to improve the efficacy of transport. Ratna returned and made me an offer, for what I had by then ascertained to be the standard industry package of INR 8,000 or approximately USD 160 a month, sans incentives. She also specified that I would have to sign a six-month contract. I had already been told that such contracts were rarely enforced and that many workers quit without giving notice. Very rarely did the organization pursue the workers since the cost of a lawsuit would far outweigh the cost of replacement. However, not wanting to be bound, I wavered. Ratna noticed my hesitation and went back into the caverns of the HR department to confer with her colleagues. She returned and noticing my continued hesitation, suggested that I apply to work instead as a communications trainer.

I persisted in applying for the position of an agent at two other call centres, where a new set of obstacles arose. On being informed that the work I conducted would also help my doctoral work, managers at both places demurred and withdrew their job offers. Realizing that my educational qualifications and research mandate put me at a disadvantage in relation to being offered call centre work, I suspended fieldwork, and began to work actively at being recruited as a voice and accent trainer. I managed to successfully apply to be a trainer at another large call centre in the city, one that I call Systematix Ltd.

---

While I am not convinced that this is tantamount to Sennett's account of a loss of character, I do see its relationship to flexibility in two ways. One, being flexible entails superimposing modes of polite address and empty communication upon one's 'real' self; and two, the very reason homogenized speech exists in interview situations is to enable flexible movement between corporations.

### Orientation and Disorientation

At Systematix, the HR personnel similarly tried to coax me into
getting started with work at the soonest possible opportunity. I
postponed my 'joining date', pleading logistical arrangements, in
order to move house closer to the call centre. Within the fortnight,
I was asked to attend a two-day orientation session. These sessions
were held at regular intervals and were the purview of HR personnel appointed specifically to coordinate such events.

I arrived at the given location at 8 in the morning on a Monday.
Two hundred odd young workers milled outside Aurora Towers. It
looked as though the audience for a rock concert had gathered at the
wrong time of day. Young men and women, most of them casually
dressed, waited, chatted, smoked, and drooped against store shut-
ters and building walls, scooters, and motorbikes in various states
of excitement and boredom. We had all been summoned. Having
passed psychometric, aptitude, and up-close and personal tests and
interviews, we were the chosen many who could now enter the
hallowed portals of the corporation. Unlike during our job interviews, when we walked into the company premises with temporary
identity cards and guest passes, we were now awaiting branded IDs
and a clearly readable employee number. We would soon genuinely
be. I stood there rubbing my eyes, half-asleep.

Aurora Towers was a five-star hotel situated prominently at one
end of Mahatma Gandhi Road (M.G. Road), a main thoroughfare
and shopping destination. Mahatma Gandhi Road was part of the
larger suburb known as Camp, made up largely of land belonging
formerly to the Indian Army. This area was also populated by personnel working at the Army cantonment. Camp formed one half
of the tradition-modernity dichotomy mapped onto the geography
of Pune city. Its army antecedents rendered it cosmopolitan and
ethnically diverse. Mahatma Gandhi Road, unlike the frugality of
its namesake, was dotted with upmarket stores, eateries, cafes, and
pubs. It was a well-known youth hangout. Most of the new employees were familiar with M.G. Road and would have known how to
find their way to Aurora Towers. I teamed up with two other girls
and we promptly lost our way once we entered the hotel. Aurora

Towers was a maze of conference rooms, each advertising its own orientation, training, or reunion. The sun rose outside as we made our way inside the hotel from one dimly lit room to another before finally stumbling upon a hand-printed sign with a definitive arrow that said 'Systematix'.

For some it was a first job. Others were far more seasoned and trooped in confidently, knowing what to expect. The orientation was held in a large conference room on the fourth floor. Velvet drapes helped maintain a solemn air while upholstered dingy chairs stood waiting, twenty to a row, straight-backed and armless, hoping to prod employees into participation. The workers arrived in ones, twos and threes, seeking to get through the next two days so they could get to the job. I found the idea of the orientation session a welcome preface to the actual job, since it seemed to demand no labour and was ostensibly a rudimentary and bureaucratic exercise. Many other employees seemed to have similar thoughts. Walking into the room, I heard cavalier comments about how it would be wise to find seats at the back of the room and catch up on sleep. Shweta, Meenal, and I seated ourselves somewhere in the middle. For Shweta, this was all new. She had never been to Aurora Towers before, she said. Neither had I. The hotel was one of the first five-star hotels to be built in Pune. As students, she currently and I, in the late 1990s, neither of us had possessed the resources or the reasons to venture here. As employees of a company whose shares traded on the New York Stock Exchange, we had however, now been invited.

As I looked around and chatted with a few workers, it became clear to me that the majority of attendees were customer service agents. As the manager read out a roll call, I gathered that I was one of the two trainers attending this orientation. We began the proceedings with a talk from the HR manager on the benefits of outsourcing. As the day wore on, we were taken through the logistics as well as ideologies of quality and integrity that needed to be absorbed before becoming part of Systematix. The narrative was sustained by representatives from various departments, who testified to the company being exactly the kind of behemoth that could absorb the teeming numbers that occupied the room.

Financial accountants led us through tax planning, bank account logistics, and incentive structures. The IT department educated us on our computer access privileges, electronic cards, and computer account usage. Human Resources sang paeans to the founder and the company's 'mission, vision, and values'. The sales team spoke about the company's position in the market and its projections for the future. Operations managers lectured us on work ethics, and the importance of the functions that the company performed. Infrastructure personnel took workers through the fascinating, complex, and chaotic organization of nightly transportation. By the end of the first day, the two boys seated behind me who had kept up a stream of inane comments through it all had let their heads drop. One of them snored and was sharply nudged by his friend when the orientation coordinator said goodbye. At the end of these first sessions I walked out worried for myself, the company, and the hundred and eighty odd teenagers crammed into the conference hall.

The majority of the second day was devoted to a detailed check-list of requirements to be fulfilled before we could all receive our first paycheck. The human resource manager emphasized time and again that we needed to provide notarized copies of our undergraduate certificates before we could receive employee numbers. This insistence, I discovered much later, was because many engineering students used to temporarily enter the call centre while in the process of clearing backlogs on their engineering term exams, after which they would promptly return to college, thereby contributing to skyrocketing attrition rates. One of the tasks to be performed by gatekeepers during orientation was to weed out such itinerants. The rule used to reject such applicants was that the organization did not accept workers who did not possess an undergraduate degree.

Although seemingly enforced during orientation, I encountered numerous instances when young boys and girls just out of high school, were able to slip through the cracks by pursuing long-distance undergraduate degrees or even by faking certificates. The former worked in favour of the company because such workers were unlikely to quit given that they had no time constraints with respect to being physically present at their college premises. The latter were more difficult to filter. On the whole, while the appearance of order and rules seemed to indicate a will to retain a certain kind of worker—the laxity, ambiguity, capriciousness, and looseness of the so-called rules of recruitment did, time and again, bring into the call centre many trespassers.

## Recruitmentology: Good Recruiter, Bad Recruiter

*During certain periods there appear agents of liaison.*

— Michel Foucault (Foucault and Gordon 1980: 62)

The recruitment process for the call centre industry was also in many ways a decentralized one because workers were channelled in through a diverse set of institutions. The large volumes of workers entering the call centre were brought in not only by word-of-mouth, advertising, and publicity sponsored by the company, but also through a parallel network of organizations functioning independently of the call centre industry. These were called recruitment consultants. The human resource function of the call centre industry had itself been outsourced.

Call centre consultancies were smaller outfits dotting the city landscape, which functioned as points of access for young workers and organizations alike (Figure 2.3). Offices for such consultancies ranged from makeshift one-room apartments to outhouses or single-room facilities located in the backyards of bungalows owned by genteel Pune residents who found such rentals an easy income supplement. Many that I surveyed had hand-painted signs with desks manned by a single person who was responsible for all administrative functions. Most functioned on the franchisee model, with a parent organization providing a brand name that was farmed out to entrepreneurs for a fee. Each of these franchisees, whether employing a single person or a team of people, was responsible for ensuring the quality standards dictated by different call centres. These could vary not only across organizations, but also across specific industries that required additional workforces at any point of time. For example, while Reservoir might ask for thirty candidates within the day, fifteen of them would be required for credit card

**Figure 2.3**   Training and Recruitment Consultancies
*Source*: Author.

sales, necessitating that they be garrulous and quick on their feet while the rest could be for positions in the technical support field, requiring that they be graduates with sufficient computer expertise to comprehend and resolve hardware queries.

Consultancies therefore worked on a pay-per-assignment basis with only a limited amount of information and involvement in the recruitment process. While they could hire agents, they were not invested in their tenure. As a result, in the words of one HR manager, they 'played havoc'. He further added that these consultancies would 'pick up a hundred and a fifty people', receive their commissions, and then approach the very same agents for other call centre job openings. Only trainers and managers directly employed by the call centre were held responsible for loss of workers or labour turnover at the end of every month, and recruitment consultants were not concerned with attrition.

Ajay Sinha, the CEO and founder of an outsourcing consultancy in the city, was convinced that recruitment processes needed a radical revamp in order for the industry to have stability in its workforce and output. During his early experiences as an HR manager in one of the first call centres to open shop in Pune, he claimed to have dismissed all consultants in favour of recruitment through employee referrals:

> So I chucked away all the consultants. Just threw them out. Each and every recruitment event of mine was referrals. That's their [HR's] bloody job. To get those people. We used to just do community exercises. We used to go to the nearby society. We put posters there, we used to say come and visit the call centre on a Saturday. See what a call centre means. If you have somebody willing to work there, come and work there.

He also sensed that attrition might be curbed if managers changed the ways in which they addressed workers and their relationships to work:

> Working in a call centre meant, number one, you needed to have a ponytail [for men] ok. You needed to be pubbing every night. The girls would be having all the trendy clothes on. Ok, these are the people who are having a lot of cash in hand. They blow it up on trance parties on pubs. Invariably on the BPO notice board, there will be free entry at so and so TDS [Ten Downing Street]. Collect your pass for this rave party and all that bullshit. And that's what exactly BPO used to be at that particular place. Now who created this particular culture? You think people created this on their own? No. It's not the people. People like me as managers actually created that culture. And when I entered, I came from a very serious industry.
>
> When I came into BPO, I said this is all bullshit. We used to challenge the entire thing.

Measures like Sinha's began to be adopted piecemeal by various other call centres in the city. Organizations and management began to wonder if partying and creating a 'fun' atmosphere would disallow serious aspirants, and hence began to engage more productively to create a long-term worker pool. The lure began to be modified by including educational incentives such as a company sponsored part-time MBA in return for a bond agreeing to work with the call centre for a few years. Workers were promised opportunities or 'Internal Job Postings' (IJPs) at the company's collaborative units, which dealt with far more 'serious' IT work. The message seemed to be that all workers needed to do was prove their loyalty, and indeed, their seriousness towards their own future goals by staying within the organization. Similarly, employees that were dispatched on assignments to the US or the UK for purposes of training were required to sign agreements, wherein, they contracted to stay with the organization for periods varying from a few months to three years, as a sign of loyalty or indication of gratefulness for the company's investment and faith in the worker's abilities. Such opportunities served two purposes. One, they established incentives that would help retain workers; and two, by highlighting the workers that might refuse such opportunities, they helped weed out those who were ostensibly not willing to stay in the long term. Many workers who had signed such bonds shared feelings of uncertainty as to the costs of their upward mobility within the company. Despite measures like this, recruitment continued to be a hit-and-miss game, in part because, 'suitable' populations were in themselves elusive.

The word recruitment acquires different meanings across contexts, and it has come to mean not just the end product, but also the process in itself. Steven Epstein chronicles the mechanics of what he calls 'recruitmentology' (2007) in his account of the politics of bringing in diverse experimental subjects for the purposes of American medical research. This, he describes, as 'an empirical body of studies scientifically evaluating the efficacy of various social, cultural, psychological, technological, and economic means of convincing people' (Epstein 2007: 182) to become and remain human subjects. In other words, it is 'an explicit attempt to transform the art of recruiting into a science' (Epstein 2007: 319). A similar professionalization of recruitment in call centres indicated a faith, not only in the efficacy of such processes, but also in the future of outsourcing. In other words, the need for 'recruitmentology' was prefigured by an understanding that the work of recruitment was at the outset voluminous, and continuous in the long term. In the medical research industry as in the outsourcing industry, the recruitment function became 'outsourced'. This focus, on what one HR manager I interviewed called, 'quantity not quality', resulted in the recruitment of subjects who were either unsuited to the task at hand, or would leave. The similarities in medical research and the call centre milieu are striking. Subjects are 'subjects' in both senses of the word; 'at times subjects to the will of the experimenter, at times endowed with subjectivity, agency, and a capacity to pursue their own interests' (Epstein 2007: 185). In both, the medical research and the call centre industry, the incentive for recruitment was often cash. While in biomedicine and pharmacotherapy this underlines the clear commodification of human bodies and body parts, it is no less a version of biocapital (Sunder Rajan 2006) in case of the call centre industry.[8] If one were to pause to view the bodies being corralled into the call centre, the memory of a Fordist assembly-line chain might flash past as if this be 'a moment of danger' (Benjamin et al. 1968: 255). However, I argue, that while this mode of analysis might expose the workings of capital in familiar and repetitive modes, also at stake here are the very cracks and frictions at the heart of this mode of flexible capital. Recruitmentology in this analysis functions as a tool to excavate how the call centre's increasing need to institutionalize and rationalize recruitment was a reaction to the very uncontrollability and the radical flexibility of the working bodies that it sought to legitimize, and the business processes it tried to streamline. The frenzy of recruitment laid bare an unsure and nervous regime that was unable to deal with the flexibility of mobile labour, a flexibility, as I have argued in the first half of this chapter, of its own making.

### The Daily Battles of Recruitment

Weekly recruitments at Systematix ranged from 50 to 500 depending on the level of activity in the business. Rapidly increasing

---

[8] The analogy comes full circle in the fact that India is now considered an apt location not only for medical subjects but also for well-trained, English-speaking researchers, nurses, and staff at cheap wages. As the *Financial Times* article that Epstein quotes states, 'some executives believe India could become as prominent in pharmaceuticals as it is in information technology' (Epstein 2007: 199).

business volumes required hiring activities to go on overdrive through 'ramp-ups', or increases in the scale of the organizational manpower. For example Zinax, a computer manufacturer based in the UK and an existing client of Systematix, decided to additionally outsource its technical service operations to the company. This was what human resource managers termed a 'ramp-up', hence demanding that a hundred new agents be recruited within the week. Agents were distributed across various industry verticals such as insurance, credit cards, and airline service processes. In a single day, anywhere between 50 and 200 applicants were interviewed at the Systematix premises and its corollary recruitment offices.

During my four–month stint as a voice and accent trainer at Systematix, I participated in the recruitment process in many ways. As a new recruit, I had to undergo the interview and orientation process, which was common to both trainers and agents. Further, trainers were integral to the recruitment of new workers because they needed to examine their linguistic and communicative abilities in the English language.

I walked out of my training session one sunny Tuesday afternoon in March 2007, and attempted to chart a path through a crowd of young men and women clustered around the reception area. They were all waiting for results from their psychometric tests. These were candidates who had successfully cleared their aptitude tests, personal interviews, and group discussions. Aptitude tests were written tests given to determine general ability at language, logical thinking, and basic mathematics. They tended to be designed on the lines of scholastic tests for college and graduate school. Personal interviews and/or group discussions were held to examine workers' abilities to construct sentences and express themselves. While a seemingly effective set of processes, the large number of interviews conducted in a day ensured that these tended to be often perfunctory and conducted indifferently by human resource personnel under enormous pressure to increase the number of employees. Workers who successfully made it through the aptitude tests were then administered psychometric tests. These tests were designed on the lines of personality calibrating mechanisms, seeking to determine possible behavioural patterns in worker's responses to people, and work and life situations.

One of the most widely used psychometric tests in the call centre industry was the Myers Briggs Type Indicator (MBTI). This test was developed during World War II to categorize women who were entering avenues of paid work for the first time into appropriate work categories. The personality indicators, as identified by this test, were often familiar shorthand to many BPO workers. Workers were further aware of the kind of ideal personality types for BPO work that fell under the purview of this test. They were therefore capable of manipulating their answers accordingly. Many BPOs administered these tests in order to ostensibly identify workers or worker 'types' that could handle high stress, flexible and long work hours, and nightly schedules. Typically, this test was a multiple-choice questionnaire asking interviewees to answer a large number of questions spontaneously within the span of thirty minutes.

Questions were often repeated or phrased differently in order to ensure consistent results. It was not difficult to imagine what one would ideally do in any given situation in order to be considered an appropriate BPO employee. For example, it was desirable to display leadership skills, show that one could be calm under stress, and display enthusiasm for work. It was not desirable to refuse positions of responsibility or display introversion in general life situations. Once workers passed these tests they would be asked to wait or come back another day in the coming week for their voice profiling interviews.

Passing the young men and women, I sneaked into the training department hoping for some respite before my next training session, only to be told that I would be conducting voice profiling sessions. These interviews were ten-minute conversations conducted by voice and accent trainers who then classified workers into categories titled A, B, and C in order of perceived language capability. Workers in the C category were assigned additional training sessions. Workers who did not fit into any of these categories were flagged, and could not continue working at the call centre. Voice profiling exercises were often conducted even while the workers were undergoing training. A quasi-scientific form of filtering the willing hordes, the process entailed that trainers train their hearing to listen for 'mistakes' such as individual syllables inflected differently, and then wait for the pattern to repeat itself. They were guided by a sheet, listing parameters such as clarity of speech, analytical ability, and sentence structure, and provided five-hour training sessions by a senior trainer to make clear the form of assessment. These last were called calibration sessions.

Each trainer conducted an average of two profiling sessions a week and each session lasted for about two hours. During this time they interviewed between twenty to forty current and potential workers. From my notes during this period, I notice in myself an intense fatigue. Profiling was far more demanding than conducting training sessions. Young men and women filed into the rooms one by one, nervousness writ large on their faces, limbs and voices shaky, willing themselves to perch on the edge of the seat. Haltingly, sometimes confidently, they attempted to condense their worthiness and their life history into a few short sentences. My typical opening question would be, 'Tell me something about yourself'. Often the answer followed the format, 'Myself abc, I have completed my schooling from xyz, my hobbies are reading, netsurfing, and listening to music'. I would then coax the unwilling ones into some form of conversation so their speech patterns could be 'uncovered', and attempt to curb the more garrulous ones so that I could move on to the next interviewee. After eight to ten interviews, the voices would all begin to resemble one another and it became easier to uncritically characterize them as an A, B, or a C. Flagging took a little more effort because trainers knew that additional candidates would have to be interviewed in lieu of flagged candidates in order to ensure that the required number of workers were inducted into the organization.

Herein lay the central paradox of recruitment processes in the call centre. Since management and the human resource department require that the number of open positions be filled as soon as possible, the paucity of skilled labour led to a large number of workers making it through the filters even when their performance levels did not match organizational requirements. Trainers were constantly at war with human resource personnel, each negotiating to ensure their disparate priorities. In the event that trainers succumbed to pressure, they would have to bear the additional burden of training candidates with linguistic inability to conduct work. With such workers, clients would often come back demanding crisis management, because of complaints from end-users/customers in the US or UK about the quality of service.

However, this seemingly counterintuitive process worked in the short term because the workers could be retrained while holding down their positions. The organization could therefore show and bill for the requisite number of workers on its roster. Also, the management hedged its bets, hoping that clients would not complain until later in the work cycle, during which time, the quality of work could be addressed through repeated training modules. Agents thus told me during one such training session, as to how they had undergone at least four language, voice, and accent modules with different trainers and had yet continued to be at the receiving end of management and client complaints. They were, as a result, suitably nervous about the possibility of losing their jobs. Training had thus become an end in itself, a process repeated sufficient number of times to register marginal change that could then be converted into statistics to prove to the clients that their complaints were being addressed.

Calibration sessions or training modules, meant to ensure the consistency of standards by which trainers evaluated and recruited applicants, might shed some light on the ways in which the corporation attempted to mitigate this paradox. Trainers graded job applicants on the basis of a five to ten minute conversation during the course of which the latter were asked to talk about themselves. In an effort to ensure the uniformity of quality for applicants who made it through this interview, the training department attempted to standardize evaluation by way of organizing training sessions for trainers. These calibration sessions involved six to eight trainers evaluating a set of ten applicants over a telephonic interview.

Trainers gathered in a room and clustered around a telephone on loudspeaker mode. Applicants would be directed to another room in the call centre office and asked to speak on the phone with this panel of trainers. Ten applicants would be interviewed per session, and each session lasted for about two hours. All trainers were

required to grade the voice on the phone for clarity, tone, sentence
structure and so on, based on a carefully worded grade guideline
sheet that gave operational definitions of errors or problems. For
example, errors in case of sentence structure included instances
of subject verb disagreement ('they plays' instead of 'they play'),
incorrect prepositions (he is 'in the phone' as opposed to 'on the
phone'), and literal translation from the mother tongue ('Your voice
coming going' as translated from '*Aapki aawaz aati jaati rehti hai*'
or 'I have two-two offers for you' from '*Aapke liye do-do offer hain*').

The lowest score in this case could, however, only be marked
in the face of three related errors. So the interviewee would have
to make three errors of the same kind in order to be graded low.
While the form of interviewing seemed to ostensibly emphasize a
high quality standard in evaluating workers, the benefit of doubt
however, was largely theirs. Often interviewees would be asked
to pronounce certain words over and over again so trainers might
understand if the errors were a normal occurrence (and hence could
not be trained) or temporary mistakes that could be corrected. Final
scores would be tallied and interviewees classified into A, B, C, and
flagged categories. The last were then considered 'non-hirable'. A
large number of interviewees would often be classified as C candidates, who were then signed up for pre-training sessions called
'bridge training', and re-tested before being considered for regular
employment. Vendor organizations contracted specifically for language and communication boot camps provided such preliminary
training. Trainers employed with these organizations were generally
former call centre workers acquainted with the interviewing and
calibration processes. They would teach applicants to repeat certain
sentences and provide answers by rote, thereby allowing for the
system's appetite to be quenched while ensuring that the necessary
head count could pass through.

* * *

Literatures, popular media, and business reports over 2006–8
focused on a rapidly dwindling cache of call centre workers, and
falling standards of service and labour output. They also reported

resultant efforts by the industry to professionalize recruitment and control the quality of incoming labour. However, given the highly competitive milieu of labour recruitment as well as the relatively low levels of centralization in these processes, I contend that the chronic restructuring of recruitment systems should be read as symptoms of the paradoxes inherent to the creation of this labour force. I argue for the systematization of this mode of production to be seen and analyzed as a form of government or even as a regime of practices. While there was an internal consistency to the way these practices were ordered (systematic, defining goals and ends, seeking specific kind of workers), the cracks began to show through in the ways that these practices were unable to engage with the changes that they had themselves brought about.

Through publicity, recruitment, and advertisement, call centre corporations set into motion a range of governing practices that transformed the labour milieu within which the call centre industry sought to function. This mode of government, however, failed to mimic the flexibility of the subjects it recruited and shaped. As the industry consolidated and corporate governmentality sought to direct and control the quality of labour, the accelerated pace of the outsourcing economy itself interrupted such possibility of control. The forms of control—the text, the language, and the discourse—could not contend with the paucity of bodies, and indeed, their very flexibility.

Following Foucault, Hacking argues that the classification of individuals is at the heart of modern, and bureaucratically rational strategies of government and control (Hacking 1990). The call centre industry might seem to embody such modes of classification. However, its very inability to control the registers of flexibility rendered suspect its parameters and definitions for an ideal call centre worker. As a result, these definitions themselves had to undergo change. Large numbers of middle-, and lower-middle-class populations were able to access work opportunities in the call centre via the more ambiguous definitions afforded by such flexibility. Avenues for joining a call centre grew across the city, bringing in populations from nearby towns. As opportunities increased, a teeming Indian urban and semi-urban population began to be commandeered into service work.

In this chapter, I have shown how in the period between 2002 and 2008, the call centre industry created and produced a new set of workers. In attempting to validate the industry among potential workers and their extended networks, call centre management defined its work as a white-collar profession, and additionally re-negotiated and made legitimate, the act of paid white-collar work for a young middle-class population. Through exercises that initially positioned the industry as a quick moneymaking proposition, and later as one imparting professionalism and the possibility of a future white-collar career, the call centre industry recruited a hitherto unemployed class of workers. However, the changing and accelerated pace of recruitment was symptomatic of the fragile assumptions of the Indian outsourcing industry. The pace of recruitment had to become increasingly flexible in relation to workers' movements as well as to global capital fluctuations.

In this scenario, the processes of recruitment serve to remind us that flexibility as an enterprise can be both an enabler for regimes of late capital as well as an opportunity for new possibilities and openings for the labour populations it creates and fosters, in ways that capitalism cannot anticipate or fully control. While discourse around new forms of service work emphasized the need for a flexible workforce, recruitment was running up against repeated crises on account of that very flexibility. Celebratory discourse around the call centre industry was challenged through constant crises, wherein clients demanded the kind of workers that the industry had initially recruited—middle-class, English-speaking, and cosmopolitan. However, the industry could neither find such resources nor live up to claims of training potential candidates to work according to such ideal standards. Clients at the same time were loathe to withdraw investments and preferred to deal piecemeal with the issue of unsuitable labour populations. Changing recruitment practices, I argue, were the inadequate yet necessary part of such a flexible and unstable equation.

There are two sets of conclusions I attempt to draw from these processes that sought to recruit young men and women into the call centre industry. One concerns the nature of corporate governmentality, and the other concerns the role of speed and its relationship to the lived worlds of flexible capital. Firstly, I consider recruitment processes in their specific relation to the working of the call centre. However, I see these as not just logical outcomes of the mechanics of demand and supply, but as the very flesh and bones of the logic of flexible transnational capital. In setting into motion relentless hiring practices, the transnational call centre rendered visible its relation to Indian national and urban space. State and corporations together conspired to recast citizen subjects as worker subjects, resulting in the alignment of global and national visions of flexibility in the service of future prosperity.

Secondly, I am concerned with how speed works in the milieu. Reading recruitment in its will to grab every trespasser, I argue that speed in this instance is not a measure of success as much as it is an indicator of the ways in which the BPO industry ushered in a regime of flexible work practices. While constituted by the possibilities of such a labour force, call centres nevertheless did not anticipate the ways in which the flexibility of the outsourcing economy would lead to hyper-competition on one hand, while the flexibility that it had instituted in its labour force would render the very availability of such labour fragile on the other. Just like in Karen Ho's study of investment bankers in Wall Street, the call centre industry fell prey to its own voluminous spread (Ho 2009). In the same story, call centres were thus, simultaneously powerful and vulnerable. Nigel Thrift has argued that what is common across corporations now, is that they are in a permanent state of emergency (Thrift 2000). In the context of the call centre industry, I argue that such a state of emergency was merely the corollary to an increasing call for 'flexibility'. The ability to be flexible, even on the part of the corporation, was a process fraught with unexpected possibility, leading to a widening gap between the corporation's definitions of ideal workers and its actual labouring subjects. In reading this emergency as it played out in the recruitment processes of call centres, I argue that flexibility can be best understood in its relationship to both crisis, and crisis management. I argue for these continuous processes as dialectic, led by the vision of a future, only capable of being secured by the will to be ever flexible.

# 3

## NOCTURNE

*The alarm goes off. For the third time. And it's still difficult to wake up.*

—Anil, call centre agent
Shift timing: 4:00 a.m. to 3:30 p.m.

*Landlords are constantly creating halla [noise] saying why do you work so late? As if they didn't know first.*

—Reena, process trainer
Shift timing: 1:00 a.m. to 10:30 a.m.

### Nightly Labour

There is a state of physicality that has to be learned in the process of working in a call centre. Such learning involves the practice of instantly disinterring the awake self from the asleep self, no matter the time of evening or night, and conversely coaxing the body into sleep irrespective of the break of dawn or day. For four months, I inhabited such a form of 'unsleep'. Unsure of span, uncertain of calm, now awake and now comatose, I meandered between states of extreme alertness in the nights, staying awake through coffee, exercise and work, and wakeful sleep in the day, combating light, noise and the day-dwellers with heavy curtains and the blinkers I had stowed away from airplanes and hotel rooms. For four months, I was called upon to be awake on demand, changing my sleep schedules week after week. For four months, I dreamt of sleep.

It might be argued that I was one of the inflexible ones, unable to realize that staying awake in the night is merely a 'mind-game', as Preeti put it. 'Just train your body to work differently', she said, 'because after all, don't farmers wake up before sunrise? And so many people work night shifts anyway—in the factory, truck drivers, doctors'. Preeti was 21 during the time of this interview and had moved to the city from Mumbai in order to be away from family. Her examples were relevant and her attitude exemplary. Preeti had truly learnt how to be a good call centre worker. But just like the other night shift workers she referenced, Preeti's call centre job came with its attendant costs. Her ability to be a good worker was won not only by fighting against the body, but also against parental norms, societal judgement, and daily life. Six months after this conversation, Preeti quit her job at the call centre due to acute health issues that mandated a six-month leave from work. She narrated this 'problem' of health as having necessitated her taking time off on her doctor's orders, and wondered aloud as to how it would affect her prospects for upward mobility should she return to the company after her sabbatical.

Call centres in India ran processes and shifts on a schedule suitable to American and British workdays. While back-office and data-entry work could function in the day as much as the night, most international voice-based work necessarily ran through the night. Hence, for call centre agents in Pune, willingness to work the night shift was the ubiquitous condition of employment. While latitude was possible in terms of when the shift began (earlier in the evening as opposed to the beginning of the night), or ended (mid-morning or late in the night), workers had to be prepared to work through 'graveyard' shifts that ran from 9 or 10 p.m. until early in the morning. The night shift was nine and a half hours long. In most call centres, this shift included two fifteen-minute breaks and an hour-long recess for a mid-shift meal. Additionally, workers had to factor in the time it took to get to the call centre, travelling in the night for at least one half of their commute. Workers' shifts tended to rotate on a monthly basis and many of my informants had moved between various combinations of evening, night, and morning schedules over the course of a call centre career. Shift timings became something eagerly anticipated and planned for, as much as dreaded and worried about. For voice and accent trainers, as well as middle management, shifts often changed every week. Workers' relationship to daily life was therefore dependent upon their management of nightly life.

Call centre work bore a constitutive, intimate, and tortured relationship to the night. Both banal and transgressive, the night sustained and fuelled the possibility of outsourced customer-service work, while simultaneously corroding its performers' bodies and rendering them suspect and degenerate. This chapter attempts to unpack the concerns and affective states of nightly work in the transnational Indian call centre. Popular media and scholarly work have examined this issue in terms of transgression, the colonization of time, the machinations of transnationality, and the politics of sleep (Aneesh 2006; Babu 2004; Mirchandani 2004; Poster 2007a). Borrowing from and building upon these literatures, I focus on the question of the night as both the axis of experience and the object of discourse, surveying nightly call centre work through the plea-sures, dangers, and anxieties of inhabiting the night. I am interested in the positions that workers navigated, negotiated, and owned when working at night. In other words, I ask: How and why did the worker go to work at night?

Underlying both the physical and affective qualities of transna-tional service work, the night was what indexed the time and space of the call centre. It allowed the call centre to sustain its business model, and it is was in the night that Indian workers became trans-national. The bridge that cut across the distance between India and the West only magically came into view, by turning inside out the relationship between night and day. When I was a child of six, and asked to describe the country that my father was away working in, I would say, 'When it's day for us, it's night for them; when it's day for them, it's night for us'. Like a magic chant that can make things visible, I could grasp US through a clearly demarcated inversion and opposition. This was in the early 1980s. In the twenty-first century, the inversions still apply, but the oppositions are expected to break down. David Harvey (1990b) argues for such time-compression as the driving force of late modernity, and suggests that the hallmark of forms of subjectivity that take shape in the wake of new forms of organizing production is the ability to go along with this world-view. Distances are smaller and communication channels faster—time differences are claimed to be incidental (Friedman 2007). I argue that this ability to be incidental was hard to maintain, and acutely felt by the workers most subject to its inversions. While these inversions have become the condition of transnational work, the efforts of workers towards inhabiting this inverted order are, I argue, key to understanding the discourse of globalization.

In the process of examining such inhabitance, I am however, not concerned with agency, or lack thereof. The question of whether nightly work allowed for mobility in relation to life as lived in a different space-time, and consequently agency (Patel 2010) is no doubt important. But in this project, I unpack the act of waking up and going to work when it is dark, by simultaneously foregrounding societal transformation, urban culture, individual experiences, and the transnational corporation. All of these, I argue, exert an influence at the same time. The flexibility of nightly labour, therefore I argue, emerges not in terms of individual effort, agency, heroism, or victimization on the one hand, and societal pressure and globalization on the other, but as a mode of collective enunciation that upheld call centre work. This enunciation is also part of the complex that I term 'flexibility'. The collective was, however, composed of individuals that inhabited this work of flexibility differentially; through age, class, gender, and other social positions. This chapter will also show how such difference bears a relationship to the amount and kinds of work that were performed in order to become ideally flexible.

I argue that night work in the call centre and the landscapes fostered by this nocturnal time schedule formed a 'secret public' in the context of urban India. Michael Taussig's 'public secret' (1999) posits the nature of something which is generally known but cannot be spoken about. In performing a theoretical inversion, I speculate upon the ways in which normality is achieved by glossing over something, and by making public a description rather than an experience. In other words, I look at the implications of grasping a phenomenon as merely a set of surfaces. The fact of working in the night both in the context of the call centre and in case of other blue-collar work was not a secret. It was widely spoken about, commented upon, and discussed by both workers and bystanders. However, in the case of the call centre, those who performed this work expended considerable effort normalizing their lives and routines in spite of having to work at night. Both verbally and in actionable terms, they performed labour in order to ostensibly render normal that which others called abnormal. My intervention then asks about the costs of such normality, and argues that what was considered public knowledge was in fact a secret, purposefully erased by those who inhabited this landscape, and discursively flattened and therefore disregarded by those that did not. The perpetuation of call centre work depended on the stability of this equation, this 'secret public'. Yet, social inequality and acts of violence ruptured and broke down the possibility of its maintenance. Here I turn to Taussig's 'public secret' and ask if acts of violence that erupted sporadically and threatened to upset the careful routines of night-time work can be read as a form of 'defacement' (Taussig 1999). I argue that such a formulation can help draw crucial connections between the violence carried out on the bodies of call centre workers, even as they were exposed to the dangers of the night, and larger rents in an unequal urban Indian social fabric transformed in no small part by globally oriented white-collar promises, such as those offered by call centre work.

In the first half of this chapter, I look specifically at the ways in which the night figured in the imagination and experiences of workers. Simultaneously pleasurable, painful, stressful, dangerous, and necessary in the context of the call centre, the night demanded a reconfiguration of wakefulness. It also brought to the experience of being awake a different repertoire of sensual stimuli. The time and the space of the night became an introduction to the city, as both an exciting and dangerous realm, one inhabited by multiple denizens of the night: criminals and customers, fugitives and corpses, murderers and policemen, revellers and insomniacs, dogs and rats, and small stores lit by paraffin and kerosene lamps.

Throughout this section, I illustrate the tactile and sensual experience of working in inverted time. While accounts privilege the night as either deterrent or obstacle, requiring bodily and cultural adjustment, I look at the night in its various experiential and affective facets. Service work and transnational corporations demanded a transcendence of barriers between night and day. In order for this demand to be met, these entities sought to transform, erase and/or reify the very experience of the night. The night thus stood central to the endeavour of the Indian transnational customer service industry. Concurrently, I argue, this experience gathered workers into a community of note—a set of people with a different relationality to space and time. I build on this argument to examine the meanings of work in this context. What did work then become? How did it take over daily/nightly life? I also ask if the experience of life itself became reconfigured in its wake. Further, I look at the ways in which workers explained away the act of toiling through the night, and sought to make it incidental. In these explanations, I locate the work of transnationality.

In the second half of the chapter, I detail the pragmatics of nocturnal work and the political mechanisms that were deployed in order to bring the call centre's nightly workforce into being. While night shifts were not new for many manufacturing industries in India, they were a relatively unfamiliar phenomenon in the context of white-collar service work. I look at amendments in Indian labour laws in this context and examine the class and gender dynamics at play in such legislation. Central to this discussion is an examination of how, in this instance, responsibility for space and time came to be divided between the state and the corporation (Brenner 2004). I look at call centre night work as signifying the complex relationship between the Indian State and the corporation.

In this analysis, gender emerges as an important sleight-of-hand for both the socio-political milieu of the call centre as well as the management personnel. On the one hand, such work was posed as a liberating opportunity for women, one where gender did not figure in the question of employment or upward mobility. To illustrate this, the industry often boasted of its ability to accommodate a large percentage of women workers. However, periodic episodes of violent crime played out on the bodies of women call centre workers presented an obvious refutation to such claims. In this chapter, I am interested in reading the bodies of female workers in a way that does not merely tell us the almost clichéd truth about Indian public space and its misogyny, or even about the traditional division of labour between the sexes—the transgression of which provokes violence. Here, I propose understanding the body of the female worker in relation to the classed and gendered politics of urban middle-class India, the space of the city, and the discourse of the state.

The popular understanding of the call centre was as a portal that invoked and provoked the sexual urges of workers and passers-by alike. The women and men who worked there became blasé and promiscuous, and young girls and vulnerable women were subject to rape, molestation, and damage to their reputations. However, such accounts distributed the responsibility for regulation unevenly and in a classed and gendered manner across constituent populations. Looking at a case of sexual crime and homicide in relation to a Pune-based call centre, I examine media accounts in tandem with my own experiences of regulatory mechanisms in the call centre.

## Life in the Graveyard Shift

Imagine 5,000 voices in a single office campus, arguing, talking, and bantering with voices from the other side of the ocean. Imagine the buzz. No wonder they called the night as the time of 'real action'. Customer service agents and managers both displayed a similar understanding about the night shift. The terms that were used to describe the experience of working in the night were often about pace, noise, chaos, people, fun, and excitement. The call centre always came alive with activity in the night. While seeking to be as orderly and mediated as day work, the night promised more excitement. The organization was inhabited with more people, the decibel levels rose, and one could be forgiven for thinking this to be a brightly lit college campus, awash with the excitement of young adrenalin.

Managers, while complaining about the toll that the graveyard shift took on them, nevertheless stated a preference for working in the night. They could be part of the action and oversee bodies and voices, thus ensuring their own professional growth in an industry where night work was *de rigueur*. Trainers preferred working in the night because there were no bosses supervising them and there were far more people at work to chivvy around. The night added to the challenge of the training process since it often involved not only coaching young workers but also being performative, loud, and maniacally energetic in order to cajole this workforce out of sleep and into productivity. Agents, and simultaneously the consumers and producers of the call centre and its practices, found themselves oriented towards the space and time of the call centre in curiosity, wonder, and transgressive action.

The graveyard shift, which mainly catered to US-based processes on account of the twelve-hour time difference tended to run through most of the night. But night shifts serving the UK and other geographies functioned anywhere from between 8 and 1 in the night to 5:30 and 10:30 in the morning. Workers were ferried from their homes to the call centre in cabs contracted by the company. Call centres suffered a dubious reputation in the early days of the industry and hence, in order to ensure safety of all, and especially women workers, companies had to bear responsibility for their commute. Legislation allowed for the participation of women workers in nightly call centre work only under these conditions.

Danger came from the night and the nightscape. The roads were empty, policing sparse, and the landscape barren. Since many call centres were located at the periphery of the city in state-subsidized IT parks, access to them was fraught with the kinds of danger not associated with a far more stringently governed central urban space. Corporations attempting to escape the high real-estate prices within the city were simultaneously also considered responsible for supplementing the attenuated reach of the state in terms of both public transport and regulation (Miyoshi 1993; Sassen 1996).

As a call centre worker, I found myself most cognizant of the night when traversing this landscape on my way to the company precincts. Every night I would wake up groggy at around 11 p.m. My alarm would have gone off a few dozen times already. Every night, I would receive a call from the cab driver—or rather, a cab driver. The call centre's transportation system was configured thus that a different cab would be on call for every employee. Cab drivers were entrusted with workers' addresses and phone numbers two or three hours before workers were due to be collected. Drivers would then call and ask for detailed directions.

In Pune, many streets were unmarked, apartment names unclear, and roads unlit. It was common practice to make your way in the day not through an online search for addresses or maps, or by following clear road-signs, but by asking passers-by and vendors at street corners for directions. This unique form of navigation was unavailable in the night, therefore placing the onus on employees to repeat directions night after night. So every night, I would repeat the familiar conversation, detailing my address and negotiating to be picked up last, after the three other workers on my cab route had been scooped up from their respective dreams. 'Take a left from Hotel Sarjaa, come all the way down the street and stop at the bank sign', I would reel off by rote in Marathi.

Grabbing a few more precious minutes of sleep, I would pull myself up, stumble to the light switch and will naked, harsh, fluorescent night-light and wakefulness into my sleep-deprived body. Making my way to the stove, I would put on a pot of coffee and call a friend hoping that he might get to work at the same time and we could catch up, over his smokes and my second coffee, on the terrace of the office building where we both worked. I would then pick up my bag, lock the balcony gate, check the cooking gas knob, switch off the water heater, manage the general state of cleanliness of the apartment, grab my water bottle, and leave. The bottle was essential as nightly work and the air-conditioned offices demanded constant hydration. Many young workers were cavalier about it, leading to throat trouble and fatigue. The corridor of my apartment building would be dark, and I would stumble down the stairs. I would tiptoe past the snoring watchman and open the rusty gates as quietly as possible, praying hard that the neighbours would not notice the sound. It had been hard enough to find landlords that would rent an apartment to a single woman, and the last thing I needed was for neighbours to complain about noises in the middle of the night. Standing at the corner of an eerily quiet road, I would fend off barking dogs and wait for the white

Tata Indica cab's headlights to direct the driver to the end of the street. The other occupants would often be asleep. The driver, if new to the route, would sometimes ask me the best possible way to get to the company premises.

Cab drivers would invariably speed, taking advantage of the empty roads and sparse traffic. The drivers were paid according to the number of trips they made to and from the call centre. They sped because the sooner they dropped one set of employees, the sooner they could be available to pick up the next. Every other day, one would read newspaper reports of speeding call centre cabs injuring their occupants, or people on the road. In the night, it was more likely to be the former just because there were hardly any pedestrians. Drivers were mainly from lower-class backgrounds; a number of them who I chatted with were not from Pune, and had moved to the city to gain a better quality of life for their families and themselves. Many were also drivers with private transport companies and held down two jobs. They found call centre work tedious, but had discovered that the call centre business was booming and that these jobs seemed to be the easiest to find.

The time-space compression of globalization seemed to permeate every level of transnational call centre work, including the cab ride. The hyper speed of work demanded efficiency, presence and constant manpower, and was served by building tireless, incessant corridors of communication between work and home. Like call centre workers who took phone calls, cab drivers too were subject to the time discipline of this industry and its attendant burden of monotony. Boredom played out at every level of work, and the call centre and its corollary veins became microcosms of the routinization of labour processes. Speed was one of the few ways to shrug off the tedium of the endless dark road. Drivers spoke of placing bets with other drivers on the time their trips would take, and of racing one another on dark, desolate roads. Such empty roads and the consequent licence to speed could hardly ever be experienced in the daytime, given Pune's high vehicular population, narrow roads, and the increasing influx of migrants in search of white-collar work in the IT and call centre industries. The night facilitated speed. But speed is of course the other side of danger. When interrupted,

it can only end badly. A page from my field-notes during this
time reads:

> The roads are empty. We travel through side roads before getting to the
> Mumbai-Pune highway. The driver accelerates and we are zooming at
> 80 kilometers an hour. I am worried that we will run over the dogs and
> ask him to slow down. He responds saying that if he drives at the speeds
> I want, we will probably only get to work the next day. I sit back. He
> assures me with a motivational speech, saying I should hold tight and
> tell myself it will be alright. The girl next to me giggles.
>
> I watch the landscape whoosh past; construction sites, hovels, huts,
> a building called Wakad Poshville, another called Montvert Finesse;
> Bellagio looms up ahead. Dogs run amok over Pune's Las Vegas. One
> could be forgiven for thinking that all this unmooring is distinctly
> postmodern. Poshville looks distinctly un-posh. We meander in and
> out, the night brightened by headlights and street lights and often,
> just dark.
>
> I remember nights in Pune in the mid nineties, when my friends
> and I would often ride motorbikes on lonely roads, switching off the
> headlights to be guided by moonlight. The moon is hidden tonight, the
> streetlights intermittent. Radio Mirchi plays loudly. The city looks alien.
> The streets are empty, the dogs come forth from subterranean tar, chas-
> ing us, the intruders of the night, away into someplace else. The radio
> continues to play. Sharad asks the driver to stop so he can pick up a
> cigarette. A faint glow alerts us to the stall approaching to the right,
> just before the flyover that will lead us into cybercity, electronica and
> otherworldliness. Sharad buys a pack, lights one, slides into the seat next
> to mine and rolls down the window to let the smoke out. It swirls into
> the night as I attempt to drink in the suddenly revealed landscape. The
> office looms ahead and is awash in fluorescent light. The lights are harsh
> and I am now awake.
>
> We speed ahead and pull up to the office, all intact. It is the middle of
> the night. I swipe my identity card and walk into the training area. The
> lights are on, and the work area is tranquil. On the floors above, agents
> are on call. If I were to walk up, I would hear them all. In the training
> office, there are no people. I start as I hear sounds. Somebody is snoring
> in cadences of sudden shrill peaks and falls. I tiptoe to the back of the
> room to find Rahul Verma, mouth open and almost falling off the chair.
> His next training session begins at the same time as mine and I try to jog
> him awake. He cusses and goes right back to sleep.

As much as the night was a strong, unifying, and definitive landscape to the notion of call centre work, there were mainly two periods during which it was inhabited—while travelling to work and back. The state and the corporation's form of tackling the dangers of the night was to reduce the possibility of the worker being outside both the space of home, and the space of work. Call centres were allowed to employ women workers only under the condition that they be ferried in company vehicles to and from the company. This was legalized by way of individual state government's amendments to the Factories Act that had otherwise prohibited women's participation in night work.[1]

One could argue that there was a conscious attempt to induce a kind of night-blindness among workers in order that these middle-class productive bodies could both be protected from the uncertainties of the night, as well as put to use despite its demands. Once inside the premises, the night was pushed back with bright lights, caffeine, and constant work, almost as if not only did the night not exist, but also it could not be tracked or felt. One was reminded of casino atmospheres, where the success of the enterprise depends on the player losing track of time. Workers did find ways to leave the premises and inhabit the nightly city, but it was precisely as a space of danger and transgression, forbidden by both the corporation and the state, that they found it most appealing. In this way, although call centre work was characterized and spoken about on account of its nightly nature, the corporation itself reified the idea of the night as not 'normal', but a landscape to be overcome through avoidance.

### Working in the Night

Once within the company premises, one might think it is just another workday. The building would be brightly lit and people would be in and out at all times of night. Reminiscent of Baudrillard's 'aseptic whiteness' (1993), workers seemed to be forever exposed

---

[1] See Aneesh (2006: 97–9) for a discussion on the various legislations that were amended in order to allow women's participation in night work. Also see Patel (2010).

to light through technology and its glare. Trainers moved in and out of classes, cabs expelled their sleepy contents, and agents milled around the tiny cafe counter before leaving for their work and training sessions. While agents monitored calls, team leaders supervised performance, and trainers led yet another batch of new workers through voice, accent, and work process lessons. New workers, especially those assigned to US processes were trained on night shifts in order to acclimate them to working in the night. When I asked Hari, a call centre veteran of over five years, about the problems of nocturnal work, he exasperatedly said, 'What's the big deal? After all, the game must go on'. I interrupt such a 'game' to emphasize the philosophy of the multinational corporation, and in turn globalization—a game that continues day and night with no regard for 'normal' human schedules. The organization overcame time by traversing space, and Hari was part of this effort.

Rahul Verma, a voice and accent trainer, would incessantly complain about the night shift, while simultaneously admitting that only the night shift promised excitement and action. The night was the time when Rahul, a consummate gossip, could find the most material for his stories and sagas, all of which would then circulate through the training department the following day. Rahul also found excitement in training agents during the night. New trainees tended to be lethargic and often used the training sessions as ways of catching up on sleep. Trainers therefore needed to be on their toes for eight hours, not only teaching, but also entertaining. While tiring, it nevertheless was a challenging job.

Agents also enjoyed inhabiting the nightscape, seeking out 24-hour dives and roadside restaurants alongside the adjacent national highway. Even though cab drivers had been given instructions to ferry workers straight home and not halt along the way, young workers found ways to inhabit and prolong the experience of the night. Alcohol and drugs were frequent indulgences before and after work, as were house parties and rave sessions. While over-emphasized in popular accounts, they were nevertheless common modes of leisure around the call centre. While the brightly lit corporation, and its rules and regulations seemed to be institutional attempts towards keeping darkness and sleep at bay, the night was but a picture window and a light switch away. Beyond the pale, lay people and things that came out at night.

## Tales of Night Work

Nightly work has long been the lot of the disempowered, the marginalized, and those without voice and visibility. It is a gendered bastion, one populated by those for whom the night-time is not a 'fleeting but regular period of modest but cherished freedoms from the constraints and cares of daily life' (Palmer 2000: 19). However, it is difficult to speak of call centre workers in the same breath as factory labour, janitors, night watchmen, and prostitutes. While they share a common condition of the night shift, the salaries that call centres offered and the kind of white-collar status that workers enjoyed, rendered them differently positioned. Ostensibly, such white-collar status begs the question of choice. Why did call centre workers seek to work at night? In order to explain the ways in which the process of night work was desired, sought, tolerated, or performed by workers, I turn to four different case studies of men and women at various stages of their call centre careers.

### Ashwin

'But why?', I asked Ashwin, 'Why are you ruining your health like this?' Eyes bloodshot, clothes rumpled, and hair dusty and unwashed, Ashwin had been lolling on my daybed, rolling a joint. '*Mazaa aata hai* [It's fun],'[2] he said, 'It's great.' 'I get on my bike, the roads are all empty, I go to work and I can stay as long as I want.' '*Koi poochnewala naheen* [Nobody can nag me].' Ashwin was a few months short of his twenty-first birthday and was often the subject of playful ribbing by his friends for not being able to walk into a pub and buy alcohol. However, he had all the other trappings of adulthood. He earned between INR 15,000 and INR 25,000

---

[2] While *mazaa* translates easily as fun, it also functions as shorthand for various kinds of feelings. It can mean excitement, taste, flavour, enjoyment, libidinal high, hand-rubbing glee, and wilful pleasure.

a month and had once taken home INR 57,000 for working five consecutive days straight without a break, he claimed. At the time of our conversation, he was juggling two different relationships and would keep glancing at his cell phone to screen calls. 'Girlfriend *se kab milta hai phir* ? [When do you meet your girlfriend?]', I asked. '*Ek tho office mein hi hai* [One of them is in the office itself]', he mischievously replied, '*Aur doosri Dilli mein* [And the other in Delhi]; *sab setting hai* [It's all set]'. I shook my head and smiled.

I persisted in my line of questioning and asked him why he liked working at night.

> *Yaar fark naheen padta* [It doesn't matter]. It's all work. My father used to be in the army, then he went to Saudi Arabia and then came back to start a travel agency. I used to go to my dad's office everyday and eat and come back. Then one day, one of his friends told him when they were having a few drinks as to why don't you make your son work? So he forcibly took me to a call centre interview saying that you'll know what life is.
>
> I got selected, but initially I hated work. I used to run away and my TL would come home and then pick me up to take me to work. My dad used to drop me to office, I'd cry. Then my dad told me to stop, but I said no. I started liking the job. First I only knew how to check my email. Then I started liking operating systems and all that. I used to stay there for 18–20 hours taking calls. I was 17; I used to feel good.

To Ashwin, as he grew to like work over time, the night became a mere occupational condition. It did not matter that he was working at night. It was necessary to work in order to know the world. The content of his job and the recognition it accorded him, which was otherwise denied to him by his father, were also instrumental in rendering the workplace attractive. When I asked him how he managed his sleep schedule, he said:

> I used to get drunk and go to office all the time. Every alternate day, I used to get drunk and then go to the office and take calls. I'd go to work, then sleep at my manager's place because it would take me three hours to get home. People at home used to tell me not to work so much for so long. My manager would say, just come and sleep at my place and go back to work. And this was only for seven thousand rupees odd. And when you are working very hard, then the manager sometimes lets

you sleep. On the floor. During work times. I used to sleep for two hours, wake up, have a smoke, take calls, then go to sleep again. One week, I took a hundred and ninety calls. I used to have underwear, t-shirts in my manager's locker. After those five days straight of work, I slept straight for 32 hours.

Ashwin's relationship to the night was managed partly by reducing the amount of sleep he subsisted on, and partly with the help of co-operative managers who ensured that he could get to work on time, or even better, did not have to leave the workspace at all.

Many young workers that I interviewed similarly took pride in being able to manage on very little sleep and stay long hours at work. Conversations around the coffee machine at work often revolved around competition over the number of hours of sleep that one managed to subsist on, thus maintaining the active and awake body of disembodied call centre work at all times of night and day. Male respondents often led me through their routines of sleep and eating, that included cigarettes, Red Bull, and marijuana, specifying that it did take a lot of effort to be able to maintain a call centre lifestyle. However they also peppered their awareness of this effort with a matter-of-factness. Styling themselves as the new 'flexible' citizens of a global age, many respondents shared their macho nonchalance with a shrug of the shoulders and a smirk, indicating their amusement at my obsession with the question of the night.

Such flexibility, however, was not without direction given that it was employed in the service of work. Ashwin narrated how his father would call him every month and mock his salary of INR 24,000 saying it took him merely an hour to make that much money. When I asked Ashwin how he reacted to this, he said, 'I tell him, fine. But I work, I like it. I don't go to an office and sit there and do nothing and make people work'. The night, to Ashwin, was part of the contractual obligation of work. Work, to him, was part of a rite of passage, one initiated by his father and now in turn, played out in defiance and stubbornness. The night merely formed part of this complex of both rebellion and adulthood.

Work was not just the task at hand, but also the ability to last through the shift, to stay beyond the time of duty and to push the limits of physical and mental endurance. To work meant for many to be permanently in a daze, to not know how time progressed or the way the hour chased the one preceding it until it all melted into a long night and a fitfully sleepy day. Days became months, and months became years, and life stayed tightly bound within the movements of the call centre. Sleep disorders would ensue, and the stomach would rebel. But workers were young and believed in being able to endure. The body would not be reason for abandoning work. A litany of maladies might build up like a roster of war wounds. But to work was also to test knowledge of self. To such workers, working was tantamount to both, rebellion and attaining adulthood/manhood.

### Rohan and Arun

For every worker who could endure, fight, and perfect the ability to work through the night, there was another who did not know how to deal with this inversion. While aware of night work as the condition of call centre work, the reality of the experience for many workers did not register until a month or so into the night shift. Rohan was a 23 year old who had moved to the city of Pune from Calcutta in eastern India. He did not know anyone in the city. He had decided to start working in the call centre against his parents' wishes and had found the initial phase of work quite fulfilling. Much like Ashwin, Rohan considered the call centre an exciting space and he supported himself with the money he earned. However, unlike Ashwin, the allure soon wore off for Rohan. He narrated being perturbed by the physically demanding schedule:

> Then I started working on the floor, it was all the shift timings. You get up at around eight in the evening, get to work all zonked up, listen to abuse, and the sun rises, everybody is going to office, you go home, go to sleep, don't get enough sleep, it was all a mess. So, three months, I'd say and that was it. I was not enjoying it. I thought I could do it in all *mauj, masti* [fun and games] if I may say it, and just grow. It doesn't happen that way. It's serious business. It's very serious business. But then I had joined a job against my parents' wishes, I had to continue. One year later, I got a good opportunity with a UK process and I moved.

Frustrated, that he could neither tolerate nightly work nor admit to his parents that it hadn't been a good idea, he attempted a compromise. Rohan changed jobs and moved to a UK shift because it allowed him to work from 1:30 in the afternoon to 10 at night. He was unable to become the consummate flexible subject and instead resorted to a partially tenable option. Many were not able to access this option and ended up leaving the industry a few months into work. Labour turnover was therefore a chronic problem faced by call centres in India. Companies confessed rates of 30 to 40 per cent, while unofficial estimates ranged as high as 70 to 100 per cent. The reality of working through the night only sunk in for new workers once they began full-time work after a relatively lax training period that was meant to be light on the body and schedule. Attrition was calculated to occur most often at this point of transition. Ratna, a Human Resources Manager shared her experiences on the challenges of retaining young workers:

> Eight week attrition, he is done with training, he is done with all types of quality, now he thinks call centre is not his cup of tea because he has to start working night shifts, he leaves. Challenge is US shift, US timings; not everyone is able to adjust with the timing. On an average, we have people of 23–24 years average. For 23 years, he has been sleeping at night and working in the day, now suddenly you ask him to work at nights and sleep in the day.

The US shift or rather the graveyard shift perplexed workers who had otherwise thought it would be a 'piece of cake'. While they imagined that the routine they had followed for twenty odd years of their lives would be easy to manipulate, the limitations of their bodies and daylight society bested any such intent. A number of workers in their first few months at the call centre reported experiences of disorientation and fatigue. Many never overcame this experience. Arun, a 24 year old worker in his second year in the industry, continued to be overwhelmed by the sense of an automated and chronically tiring life:

> Night shifts, you get really zonked. You go and sleep at around eight in the morning, all sunlight. Mentally you get depressed seeing everybody going to work. Then your *bai* [maid] comes at ten and then your

*doodhwala* [milkman] asking for a bill, so you don't get to sleep. Your food patterns go for a toss. Cause you never know when to eat. Then six o'clock, people come home, you go to work. It's a very depressing thing. It's a very monotonous thing; get up go home sleep, get up go home sleep. It's one machine thing, constantly. Then the leaves that you have, you tend to sleep. It's a bad thing, to be very honest, very very bad.

For young call centre workers, working in the night connected to their understanding of transgression, rebellion, and early adulthood. However, this experience was short-lived, and the body and the world outside the call centre proved to be powerful deterrents to night work. At this point, many workers took a break, often returning to the call centre as the only available avenue for work given their minimal educational qualifications. Returning to work disabused of their romantic notions of the call centre and its excitement, they found themselves giving in to the nightly requirement of the job as merely an occupational hazard. As night work became normalized, and call centre work professionalized, it lost it aura, and both attrition and job dissatisfaction came to the fore. Work and its attendant benefits, however, continued to exert a powerful pull.

### Prachi

Prachi was twenty-two when I spoke to her. She had moved to Pune after her marriage. Even before coming to the question of the night, the first thing that she shared with me was her 'love story'. She said, 'Have you seen *Saathiya*? That's my story'. The plot of *Saathiya* [Companion] (Ali 2002), a popular Hindi movie, revolves around a young couple whose families are against the idea of their love. In spite of parental dissent, they get married in secret but continue to live apart from each other with their respective families. Similarly, Prachi and her husband revealed their marriage *post facto*, and left their hometown, a small town in the state of Maharashtra, for Pune in the face of her parents' ire. Prachi's parents were of a higher economic class than her husband's family, she said, which was the reason for their disapproval of the relationship. Prachi severed all relationships with her family after her marriage, and she and her husband moved to Pune to live with her husband's family.

After they moved, her husband faced financial problems, and Prachi began working in order to support the family. Her in-laws were against the idea. In their words, 'The daughter-in-law of the Mhatre family need not have to work'. However, her husband supported her, and she also asserted her desire to 'know the world' by working. She knew nothing about the call centre job except that she would have to take calls. On her first job, which lasted six months, she suffered stomach problems, headaches, and sleep deprivation. In her words, it was 'horrible'. She wondered aloud how she had managed six months in a job where managers treated workers like 'slaves', and where she was paid 'peanuts'.

She quit and moved to another call centre where she had a much better experience. Even though the organization had stringent quality standards, she enjoyed her work and preferred her colleagues at this place. However, after six months, she quit work again and moved to a smaller organization with daytime work hours in order to be able to spend more time with her husband. For the year that she needed money and experience, she tolerated night work. To her, it was an essential part of growing up, and attaining adulthood and maturity. She said that she would weep when working at the call centre, unable to deal with lack of sleep or illness. But her husband would console her, assuring her that this was how she would gain strength to face the world. 'You go tough', she said, 'but I wouldn't advise that anyone work at a BPO for more than six months'.

### Simran and Jaya

For those who stayed longer in the industry, night work had necessarily to be normalized. Simran, a 27 year old woman, whose husband also held a call centre job spoke of the ubiquity of night-shift work:

> It's not like I didn't had an idea of night shifts or something. My Dad used to do it. My husband used to do it. So definitely I knew what a night shift was. So how to change your body cycle, I knew that. You have to actually think that evening, when you wake up, that's your morning. You cannot think that, *naheen che baje* [It's six now], not like that. The kind of body cycle I was able to adjust. Once you wake up, just put it in

your brain that it's morning. Don't look outside. I was able to manage; that was the main concern of my family and my in-laws' family. But I was able to manage it, probably because of will-power or the way I have taken things.

Here, Simran drew upon earlier memories of night shifts in the factory that her father worked at, and normalized work according to her understanding of herself as a modern woman who could also inhabit a man's world. Drawing upon existing pragmatic knowledge, she resorted to mapping the change required of her schedules onto a malleable, governed, and disciplined body and mind. Many of my colleagues shared her view that it was a matter of willing oneself to invert common wisdom and think of the night as day. If one could do away with the orthodox separations of day and night, and think specifically and minimally in terms of things to be done and hours to be slept, one would be alright.

Jaya, a Human Resources Manager, often required to work long hours on the night shift, shared her views on being a working mother in the BPO industry:

> Of course, as I mentioned, it's all about time management and how the person takes it. So what if I have to work night shifts? I have to give the evening time or morning time to my child, so … See, it's about working 9 hours in the whole 24 hrs, so you will have to adjust with your family. I mean, if you are working, it comes by default. You don't have to give separate time or extra time. If I am working at night, I ensure during morning or afternoon I am giving time to my child. As long as I am giving her three to four hours. It is a lot of time management and sacrifice, but it's ok.

Jaya and Simran clearly worked within a very routinized under-standing of flexibility. In other words, all change would be possible only by devising and sticking to a schedule. No male worker, who I spoke to, shared this sense of routine or adjustment. The married men spoke of their troubled wives who were frequently annoyed by their late hours, but hardly ever narrated adjustments or efforts they made to compensate for such ire, except perhaps in gifts or sometimes, by taking time off from work. On the contrary, they seemed to take joy in their dedication to work.

## The Gendered Corporation

Linda McDowell (McDowell and Sharp 1997) and Mary Beth Mills (1999) point to the study of masculinity as essential to understandings gender dynamics in the context of work. As Rosabeth Moss Kanter (1977) notes, the manager is always an authority-laden, masculine figure, and this masculine aspect must necessarily be adopted by women wishing to break through the gender ceiling. Organizational logics make a naturalized connection between responsibility, job complexity, and hierarchical position within the environs of the corporation. Hence child-rearing, emotional responsibilities, and various other commitments outside the workplace are not taken into consideration in the evaluation of employee performance.

The corporate evaluation of performance follows an unproblematic and seemingly neutral meritocracy, where all other conditions being constant, productivity has no gender. What it conveniently glosses over is that all other conditions are not a constant. For example, performance reviews purport an ostensible equality between men and women, requiring that both exhibit equal commitment to the organization. Family, housework, and responsibilities are often considered deterrents to a successful career and this is often ossified in the literature on economic and business logics. As Acker points out, the closest that the disembodied abstract ideal worker comes to, is the male worker 'whose life centres on his full-time, life-long job, while his wife or another woman takes care of his personal needs, and his children' (1990: 149). The disembodiment of the organizational role is thus a double sleight-of-hand, privileging men and erasing the space and work performed outside of the corporation in the same stroke. The individual is successfully abstracted from the body (Pateman 1986).

Across the stories of men and women in call centres, one could identify a tendency towards a kind of implicitly masculine 'objectivity' in the service of a nightly routine. There was a partial will or at the least, an intent to refuse the abnormality of night work. Whether as a masculine rite of passage, an act of carefree rebellion, or a pragmatics of corporate mobility workers attempted to render possible the inversion of night and day. One would think obsessive newspaper coverage of the ill-effects and disturbing experience of working at night in the call centre to have been manufactured by globalization's critics, those who find work to be uniformly exploitative and unfair, unwilling to recognize that one of the ways in which people interpret daily, unimaginative work is by performing what I call the heroics of banality. However, I contend that banality itself is a performance that needs to be analyzed as an effect of globalization and its demands. These demands for banality do not account for the different positions that workers occupy by way of age, class, and gender, and how these differences affect the navigation of nightly work and its cautions. The only thing that they account for, is the constitutive condition of work—being asleep and awake on demand. This management of self and sleep, while presented as achievable, is shot through with differences that are undercut and erased by the discourse of presumed uniformity that workers feel compelled to inhabit.

## How I Became Flexible and Learnt to Love the Night

One of the first questions asked during the course of the call centre job interview was whether the applicant was prepared to work at night. A 22 year old woman, called Shilpa, told me that she had declared her complete willingness to do so, because if she hadn't, the organization would not have considered her application seriously. She had applied for the job without informing her parents, with whom she lived. She said that letting them know would have definitely jeopardized her chances to even apply. Indeed, many workers shared stories of negotiating with their parents, for permission, only after receiving an offer from the corporation, for fear of being refused even the opportunity to apply. Parents' main concerns, workers said, had to do with working in the night and how such schedules might take a toll on health, values, and their educational trajectory.

One of the earliest studies on the biological and social effects of nightly work was commissioned by the International Labour Office (ILO). Titled 'Night Work: Its Effects on the Health and Welfare of the Worker', it defined night work in two ways—either as part of a continuous work schedule such as in process industries, or as exclusive as in the case of night watchmen (Carpentier and Cazamian 1977). It also acknowledged that it was difficult to separate night work's biological effects from its social impact, concluding that, 'Every industrial society generates—and must then settle—a conflict between its functions of production and of the protection of the producer ... between the demands of industrial growth and the quality of individual and social life' (Carpentier and Cazamian 1977: 67). Call centre work paradoxically conformed to both kinds of shift work; while exclusive in that it was mainly performed at night for many customer service processes that ran through the day in the US, it was also the transnational arm of organizations that ran 24-hour processes, indeed facilitating such continuity. I argue that call centres responded to this tension that the ILO report indexes by creating a nightly world that not only defined a workspace but also extended it into a parallel sociality.

While interviewing workers aspiring to a call centre job, managers were categorical about the necessity of functioning in the night. The corporation thus assisted in the work of transnationality by presenting the night as not only safe and hospitable, but also as the necessary condition for upward mobility. The corporation tried to ensure that the night was a self-sufficient and coherent world. Human resource managers and team leaders alike, cautioned workers about the perils of losing sleep and eating badly. Offices ran full-fledged cafeterias with a choice of meal-plans. Cabs ran back and forth picking up employees to ensure that they came to work. The company campus gymnasium remained open through the night and offices were dotted with coffee machines. Additionally, many organizations provided work incentives by way of passes to discotheques, pubs, and events in the city, and easy loans for motorbikes, cars, and apartments.

Besides providing transportation for workers, the corporation also ensured a strong communications network as a corridor to the workspace. Workers' cell phone numbers were an essential part of the information database that the company maintained. All communication between workers, managers, colleagues, cab drivers, and team leaders took place over mobile phones. Not having a phone in this milieu rendered one helpless, disconnected, and insecure. In many cases, call centre workers were not allowed to carry cell phones into work areas for security reasons, or because personal phone calls might distract them from work. However, these rules were only sporadically enforced and varied between organizations and managers. The sense of always being connected was an important aspect to night work. This connection carried into the day, and I rarely interviewed any call centre worker without his or her being interrupted by phone calls from co-workers, bosses or operations personnel.

The sales pitch, the amenities, the rules, and indeed the very understanding of the night as not only constitutive, but also possible, rendered night work at once banal and special. Here I want to suggest that the institutional, emotional, and procedural contents of call centre work rendered the night itself into a kind of 'affective atmosphere' (Anderson 2009) that fed into the sense of a call centre world. The night, nightly travels, and the community of other workers in the call centre together created intensities as a kind of atmosphere that envelopes life, 'intensities that are only imperfectly housed in the names we give to emotions' (Anderson 2009: 77). Ben Anderson argues that the 'atmosphere of an aesthetic object discloses the space-time of an "expressed world"—it does not re-present objective space-time or lived space-time' (Anderson 2009: 80). The night as not only a discursive, but also an aesthetic object and a sensual experience, was then apprehended precisely through such an atmosphere and became an important element of work.

Therefore, this nightly 'secret public' of call centre workers was not only cohered by the fact of work, but also by the aesthetic atmosphere of night. Its travails, routes, darkness, alleys, neon lights, absences, and presences became part of the ways in which the worker was attached to work and the workplace. No matter the banality of work and the sleeplessness of routine, this was nevertheless a community that came alive at night.

One of the main acts that bound workers together was their management of sleep. The skill of not only managing waking times but also surviving on sleeplessness helped move call centre life. In many accounts, sleep became a casualty of work and sleeplessness a mark of valour. 'I slept four hours only' or 'I didn't sleep at all', were casual comments that I heard many times during the course of my interviews. The politics of sleep or lack thereof were a strong structuring force in the call centre milieu. In emphasizing that one could strive to normalize night work, the organization and its workers also sought to re-inscribe sleep as a modular function. By modular, I mean the ability to detach sleep from its deterministic attachment to the darkness of the night and instead, define it as a bodily property that could be trained to be exercised at will. By repurposing both bodies and the time of the night, the call centre made possible its conceit of the continuous work night.

The eight-hour workday, as many scholars inform us, is a product of a relatively recent history of the Industrial Revolution and its labour requirements, and in reversing this, workplaces may be arguably harkening back to a modular notion of time as regularized by pre-industrial forms of vagrancy and work (Palmer 2000; Wolf-Meyer 2012). However, this modularity did not really produce new forms of time-discipline as it did a simple reversal. The eight-hour continuous workday was now the eight-hour continuous work night, necessitating absolute opposition to the time-disciplines of the rest of the urban milieu. The flexibility that the call centre demanded thus fundamentally required workers to maintain an inverted notion of time, one that needed to be ordered around night work, while not acknowledging workers' continued engagement with the world of daylight. In response and due to an inability to function completely out of synchronicity with the day dwellers, many workers functioned with a fatalistic notion of chronic sleeplessness and/or sleep deprivation. Sleep was subsumed by the demands of work and livelihood. 'Show me a person with bags under his eyes and I'll show you a call centre worker', Varun said. He claimed to have been functioning on four hours' sleep per night, during the week that I interviewed him. I asked him how he managed. He said, 'The body goes for a toss. I sometime don't know how I get home from work and I just sleep'.

Through a variety of tactics meant to heighten and prolong the experience of being awake, call centre workers, I argue, accumulated what has been called a 'sleep debt' (Dement and Vaughan 1999: 60) and sought to manage the situation by becoming what Matthew Wolf-Meyer has called 'pharmakological subjects' (Wolf-Meyer 2006), consuming stimulants and alertness enhancers to prolong the waking state. I argue that the call centre perpetuated and encouraged a flexible understanding of sleep (Martin 1994), an understanding that was nevertheless incomplete and difficult, and which showed up in bags under the eyes, sleeplessness, dissatisfaction, and never enough flexibility.

## Amoral Nights and Improper Subjects

Newspaper coverage on call centres tended to follow a few predictable themes. It invoked business volumes, questions of information security, promiscuity, sexual crime and excess, and violence. Trepidation in society around the 'issue' of night work seemed to inundate the call centre milieu. While safety was the prominent rubric around which the night became coloured with anxiety and doubt, there was also the intertwined and often equally looming question of sexuality. An outsourcing consultant I interviewed spoke about the early days of the industry when parents of young workers hesitated to allow their children on night shifts. He shared that as part of the recruitment process, he would hold sessions in the organization so that parents could see for themselves the kind of corporate environment that would ensure their children's safety. However, he himself was determined that none of his family members should ever work as customer service agents.[3] When

---

[3] I remembered thinking of the old joke wherein a man is asked to choose between heaven and hell. When he asks for a sneak preview, he is shown a placid and pastoral heaven with people praying and soothing background music. Hell on the contrary seems to be a place where everyone is having fun, partying, drinking, and listening to loud and raucous music. He chooses hell. Promptly transported there, he then discovers that hell is actually fire, brimstone, and sulphur. Perplexed, he asks the gatekeepers as to what happened to all the parties and is told, 'Well that was our PR department'.

I questioned him further, he said that this was because he had noticed that call centres had become zones of abortion activity. 'With all these young boys and girls working together through the night', the atmosphere around call centres seemed to him to have spiralled into dubious sexual excess. I was struck by these paradoxes and the consultant seemed to be a trickster of neoliberal proportions to me. Yet, the paradoxes articulated in his statements lie at the heart of questions of gender and gendering at Indian call centres.

A 21 year old agent, named Manasi, and I were chatting over coffee right after her training session. Manasi was in her third year of college for an engineering degree. During the time of our conversation, the two weeks of training she had undergone were already taking their toll on her. She had been experiencing chronic back problems and looked ill and wan. Manasi mentioned that she would have to skip her training sessions for the next few days, as she needed to move out of the apartment that she had been sharing with two other girls. When I asked her what had prompted the move, she told me how her landlord, after two weeks of prying and directing snide remarks, had finally given her notice since according to him, she had been keeping irregular hours. I surmised that Manasi was actually living in paying guest accommodations, since the room she mentioned was in the house where the landlord lived. In such accommodations, which are fairly common in Pune, the tenant is more likely to have to conform to the landlord's demands of time discipline since access to the house is restricted and controlled by the owner of the house. The tenant is not a roommate but merely a guest, albeit one who pays.

Numerous agents similarly related being subjected to scrutiny and questioning over their hours, occupation, and friends. I remembered my own experiences of renting my first apartment in Pune, and being told by the landlord that he would not be comfortable with men visiting me in the apartment. Neighbours, who I did not know, would not hesitate to call and demand that I lower the volume of music when I had friends visiting late at night. The city of Pune has a long history of curmudgeonly landlords and landladies. Many considered it a particularly worrisome responsibility to have to deal with young, single women, and consequently the burden

of good behaviour was most often laid on the women, with consequences ranging from expulsion to nightly quarantine if found
wanting in decorum and behaviour.

While young women often found ways to circumvent these
strictures, they were nevertheless the subject of gaze and talk. As
workers in the call centre, young women had to navigate a tenuously
thin line. While discourse had already labelled them suspect, their
living conditions and support structures were greatly affected by,
and were vulnerable to idle talk and speculation. The financial independence that work brought, however, allowed them to broaden
their range of options and thus circumvent the moral standards of a
city whining unto itself. In this instance, the task was by no means
easy and single women had to perform large amounts of work to be
able to bear the burden of multiple discourses.

Many of the women workers that I spoke to, categorically stated,
that they would quit working on the night shift once they were
married. Many of them were planning to do so in the next few years.
Sometimes women workers functioned as their own policing force,
pointing at other women who did not conform to moral propriety
and middle-class sexual norms. Prachi, for example, posited that
the call centre world incited transgressions of various kinds mainly
because of its unregulated nature. 'People get carried away when
they are into call centre world. In terms of money, fashion, sex. This
is because, first of all, they are out at nights. So parents don't bother
and most of them don't live with parents'. Prachi and other women
who expressed similar views inhabited the same milieu as their
so-called amoral compatriots. Their fears, I interpret, as what Robert
Stoller (1975) has called a 'symbiotic anxiety', the sense that the
tenuous virtue of propriety is ever in danger of succumbing to the
pull of vice all around.

While single women were particularly suspect, married women
were hardly exempt. Simran spoke about how her mother-in-law
had been quizzed by a neighbour regarding Simran's work hours:

The way people look at BPO is definitely these things. Where I used
to stay earlier, there is a female who stays just below on the first floor.
My mom-in-law came and this lady started talking to her and said,

*Aapki bahu raat raat tak bahar rehti hai, aapko problem naheen hoti*
[your daughter-in-law stays out all night, don't you have a problem with
that?] ... I was like excuse me, at least use the correct word dammit,
night shift.

I was so bugged up with that language. And this female is not a
Marathi, she is a Hindi speaking female from UP, so you know exactly
what you are talking about. *Galti se naheen bola* [she did not say so
mistakenly, she meant certain things]. If you are from UP, then *raat raat
bhar bahar rehna ka kya matlab hai* [what do you mean when you say
'staying out all night long']. My mom-in-law said, *ab kya karein na,
night shift hai tho kuch kar naheen sakte* [it's the night shift, we can't do
anything]. After some time, she said, *haan unko tho gaadi vaadi lene aati
hai araam se, par bahut ladke log hote hain usme* [she is often picked up
and travels in nice cars, but there are a lot of men in the cars]. I was so
frustrated and I was thinking *Kitna taak jhaak karegi, aap raat raat bhar
apne balcony mein kya karte ho?* [Why do you peep and pry so much?
What is it that you do out on the balcony all night long?].

While Simran's mother-in-law seemed comfortable with her odd
hours, she nevertheless had to defend Simran to her neighbours.

The integration of women into the rapidly changing political
economy has necessitated concurrent ideological adjustments
by both society and state. These translate into a double bind, in
which the demand for women's work as duty and right runs up
against intensified modes of control on their sexuality and conduct. Numerous discourses have traced the framing of the woman
within this rhetoric of nationalism and moral identity (Chatterjee
1990; Grewal 1996; Kandiyoti 1991; Puri 1999) through representation, discourse and practice, and the maintenance of middle-
class-ness through control over women's sexuality (Mankekar
1999). Purnima Mankekar's argument, for example, is that in
postcolonial India, social control of women's behaviour and bodies
was achieved through hegemonic processes of naturalization and
normalization, and through consent rather than through force.
Radhika Parameswaran's ethnographic study argues on the side
of resistance. She reads young girls reading Western romance
fiction in urban India in relation to their desire to escape from the
' ... burdens of preserving the honor of family and community'

(Parameswaran 2002: 832). In this respect, call centres can certainly occupy pride of place as zones of simultaneous transgression, recasting, and control.

Across a range of sites such as these, questions of middle-class values are seen to be configured around sexual propriety and modesty as responsibilities of modern, female subjects. How then, does one accommodate for subjects' own sense of desire and pleasure? Is it possible to look at 'recuperating and theorizing desire and pleasure as an important political project within postcolonial India' (Kapur 2002: 354; Parameswaran 2002)? Within these discourses of suspicion and denial, I argue, that there ought to be a space for considering the actual desiring actions of call centre workers, as a way to understand the possibilities unleashed by the call centre.

### Sexual Feeling

Passing the transportation department on the way back from the ladies' room, I noticed that the man I had christened 'Curly Hair' was sitting in front of his computer monitor, his back to me, and the door to his cubicle wide open, as his screen showed pornographic pictures of women. It was about three in the morning. The corridors of the office building were empty and he must have thought it safe to peruse private activity. However, his office was located right by the restrooms and surely men and women would have passed by all night long. Some of these young men and women had apparently also been seen making out in the restrooms, I was told by other trainers. Tales of amateur pornography on cell phone video cameras seemed to circulate around many of the call centres I knew at that time, and seemed to be either call centre legend or increasingly popular practice. If the latter were true, the video may even have found its way onto the pornography circuit that 'Curly Hair' was surfing.

Talk about sex was everywhere in the call centre. Clandestine relationships, extramarital affairs, public sex, and improper attire all emphasized the strongly sexual nature of the social milieu of the call centre. In many ways, the atmosphere mimicked those of city colleges, with people dressing in both casual and stylish attire to come to work. Often, HR personnel would instruct agents, and especially women workers, against dressing 'provocatively' or informally. 'No shorts', 'No spaghetti straps', 'No tank tops'—formed the content of many email messages. The narrative of the call centre's ability to bring out one's exhibitionism was often couched in tales of, 'You should have seen her when she came to work first; all she wore were full-sleeved shirts and salwar kameez. Now it's all denims and tank tops'. While some of this was gossip, in many ways, a number of the young women workers I met enjoyed dressing up for work and did not think it inappropriate to wear clothes that might be seen as 'sexy' or 'revealing'. Similarly, both male and female workers would tend to evaluate trainers in terms of their sex appeal and marital status. There were a number of times when I began a training session with introductory information only to be asked to reveal if I were single. On the flip side, there were very few tales of homosexual attention or even gossip available for consumption. The one time that a male trainer was dismissed for apparently having hit on a male worker, the stories that circulated never confirmed the gender of the worker.

In many ways, the milieu of the call centre hints at the larger heteronormative sexual landscape of urban India. Such middle-class heteronormativity included the production of the 'New Indian Woman' as global as well as local, and the naturalization of the idealized tranquility of the heterosexual nuclear family (Fernandes 2000). I suggest that the sexual atmosphere of the call centre has less to do with the profligacy of the night than with gender itself, which along with sexuality and ethnicity, is an intimate identity centrally involved in the appropriate functioning of modernizing markets (Wilson 2004). To this extent, the prohibition against sexual misconduct and the seemingly rebellious tendency to exhibitionism were all, as Ara Wilson has argued, evidence of the paradoxes of a transnational economy that inspires simultaneous desire and fear (Wilson 2004). It is perhaps possible to interpret burgeoning sexuality within the call centre as a sign of populations displaying active agency within conditions of late capitalism (Hebdige 1988). However, it is equally possible to see such agency re-territorializing either within hegemonic heteronormative expectations of settled families and daytime jobs or alternatively, as forms of consumption and consumerism that mediate such sexuality (Mazzarella 2003).

How do we understand consumption in relation to the call centre in a way that does not reduce it to a tale of consumerist, westernized, young subjects? One of the films that references college life and youth life in Pune, is a Marathi film titled *Saatchya Aat Gharat* or Home by Seven (Soorkar 2004). The film chronicles the lives of a group of middle- and upper-middle-class teenagers studying in a Pune college before and after one of them is assaulted and raped by a city policeman. The story also focuses in parallel on the ways in which the city reacts to modernity by narrating events of political protests and violence against Valentine's Day celebrations. The title to the movie invokes the heroine's grandmother and her perpetually ignored admonition to always be home by seven. However, conflict primarily emerges from the relationship between the heroine, Madhura, and her parents, who while having introduced her to the trappings of western modernity (alcohol, pubs, and clothing), try to revert to discipline and authoritarianism once sexual violence ruptures the idealized image of the city as modern, and society as safe. Here, consumption is indexed as 'Western' and vacuous; but on the other hand, tradition itself is absent and the 'local' tends to be both provincial and dangerous. Such is the modern landscape that inspires consumption on one hand, and alienation and insecurity on the other. Identity becomes suspect and one cannot depend on available cues towards any form of belonging.

I loosely read the space of the call centre and its ostensible hypersexuality as indexed through the consumption of brands, 'modern' appearances, and sexual exhibitionism to signify in this instance a similar space of confusion. The creation of the call centre worker subject is fraught with the tensions and the 'spectacle' (Debord 1970) of a particular vision of modernity, one that hopes to create a global subject while simultaneously whispering about its inappropriateness. I argue that workers, while seen as 'inappropriate' are neither giving into desperate sexual urges nor turning into rabid consumers. Instead, I suggest that consumption and sexuality be read together to construct a denser understanding of the ways in which call centre work inspires attachments of a certain order.

## Rupture

*'Tomorrow, around 50 police officers will visit WNS "to sensitise themselves on how business process outsourcing (BPOs) centres or call centres work". Many police officers do not understand, for instance, why BPO employees work at night. This visit will help them understand that', says Mukhi.*

—'Industry, Government Join Hands Against Mumbai Cyber Crime', *Business Standard*, Mumbai, 24 May 2010 (D'Monte 2010)

On 1 November 2007, Jyotikumari Choudhary, a 21 year old woman, employed as a customer service agent with WIPRO BPO, was raped and murdered while on her way to work. The perpetrators of the crime were the driver of her cab, Purushottam Borate and his friend, Pradip Khopde. She had taken the cab at 10:30 in the night, on 1 November, to report for her last night at work, since she had given notice a few days prior to this incident. While in the cab, she had been speaking on her cell phone and hadn't noticed that the cab had veered off course. WIPRO BPO is situated at the Rajiv Gandhi Hinjewadi Infotech Park off the Mumbai-Pune Highway on the outskirts of the city. The driver steered the cab towards a village off the highway called Gahunje. After raping and murdering her, both returned to work and picked up and dropped off other workers at the BPO.

Her body was discovered a day later after her family members reported her missing. The driver and his accomplice were soon arrested after which they confessed to the crime. Pune Rural Superintendent of Police, Vishwas Nangre Patil, who was investigating the case, took the accused to the crime scene for further investigations. 'Her veins were cut with a knife and she was strangulated with a dupatta', Patil said. 'The accused have confessed that her head was smashed till she died. It is one of the most tragic and barbaric cases. Investigations are on', he added (Inamdar 2007).

Software and IT services industry body, NASSCOM, lamented the incident and issued a statement saying, 'This gruesome murder reflects the need for greater safety and security and for all concerned to take every possible measure to eliminate such crime. Such incidents set back efforts that are being made to bring about greater gender equality in the country's workforce' (Sandeep Joshi 2007). T.K. Kurien, the CEO of WIPRO BPO, lamented the incident and added:

> We had put several processes in place, including 'no first pick up or last drop' of female staffers, compulsory rosters for every taxi, ongoing education of employees on personal safety, precautions to be followed during late night travel. Unfortunately, even the most secure processes get manipulated. We have initiated an audit to further tighten all processes, especially those concerning employees' safety. (Satyajit Joshi 2007)

Newspapers reported the crime as further evidence of the vulnerability and lack of safety for women employees in an industry where 'as many as 6,000 cars ferry at least 30,000 people who are part of this boom from their home to workplaces and back' (Inamdar 2007). Senior city police officials claimed that all call centres and IT companies had been orally directed time and again to beef up security measures for their staff. However, Deputy Chief of Police Chandrashekhar Daithankar, while asserting that BPO companies were not adhering to safety measures confessed that no written directives had been issued.

BPO vehicle contractors claimed to follow the directives of companies, providing drivers' photographs, bio data, addresses, photocopies of licences, fingerprints, and character verification certificates issued by the police. Besides, it was usual practice for a guard to be deployed by the company for late night shifts, they said. However, they insisted that the company should be responsible for ensuring that guards accompanied female employees. BPO executives maintained that the contractors were responsible for drivers, and were frequently inattentive or did not adhere to safety regulations.

The Pune City Autorickshaw Federation demanded a crackdown on tourist vehicles functioning as call centre cabs. The Federation said, that around 6,000 vehicles had been registered as tourist vehicles for ferrying passengers from one town to another on a contractual basis. However, these vehicles were found to be illegally operating as call centre cabs, it claimed. The Federation, led by president Baba Shinde, declared that Federation workers would stop call centre vehicles on roads and conduct checks.

Sarthi, a city-based organization, demanded that women drivers be employed by contractors for ferrying women BPO and IT employees, and that security surveillance systems be installed in each car to keep track of the vehicle. The organization also appealed to working women to wear modest and 'decent' traditional Indian clothes. Pune Municipal Corporation corporator, Kalpana Jadhav, also president of Prerna Mahila and Balvikas Pratisthan, raised the question of women's safety in Pune.

While deconstructing these reactions reveals more about the speakers than the victim of crime, together they also yield a vision of a collective denial. Safety rules, modesty, security checks, and surveillance—all attempts to fill in, rather than bring out into the open, the constitutive gap around which urban India is increasingly being constructed. I argue that this gap must be understood in connection with a burgeoning middle class, and with middle-class-ness as fast becoming the only subject position of value and worth in the landscape of urban India. Call centre workers were some of the most visible symbols of such consumerism and seeming upward mobility. To this extent then, violent acts such as these can perhaps signal some of the ways in which increasing class differentiation in urban public space is also accompanied by crime and danger, often played out on the bodies of women.

I do not want to reduce the question of heinous crime to societal inequality, rapid urbanization, and/or class resentment. However, such incidents of crime are not singular. This act of violence, I argue, can function as a point of entry into the 'secret public' of the night, and the 'public secret' that is this tenuous and widening disparity, one that threatens to make itself known at various points of friction.

Night after night, as I travelled in cabs, I would chat with cab drivers. Workers were warned against bantering. They were further prohibited from sitting next to the driver's seat. Women workers could not be picked up first, and they could not be dropped off last. The rules of separation were in place even before the fact of crime. Yet, many workers would attempt to tenuously bridge this

bureaucratic separation and gap. They would chat, cajole, and talk.
On many occasions following the murder, it would make me shud-
der to think of the possibility of violence. I had been alone in a cab
with the driver on at least one or two occasions. Other workers
had not shown up and I had sometimes missed my usual cab route.
I had wondered at the efficacy of the security guard in the front
seat who would often be asleep. Once Ashwini, my co-worker, had
jokingly said about the guard, 'Yaar yeh kya mujhe bachayega? Isko
tho main bhi maar doongi [I doubt he can save me, I could easily
beat him up]'. I once asked a cab driver what he thought of the
workers. He said, 'Madam, changle aahet the sagle, pun cigarette chi
savay na … [They are all good, except for the habit of smoking]'.
Others said that workers made them wait, were lazy, and hardly
ever chatted with them. They would be on their cell phones all the
time, the drivers complained, and lamented that these young men
and women did not attempt to engage with, or even care about the
people they rode with every day.

It is difficult to ignore such affectively laden daily instantiation
of difference and inequality. I do not attempt to draw a causal link
between workers' socio-economic positions, their relative youth,
seeming arrogance and indifference, and the anger of cab drivers.
Many drivers bore personal responsibility for their occupants, others
not so much. Many workers had friendly and engaged relationships
with drivers, others not so much. But given the company's rules, the
very enforcement of flexible routes and timings, in order to help
separate workers from drivers ensured that they shared no community or empathy and vice-versa. Women workers were especially
forbidden from contact. Flexibility was employed to help minimize
the space of interaction between drivers and workers. Cab drivers
changed every week, and routes were drawn and redrawn often
leading to longer commute times and frequent confusion. There
was no effort made towards attenuating difference or addressing it,
beyond avoidance.

I grew up in a middle class household in an industrial town
far from urban areas. As a child, I would travel 25 kilometres to
school every day on a particularly treacherous national highway.
My parents would worry about the safety of a six-year-old travelling

in a rickety van for two hours a day. As children, we would see an accident a day. Our drivers protected us, they were our extended family, and my parents' confidantes. I do not wish to pretend that this erased differences or accorded company-employed drivers the same privileges as my middle-class, white-collar salaried father. However, the drivers cared for us. Across difference, we built a relationship. We were the children they cared for, in spite of difference. They were the people I trusted and those with who I continued to share at least a tenuous bond. My relationship with them, consisting of the daily commute, lasted over six long years and I had an innate trust and respect for the people who drove us back and forth; these people who bore the responsibility and held the job of the driver.

Yet, many a time at the call centre, travelling in cabs, even with other people alongside, I would have an overwhelming sense of, what Lauren Berlant calls, a 'situation', 'a state of things in which *something* that will perhaps matter is unfolding amidst the usual activity of life' (Berlant 2008: 5). In Berlant's words, this was ' ... a state of animated and animating suspension that forces itself on consciousness, that produces a sense of the emergence of something in the present that may become an event' (Berlant 2011: 4–5). It was perhaps fortuitous that the event never emerged and continued to only be an un-foreclosed experience. No ethnographer was harmed in the making of this book, I am tempted to add. However, what was emerging in the present of my experience was a heightened awareness of fears of the night and cab drivers; in those various moments, this secret public threatened to break apart. Had violence occurred, the fear would have coagulated. In my case, it dissipated and gathered in turn. I went to work every night. I was aware of my shaky position as a woman travelling at night, yet confident of my value as a worker. I had a tenuous faith in rules and erred on the side of hope.

My analyses of both, violence in the case of Jyotikumari Choudhary and situations in my own experiences are not meant to signal the same set of circumstances or even a similar context. The only analysis I can offer is, that while awareness of the possibility of danger coloured the atmosphere of work, it did not necessarily make any of the stakeholders aware of the kinds of difference that might form the background to its eruption. I suggest that the violence that Jyotikumari suffered marks a rupture and a defacement of the seeming banality that workers, corporations, state, and capital try so hard to produce and maintain. While it is not new for work to be carried out at night, middle-class workers who were not hesitant to parade new-found global modernity either through conspicuous consumption or comportment, were visible entities that brought into relief difference and inequality of opportunity between themselves and others that also inhabited this landscape. Defacement on such a terrain, I argue, was not merely random and psychopathic violence. Rather, the attacker sought opportunity and indeed 'criminally manipulated' the processes that had been set up to respond to the very fear that such an act would happen. The processes in some ways were a self-fulfilling prophecy. The chain of events that they had predicted and hoped to ward off, had come to roost. Nobody then talks about the very fact of their prediction and the fear that it might happen. In other words, one needs to ask why some bodies 'always-for-ever turn up, in the right place at the right time' (Hall 1996: 25), and why particular kinds of violence are played out on and through the bodies of women. Here, we find class and gender coming together in ways that repeat the narrative of middle-class propriety as being incumbent upon the virtuosity of women, and if the space of the call centre were to be always already suspect, then so will its women.

## An Artist of the Floating World

*The best things are put together of a night … and vanish in the morning.*
*What people call the floating world …*

—*An Artist of the Floating World*, Kazuo Ishiguro (1986: 150)

Many scholars have delved into the question of the global and the local, and posited the transnational as the critical and hence more particular counterpoint to globalization's unmediated meanderings. The nation in these accounts is not transcended, but transformed and in many cases, re-iterated in more powerful modes, necessitating a problematized understanding of the spaces of the nation-state.

Sympathetic to these concerns, this research is located firmly in this tension between globalization and transnationality. I contend that in describing and examining the work that goes into maintaining cross-border movement, the notion of night work is key to understanding the parts that do not fit into the story of the transcendence of space and time. The night is a landscape different than the day, but one that nevertheless demanded that workers continue to operate around the varied logics of daylight dwellers. For call centre workers, the night was not merely an occupational condition, but a doubly hard task. Even as it was the substance of routine, it was also the object of efforts both to shut out the light of day and, through discourse, to render it normal.

In the introductory essay to a volume titled *Night-Time and Sleep in Asia and the West: Exploring the Dark Side of Life*, Brigitte Steger and Lodewijk Brunt (2003) ask as to why there is such a case of night blindness in sociology and anthropology. The night is after all not just a span of time but also a material realm of speculative danger; a place of unknown spaces, dark alleys, and forbidden inhabitance (Steger and Brunt 2003: 3). An account of night work in New York City, for example, examines 'the social space of the night; a social space that is highly structured and inherently subversive, as transnational as it is transgressive, and shot through with inequalities of power' (Sharman and Sharman 2008: 3). Perhaps, the lack of literature has to do specifically with the nightly city and the invisibility of the processes it sustains.

One of the first sociological works to be published on the question of the night was Murray Melbin's *Night as Frontier* (1987), which was concerned with the 12 per cent of the American population that stayed up after midnight to work at that time. Melbin coined the term 'incessant organizations' to speak about time as a frontier that was sought to be colonized by expanding its norms, as well as the capacity of working subjects to exert themselves beyond traditional notions of limited and controlled work days. He argued that, much like the colonization of spatial frontiers, conquering time happens in stages, and is preceded by lawlessness, violence, and a relatively decentralized state presence. While it is tempting to look at the space of the call centre as a similar frontier, I argue that colonization of time in case of the call centre was not only characterized by the centrality of the state in the first place, but that its experience was also dictated by the inability of its participants to be completely colonized or exhibit behavioural styles adequate to functioning in the night.

Perhaps it is wise to remember, that as much as one can hope for normality, those working in the night must necessarily be juxtaposed against those working in the day that one must rub against, and for whom, the night is still transgressive and obscure. To conclude, it might be important to consider not just how the night functions as a defining factor in the case of the call centre, but also, how time needs to be overcome in order to provide a permanent voice at the end of the line. If Britannia was the empire that the sun never set on, then can this global work regime be the new Empire (Hardt and Negri 2000), defined by the creation of a flexible worker capable of working as much in the night as the day? David Harvey's work has become a widely used rubric to understand how time and space come to be constructed and contested within late capitalist relations of production. In a 1990 article, he states:

> Each social formation constructs objective conceptions of space and time sufficient unto its own needs and purposes of material and social reproduction and organizes its material practices in accordance with those conceptions ... The spread of capitalist social relations has often entailed a fierce battle to socialize different peoples into the common net of time discipline implicit in industrial organization ... (Harvey 1990a: 419)

The workday and its battles, and the opposition of rest and work are all key to understanding the time discipline that Harvey discusses. One might argue that the act of working through the night in the call centre received undue attention only because it was the reaction of a 'different' society to its incorporation into an increasingly common net of worldwide time discipline. I argue, however, that it is precisely the night that makes visible, the un-commonality of specific forms of time discipline, that are only selectively imposed on certain sections of the population and in certain parts of the world. There are implications of power in the flow of work-time in one region of the world as against another.

Transnational call centre work rendered necessary the space and time of the night. Temporal and spatial organization around the industry then sought to constitute the social order through the assignment of workers and activities to distinctive places and times (Bourdieu 1977). But in the re-assignment of people to new orders and the continued co-existence of older ones, we begin to see the effects of transnationality. In the process, all orders are exposed as incomplete, incompetent and transitory. Things escape, secrets are let out, and people become corrupt. Orders become corrupt.

While accounts privilege the night as either deterrent or obstacle requiring bodily and cultural adjustment, I look at the night as initially experienced by workers as a hitherto unavailable experience. Concurrently, I argue that this experience gathered workers into a community of note, and a set of people with a different relationality to space and time. Call centre workers were young, and working in the night, connected well to their understanding of transgression and rebellion. However, this experience was short-lived and the immediate world of the nation-state and the cityscape outside the call centre proved to be a powerful deterrent to long years of night work. The work of transnationality was, I argue, difficult to maintain and I found this effort rendered most poignant in the narrative of a 25 year old call centre worker named Sam, who shared his view of an ideal day that he hoped to be able to experience in the near future:

This is the primary stage of my career. In the near future, secondary phase of my life, I won't be working night shifts. I can't do that. Making some breakfast, by 9, I should be ready, get out, take my car, drive to office 10 to 15 kilometers away, I should get lunch by 1:30, get back to work by 2:30, leave office at 6, go to get fresh and do some buying from the market. At 8, go to the local bar, have a couple of drinks, with your friends, or your office colleagues. Come back by 9:30, get your food prepared and have it by 10:30 and go to sleep by 12. Ideal day.

One night, a cab driver I was chatting with on my way back from a night shift, told me, that a ghost haunted the bridge between the organization and the area where we were headed. He had seen her often, he said. We were both slightly delirious at this point already;

he from endless trips to and from the city to the call centre and I from lack of sleep and endless bouts with the English language in the call centre. I had heard about this ghost from other drivers as well. He told me that she had long hair (of course!) and wore billowy clothes. This story, to me, continues to be a metaphor for all the hauntings that plague the night outside the call centre, ghosts that precede the light of day.

In Kazuo Ishiguro's novel, *An Artist of the Floating World* (1986), the protagonist abandons the sensory and transient pleasures of the night as vacuous and transitory objects of art, and seeks to move onto things more concrete and in keeping with the realities of the world. Call centre work, one would assume, is part of this landscape, this transient world. The work of transnationality lies, however, in refusing such transience. Sleep must be managed, lights must shine bright, and the show must go on. The night merely shows up every now and then as a ghost.

# 4

## ELIZA DOOLITTLE

### Finding Eliza

*I know your head aches; I know you are tired; I know your nerves are as raw as meat in a butcher's window. But think what you're trying to accomplish. Think what you're dealing with. The majesty and grandeur of the English language, it's the greatest possession we have.*

—Henry Higgins, *My Fair Lady* (Cukor 1964)

*The biggest obstacle is that you have to make them speak in English. English is a major problem for these people. They are reluctant towards a new language.*

—Bipin Deo, call centre consultant

In 2002, I worked for a corporate design and advertising firm in Pune. My network consisted of various people associated with the advertising, copywriting, design, and communication industries. We all worked long hours and consequently our social events extended late into the evening. During one such networking event in the wee hours of the night, a friend had to leave because he had to give his girlfriend, Vidisha, a ride to work. The reason this incident stands out is because I can remember, to this day, how different Vidisha sounded from the rest of us middle-, and upper-middle-class professionals. While English was our common mode of communication, she was the only one who sounded, what was in general a derogatory parlance termed, *firang* or foreign, and more specifically, westernized. However, it was not a foreignness that we could easily place. It sounded like an imitation, but the attempt was continuous, and it sounded affected, but it was comfortably so. At times, I had the sense of hearing a caricature out of a spaghetti western film. But at others, I could have closed my eyes and imagined a clear foreignness, notwithstanding the unmistakably Indian body in front of us. Of course, these linguistic ruminations are products of hindsight. At that time, it remained a matter of pigeonholing her into the category of the imitators—purveyors and worshippers of all things foreign, and more specifically, American. This was also because unlike the few Indian-Americans I knew, her accent slipped back and forth between what we considered a stereotypical American or foreign one, and the intonations that the rest of us middle-class, upwardly mobile, and professional white-collar workers shared. As a happy resolution, I imagined her having been schooled in an international school in the Middle East or in an elite Indian boarding school. Vidisha left for work, leaving us wondering about her strange accent, and her equally curious work-place that needed her to come in to work late at night. Even for us 'creative' professionals who prided ourselves on our cosmopolitanism and our unorthodox work hours, there was something dubious about her.

Vidisha worked in a call centre. This chapter is about Vidisha's curious talk. It is also about the fetishization of speech in the Indian call centre. In examining the terms of speech in the call centre, I am concerned with the factors that seek to create a perfectly spoken customer service professional. In other words, how does the call centre worker or agent speak. Simultaneously, I am also concerned with agents' modes of talking as speech that had effects on the ways in which they viewed themselves and sought to construct their presence in the world. The ethnography in this chapter concerns itself mainly with workers' experiences of language training offered by the call centre and its corollary organizations. It is difficult to understand such change purely in terms of language, and therefore, I locate this analysis in the day-to-day rendering of speech or in the utterance, and the caveats, directions, and compulsions that seek to govern such utterance. I use utterance in the Bakhtinian sense (Bakhtin et al. 1986), as one that is dependent on a particular language system, but also exists in a world which builds on, borrows from, and responds to other utterances around it. My memory of Vidisha's 'strange' accent, for example, was one such kind of an utterance, in response to the call centre language as a distinct set of utterances.

To further this analysis, I examine customer service communication as forming a secondary speech genre that can be identified through its typical utterances. In daily call centre parlance, this speech genre was often referred to as business communication, or often just communication. The primary genre, English language, is in itself a complex one engendered by the long history of colonial and postcolonial language education and practice in India. While briefly summarizing this history, this chapter is specifically concerned with the nature of 'business' or 'customer communication' in the call centre, and the ways in which workers were shaped into communicative beings. In other words, I am interested in the ways in which call centre management and workers mutually stabilized the genre that I identify as customer communication.

While I identify this work to have been mutual, the learning hierarchies were nevertheless acutely etched out within the training process. Managers, trainers, and American or British clients defined for workers, the standards and measures of communication skills, while workers sought to conform to them. But workers themselves brought varied histories of practice and knowledge with them, and managers then had to reconcile with these recalcitrant histories. This chapter then is also an attempt to delineate the language genealogy that challenged such imposition of uniformity. If the claim of a genealogical project is to ' ... entertain the claims to attention of local, discontinuous, disqualified, illegitimate knowledge against the claims of a unitary body of theory which would filter, hierarchize and order them in the name of some true knowledge and some arbitrary idea of what constitutes a science and its objects' (Foucault and Gordon 1980: 83), then it is this oppositional possibility that the chapter seeks to explore. Voice is implicated in this analysis, as are language and the history of postcolonial English language education in India, as is the transnational corporation and its understanding of customer service.

The title 'Eliza Doolittle' is a nod to the ways in which I view language training in the call centre, whether for men or women, to be gendered as also classed. I refer to specifically wrought messages seeking to create a well-spoken, well-trained, and acquiescent subject—another Eliza Doolittle as it were. The traits that this subject needed to attain were identified in opposition to a set of undesired bodily or cultural traits that defined the badly spoken subject, the latter often coinciding, and indeed drawn from workers' existing modes of speech, enunciation, and comportment. These standards of correctness were declared, repeated, and enforced by managers, accent trainers, and clients. By the end of the training process, while workers may have not been able to attain the measures of 'good' speech, they could enumerate the parameters by which the well-spoken subject would be measured.

Accents, for example, were configured around questions of clarity, with American, British, and 'neutral' accents being desirable whereas accents influenced by the worker's mother tongue were considered gauche, unpleasant, and ludicrous. The language of service work was often seen by agents to be both emasculating and empowering. Lastly, relations between workers, as well as hierarchies between trainers and workers, often depended on the ability to be competent communicators in English. Fluency conferred upon speakers the possibility of social mobility and professional success. This chapter seeks to be particularly attentive to the hierarchical terms around which speech skills were configured.

Conceptually, speech genres and the utterance are useful for my argument at two levels. By the time I conducted fieldwork at call centres in Pune, there was impetus for workers to be trained in an accent defined as 'neutral'. While I elaborate upon this further along the chapter, it would suffice to say that such neutrality attempted to allay critiques focusing on American and British accents as 'foreign' and therefore undesirable in the context of service work performed in India. I argue that in attempting such neutrality, call centre management and trainer nevertheless produced a customer service speech genre imbued with the assumptions of a gendered, classed, and imperialist language and communication ideology. Such ideology was not only incumbent upon the idea of strange tongues that must be subdued to the cause of customer comfort, but also sought to couch such a drive in the logic of neutrality. To speak English in certain ways, and to tame the voice to speak in an understandable fashion, were presented as logical and natural, given the pragmatic goals of global business and a shrinking world. Through an examination of training practices, I seek to deconstruct these assumptions. Second, my deployment of the utterance as a language concept also helps to complicate the possibility of achieving such neutrality. Through ethnographic research, I show how the utterance, even when asked to limit itself to a defined speech genre, was influenced and 'corrupted' by other utterances specific to the geo-political, material, and linguistic milieu of the worker.

I further argue, that the process of training workers in customer communication reveals less about the hegemony of English, than about the ways in which past histories of cultural and linguistic capital are subsumed into the imperialist agenda of global capital movement. Herein lies the flexibility and adaptability of regimes of late capital. To this extent, there is certainly a consonance in the moment I describe, with colonial and postcolonial understanding of the instrumentality of English language speech and education, and its correlation with class mobility. However, I argue that the call centre and its usage of such histories have also brought about changes in the way English language speech privileges subjects. No longer in postcolonial India is there a clear and overt isomorphism possible between forms of language, economic mobility, and class status. To this extent, the ways in which the utterance staked its claim in the call centre was akin to a moment of agency for the speaking subject.

## Talking the Talk

During my year of fieldwork in India, I worked for four months as a voice and accent trainer. My work involved teaching modules on accent comprehension, grammar and sentence construction, and cultural difference. Each of these modules was further divided into lessons detailing specific sounds, enunciation and pronunciation, and

rectifying common regional deviations in speech. The end objectives of this training were that agents begin to comprehend British
or American accents, speak according to guidelines defined by
clients, and exhibit familiarity with an ambiguously defined British
or American culture.

Travelling back home from the call centre on one bustling weekday
morning, I shared a cab with two other agents, who were talking
about work. One of them seemed to have just completed his first
day at work and was complaining:

A: *Bhai pata naheen aaj tho lag gayee poori tarah se, matlab paila teen
call tho mereko samajh mein naheen aaya ho kya raha hai,* [I don't know,
today I got really screwed at work, for the first three calls, I couldn't understand what was happening] (Imitates the customer): Can you repeat
please?

*Itna baar mereko repeat repeat bolke customer tho saala gussa
hi ho gaya, kuch samajh mein naheen aaya, sala dimaag kharab ho
gaya, bahut nervousness tha* [The customer asked me to repeat so
many times and then got really angry; I lost my mind, I was very
nervous].

B: *Kuch naheen be, pahila teen din aisaich hota hai, uske baad sab
theek ho jaata hai. Sabse bura hota hai jab woh bolta hai,* (Imitating the
customer's American accent) Can I speak to your supervisor please?
[Don't worry about it, it's always the case on the first three days, then
it all becomes okay. The worst thing is when he asks to speak to the
supervisor].

A: *Abey saala, customer chillaathe gaya.* [Bloody hell, the customer
kept yelling] (Imitates the customer) 'Speak English speak English'.

B: *Abey, kuch naheen, sorry thank you bolte rehne ka* [Don't sweat it,
just keep saying sorry and thank you].

The first agent, who had been unable to understand anything
uttered by the American customer at the end of the telephone
line, stood in direct contrast to the more experienced one who
attempted to allay the former's nervousness by asking him to take
recourse to stock and placatory phrases indicating politeness and
empathy. The nervous agent however, was referring not to his first
experience in the call centre, but to his first day on 'live' calls.
It would be safe to assume that a few months prior to this exchange,

perhaps when he had first walked into the call centre, he would have exhibited an ability to string together a few sentences in English in order to communicate information on his educational background, his hobbies, his choices of music, and his expectations from call centre work. This would have been prepared for, either from his own knowledge of call centre interviews garnered from friends and neighbours, or from a week-long training boot camp conducted at a recruitment consultancy. On clearing the call centre interview, he would have had to undergo a month-long training process consisting of language, grammar, accent and voice lessons, seeking to polish his accent and his vocabulary, and impart a pleasant, efficient, and effective customer service voice and demeanor. Yet, all he was left with at the end of a seemingly competent and extensive process of language training was 'sorry' and 'thank you'. What explains this ostensible failure to deliver? And what does such blatant mimicry (Bhabha 1994) of the customer service form reveal about the speaking subject of the call centre?

Customer service agents in the call centre, interacting with American, British, and Australian clients were expected to speak clearly in English, while intoning a modicum of appropriate accent or markers of accent, and communicate effectively in a phone conversation that most often, only lasted between five and ten minutes.[1] The content of the conversation was often repetitive and involved providing solutions for a fairly predictable and homogenous set of issues, questions, and queries. While some clients required that workers maintain an American or British accent on phone calls, others were satisfied with an ambiguously defined 'neutral' accent.

Most workers were between the ages of 18 and 25, and entered the call centre with varying English language skills. As a result, training in customer service jargon, communication, and accent formed one of the core support functions of the call centre. In parallel,

---

[1] I refer, in this instance, to customer service or business-to-customer (B2C) communication. Often, technical support and business-to-business (B2B) communication demanded longer call times and conversations.

there had risen around the call centre, a burgeoning business in English language training, often coupled with 'soft skills'[2] variously labelled as 'Personality Development', 'Effective Communication', and 'Professional Communication'. Many large call centres, however, continued to offer in-house training with a view to producing standardized work practices. Depending on the size of the organization, and the kind and number of business processes it supported, training departments of five to twenty employees provided anywhere from a week to three months of training in communication. These were often codified into acronyms to indicate specific expertise that the training department of any one organization might claim to have developed. So for example, ECT trainers provide training using 'Effective Communication Tools' and V&A personnel taught modules dealing with 'Voice & Accent'. The difference in monikers however did not extend into training content and most call centres used similar modules of language usage, grammatical structure, sentence construction, and terminology specific to the work process. While the last was often technically specific language that referred to the task at hand—billing cycle for credit cards or phone bills, itinerary for air travel, and premium for insurance queries—clients in the US and the UK often insisted on their own specific sentences, as opening or closing lines, that were mandatory for agents to spout. For example, an agent might have to begin every call with, 'Thank you for calling A [name of company], my name is Howard. How may I help you today?' and end with 'Have I managed to address your concerns today?', and 'Thank you for calling A, have a wonderful day/evening.'

Training processes could be divided into: (*a*) Basic sentence construction, (*b*) Voice coaching (speaking clearly, enunciation, and

---

2 'Soft skills', in itself a terminology variously analyzed in terms of the attendant connotations for the gendering of labour, refers similarly in this instance to modes of speech, presentation, and workers' attitudes that are ostensibly manifest in their interactions with peers and customers. They cover both, the emotional aspects of speaking on the phone, as well as the affective and people-specific skills that the worker brings in dealing with colleagues, subordinates, and supervisors.

word flow), (*c*) Tone management, (*d*) Accent (American, British, or neutral), and (*e*) Standard phrases and specific terminology.

On any given day in the call centre, customer service agents opened their mouths wider, enunciated their syllables stronger, and sought to create out of an opaque corporate lexicon, the possibility of meaning. The worker relentlessly ploughed through training sessions on accent, tone, emphasis, and grammar. One might think these to be language immersion programs, intent upon indoctrinating willing subjects into an economy dependent upon English. What is perhaps, important to note, in addressing the efficacy (or lack thereof) of such training, is that the existence of a postcolonial English-speaking populace was responsible in the first place, for investments in the Indian call centre economy.

### English Pasts and Hybrid Presents

*Any utterance is a link in a very complexly organized chain of other utterances.*

—Mikhail Bakhtin, *Speech Genres and other Late Essays*
(Bakhtin et al. 1986: 69)

The existence of an English-speaking cache of workers in India was the result of a social structure that promoted and valorized English language competence, especially among the middle class. Since this research is primarily concerned with the call centre industry between the late 1990s and 2007, it bears very distinct connections with the ways in which English language and speech became 'cultural capital' (Bourdieu and Passeron 1990; Bourdieu et al. 1990) in colonial and postcolonial India. But in order to understand this complex ideology of language learning and practice, one must necessarily survey the literature on English vis-à-vis Indian language politics and history. English language education is considered one of the most prominent legacies of British rule in India. Rooted in the colonial dictate as famously enunciated in the Macaulay's Minute of 1835, to create a 'a class who may be interpreters between us and the millions whom we govern—a class of persons Indian in blood and colour, but English in tastes, in opinions, in morals and in intellect'[3] (Brutt-Griffler 2002; Macaulay and Young 1967), pre- and post-1947 language education policies privileged English as a medium of education for the middle class, especially for higher education (King 1997; Pennycook 1998; Sonntag 2000).[4] The grounds for creating such a hierarchy had also already been instituted through what Rajeswari Sunder Rajan has called the colonial 'instrumental' and 'integrative' (Sunder Rajan 1992: 11) motives for English language education.[5]

Post British rule, independent India's governance, as a multilingual country, was sought to be streamlined and institutionalized by the linguistic reorganization of states in 1956 via the States Reorganization Act. The critiques of this policy as well as its ramifications are many and I do not explore them here. Of interest to this chapter, are the subsequent educational measures that sought to facilitate translation between states as administrative units. I refer specifically to the three-language formula, which required language curricula in schools to include English, Hindi, and one other language (Hindi in case of the southern states and one of the Dravidian languages for the Hindi speaking northern states). The formula was contested and never consistently applied. It also led to long and unresolved linguistic battles between the Hindi-dominated northern states and the Dravidian language regions of southern

[3] For the history of British colonial language policy and the rise of English language dominance, see Brutt-Griffler (2002).

[4] Also see Sunder Rajan's edited volume *Lie of the Land* (1992) for an influential set of essays exploring the various historical, social, and reformist motivations of both, colonizer and colonized, in instituting such educational measures and the subsequent ramifications for the study of English literature.

[5] Sunder Rajan argues that the elite Indian population negotiated these functions in different ways. While quick to see the relationship between English language skills and education, and its financial and societal benefits, they nevertheless contested its assimilative ends either through outright protest, or subversion and appropriation. Questions of linguistic practice and policy in post-1947 India have always been fraught with a similar ambivalence, including the range of possibilities inherent to the doubling that mimicry brings about.

India, over the contested status of Hindi in state and educational policy. However, even in this formulation, critiqued as it was, the postcolonial state continued to understand English as central to the formation of a citizen subject. The state's machinations, and the linguistic battles between Hindi and other regional languages, allowed for English to occupy a safe middle ground, eliding questions of national language and validity. English thus came to be positioned outside the question of national and linguistic identity in order to fulfill two functions—one looking outward to the global stage, and the other looking inward to resolve the problem of linguistic heterogeneity. One is almost able to imagine a hundred frantic tongues being pushed out of the way as English calmly makes its way in a race to the finish line.

In postcolonial India, this crucial differentiation between the local languages and English, and the latter's constitutive relationship to cosmopolitanism, were further instantiated through the medium of education. In the educational hierarchy, the more prestigious schools taught through the medium of the English language. Using D.L. Sheth's article 'No English Please, We're Indian' (1990), Sunder Rajan describes the differences between English-medium and regional language based education in terms of 'the existence of (a small number of) expensive public schools where English is the medium of instruction from the lowest classes, along with (a preponderance of) regional-language schools, for the most part run by governments or municipalities, where English is taught— badly—as a subject for a few years' (Sunder Rajan 1992: 19). Given this dichotomy, it was a natural corollary that mainly upper- and upper-middle-class families were able to educate their children in English-medium schools. In the context of this co-incidence of class and education, English which was already the bastion of privilege began to be associated with modernity and upward mobility, values that adhered as a consequence to the middle class (Ramanathan 2005). Such knowledge was not just functional, but also aesthetic— in Bourdieu's terms, a linguistic marker of distinction (Bourdieu 1984). So while English education marked those more capable of taking advantage of opportunities in colonial and postcolonial India, it also concurrently became a factor for distinguishing and privileging middle and upper class populations. In other words, knowing English by itself would not necessarily render anyone privileged. However, not knowing English prevented access to white-collar positions occupied exclusively by the middle and upper middle classes. The expansion of English language speech and education, therefore affected regional social dynamics while continuing to emphasize the primacy of English to the global subject. In this middle class, national space was where the call centre located its labour population.

## What Is a 'Neutral' Accent?

*Bryan and I are chatting. He remarks, 'Your accent is so British.' He is Canadian, works for a British company and lives in the US.*

—Field notes, March 2007

*I am trying to buy a car in Austin, Texas. On the phone, the car dealer, a Texan named Jim Ernst, is trying very hard to comprehend my name and asks me where I am from. I tell him that I am Indian. He says, 'Well you sound more British. I mean, I've spoken to those guys in India in call centres and you sound nothing like them.'*

—Field notes, February 2008

*My friend, Aman, who has been educated in some of the best educational institutions in India and now works in the US, tells me, 'These fools keep calling my accent British, which is ridiculous because nobody in Britain understands anything I say.'*

—Field notes, February 2008

Conversations with many call centre workers often revolved around the question of the accent they were required to maintain at the call centre. All my interviews with workers were held in non-work settings, so our conversations were in English, Hindi, Marathi, and sometimes Tamil, if we shared our mother tongue. Workers moved confidently between languages, having no trouble articulating an opinion or expressing themselves. Interviews lasted for hours sometimes, and at no point did I ever experience a lull in conversation. In this relaxed setting, they often imitated for me, the accent they would maintain at work or while on a call. These ranged from slowly drawled American accents, to clipped British, to a minimally aspirated ('t' and 'k' sounds) set of words and catch phrases.

My respondents' accent travails often reminded of my own experience when being interviewed for the position of a communications trainer. At the two call centres I interviewed at, I was asked to demonstrate my training skills while maintaining an American accent. I remembered thinking during that time how hard it was to speak in a stereotypical 'American' tongue all the time. An Indian-American friend, who was then in the city, helped me work on my slang and drawl, and suggested I try and curb what he considered the excessive British-ness of my accent. Over the next few days, I practised for hours in front of the mirror, attempting to speak slower, enunciate harder, and milk my limited life experiences in America for all they were worth. When I played my voice back on the recorder I had bought for field research, I sounded nasal, ridiculous, and unpleasant, not to mention amateur and hammy. Vowels rang false, my tone seemed alien, and I belaboured under the fear that somehow, sometime the truth would out, and that my American accent was nowhere close to American, in whatever common understanding of the phenomenon. However, in this experience, there was also the pleasure of the performance, the hope of a successful con, and the sheer sensory joy of mimicry.

In popular literature, one of the aspects of call centres most likely to strike a controversial chord is that of the accent requirement. Scholars working on call centres have commented on both, the assumed foreign (American and British) accents, as well as the 'neutral' accent that attempted to resolve the issues created by the former but only succeeded in privileging an accent tending to upper-class or British accented English (Cowie 2007). Claire Cowie in particular, uses ethnographic work from her experiences at a training organization in Bangalore, another prominent call centre hub, to show how older trainers favoured British intonations whereas younger ones were more likely to endorse an American turn of phrase. In my own experience, the accent requirement ran the gamut, with an increasing tendency towards what was called a 'neutral' accent.

The accent requirement in the early years of BPO work in India was fundamentally locative, in that it marked origin (Urciuoli 1996: 114), and more importantly, it also masked origin. In order that customers in the US and the UK could continue to imagine a kindred voice, agents were asked to locate themselves closer to the customer through accent. By attempting to speak in an American or British accent, workers dislocated themselves from an undesirable foreign place, and relocated themselves in ways that they imagined organizations and their UK- and US-based customers would consider nearer, and therefore more familiar and trustworthy.

Accent learning was a minefield. Tales of call centres that trained workers to reproduce accent right down to geographic specificity (Texan or Boston Brahmin) were largely apocryphal, and the accent that was presented as homogenously American—a notion that is in itself a misnomer—varied between call centres, workers, and even between trainers. However, the accent favoured was specific to certain race and class contexts, as reflected in the teaching material. This ended up reproducing the class implications of a 'homogenous' white American accent. As films like *American Tongues* (Kolker et al. 1986) tell us—while there is no standard American accent, there is a mode of speech favoured by actors, and TV and radio announcers in America, which travels to other countries via media consumption as standard American tongue.

Call centres provided basic operational definitions and demonstrations of an American or a British accent through media clips and by way of demonstrations by performative trainers. A typical training session consisted of exercises meant to help workers master variously identified component parts of an accent. Ayesha, a trainer and former call centre agent, who I shadowed as part of my initiation into call centre work, made workers repeat vowel sounds over and over again, in an exaggerated, slow, and extended cadence. She would ask them to merge each vowel sound into the next to produce seamless, yet differentiated sounds. I was reminded of the hallways of schools where one could have heard children recite aloud their ABCs. Ayesha had developed these training exercises from her own performance background in English theatre. Other trainers showed film or video clips, and expected agents to successfully mimic the tones heard on screen. Still others offered up their own accents as examples for workers to model their speech. Most integrated the accent training with grammar and basic language training. So workers were asked to modify sentences, use polite phrases when speaking on the phone, learn typical ways of handling abusive or irate customers, and remedy incorrect sentence formations, all the while maintaining an accent. These attempts at accent often formed the subject of ridicule and hilarity among trainers and workers alike. While each worker considered himself an expert mimic (and these self-proclaimed performers of accent were almost always men), their co-workers were singled out as phony. '*Accent maarke dikha na* [Show me your accent]', was a common form of teasing and banter.

Workers often came to the call centre with their own understanding of American accent and slang. This tended to be a mixture of messages absorbed from Hollywood movies, Bollywood parodies, video jockeys on music channels, and friends from other call centres. Derek Thomas, one of the more experienced agents, who had at the time of this interview been working for two years, shared his experiences of being asked to speak in an American accent during the time of his interview:

> We used to watch a lot of English movies and then copy the dialogues. 'I'll be back', again the same thing, Arnold Schwarzenegger. So, copying the dialogues and copying the accent, we never realized this thing is going to help us in the near future ... on the day of the interview I was like, 'yo'. I was ready to face any damn thing. I was, full flow of accent. The person who was interviewing me for voice and accent, he was like, really impressed. I used all the US accent, and totally was like in the very happy.

To Derek, his preparation through exposure to Western media signified a minor victory, a sense of rightful admission to the 'western' call centre. Others however did not enter the call centre with any such preparation, and were often made to view Western television sitcoms, advertisements or shows. One of the most popular clips to be shown during training sessions at the call centre I worked at was Russell Peters' stand-up act. Peters is a Canadian of Indian origin, known to lampoon accents and speech, especially those of Indians and the Chinese. Of course, agents favoured Peters because these clips tended to be the most fun part of training sessions. They were entertaining in themselves, and accent training only arose as a justification for what was in essence, time off from exercises. What was absorbed from such a random selection was of course, a completely different genre of communication than that demanded by customer service standards. For example, during a mock call session meant to test workers' abilities to speak continually in an American accent, one of the trainees, Aamir, used the word 'dude' in a sentence. I was the trainer assigned to monitor performance and when I gently suggested that this might be too colloquial for a professional scenario, Aamir snapped, 'Dude, you got to watch movies sometimes. Americans say dude all the time'. Media generated understandings of American-ness often became intertwined with attempts to produce a so-called authentic accent.

Accents are semiotically complex. Drawing from the work of Charles Peirce, Bonnie Urciuoli explains how they are iconic in that they invoke images, indexical in that they are understood as causal or co-existential, and symbolic in that all this is culturally learned (Urciuoli 1996: 121). The accent in the call centre was meant to invoke the image of a typical, regular, white American. It indexed American-ness or the social identity of someone familiar to an American customer. However, the ability to culturally learn the accent was temporally and spatially truncated for the Indian call centre agent. Workers were only able to gain limited exposure to American or British accents, and partly only through images, media, and film. As a result, American 'culture' as absorbed through such reductive and stereotypical sources began to index the genre of transnational call centre communication.

However, call centre agents in urban India were habituated to people around them speaking not just many other languages, but also English in different Indian accents. Thus, even when workers were conversant in English, their speech was inflected and influenced by the local language. Scholars in World Englishes have extensively documented the hybridity of South Asian English in India, especially with reference to literary theory. While such hybridity finds place in questions of language development and change, it becomes a deterrent to transnational communication with its attendant relations of power in relation to the American or British customer. In the call centre, the tendency to Indian English was collectivized under the acronym 'MTI' or Mother Tongue Influence.

Since the organization that I worked at was located in Pune, in western India, where the language spoken was Marathi, and because a number of workers came from Marathi speaking backgrounds, the MTI had been determined by senior managers in the training department to be very specific. Instances of interchange in long and short vowel sounds ('ee' for the shorter 'i' sound and vice-versa, such as Virgeenia instead of Virginia), and inability to pronounce certain words like 'vision' (pronounced by Marathi speakers as 'vijhun') were very common. Additionally, workers were also warned against 'transliterating'. The latter here refers in call centre parlance to a literal translation from the speaker's native tongue into English. Workers were constantly instructed to pay heed to the structures of English and not indulge in liberally translating the sentences they constructed in day-to-day usage. For example, workers would often render the Hindi *'Aap ka shubh naam?'* into 'What is your good name?' which is a literal translation in this case, as opposed to a respectful form of asking for an introduction. 'They don't have good or bad names!', trainers would admonish them every time they committed this faux pas. Similarly, another common form of transliteration was the use of the future continuous tense in sentences such as 'I will be helping you' or 'I will be collecting your information'. Exasperated trainers would often react with 'What does it mean, you will be helping them? When? Tomorrow? Day after?'

The tendency to a locally inflected accent and 'transliterated' speech were nearly always ridiculed by trainers and workers alike. Many respondents ruefully confessed to having been shunted from one call centre to another on account of the excessive 'MTI' in their accents. Shilpa Mane, who was in a senior position at a small BPO unit, spoke about how she had been rejected at two places on account of the Marathi inflection in her accent. She shared how she had repeatedly worked towards perfecting her accent before being accepted at a well-known BPO in the city. Over many months of

work, she gained confidence and was able to reach her current position managing a team of five agents. 'It's a matter of dedication',
she said.

Trainers often considered correcting MTI to be one of their more
difficult core tasks. Making fun of such accents was *de rigueur* and
involved ethnic jokes and regional stereotyping. In class, Shaheen,
one of the senior trainers for a class of workers assigned to provide
customer care for a utilities company would often reprimand agents
with strong regional accents who could not pronounce the name
for the American state of Virginia. 'Vhurjeenya? Vhurjeenya? Keep
talking like this and I will send you to India Gas and Utilities. There,
you can say Vhurjeenya all day long.' The class would snigger at this
pronouncement. It became a popular refrain. Every time Shaheen
caught someone saying 'Vhurjeenya' the other workers would pipe
up, 'India Gas!' While the stereotyping of accent in speech (whether
English or Hindi) has long been an element of public and popular
culture in India, the continuous and institutionalized forms of evaluating accent in the call centre were particularly strong measures
in privileging one form of speech over many others. While there
existed a hierarchy of ethnicity in evaluating the MTI component
of accent,[6] regionally accented speech as a whole was given the
thumbs down and seen to be a mark of inadequacy in being a good
professional global worker. This further underlined the urban-rural
divide in access to education and English language skills. The dyads
referenced were in turn national/global, rural/urban, and provincial/
cosmopolitan.

Over time, the need to mask origin faded, even as knowledge
of the outsourcing industry in India became common. By the time
I began fieldwork in 2006, trainers, managers, and even workers were
advocating a 'neutral' accent. While at the least, 'neutralizing' MTI
was defined as one of the markers of a neutral accent, no one person
could put their finger on what such an accent would sound like.
A neutral accent, functioned then as an 'ideal type' (Weber et al.

---

[6] Workers who spoke Gujarati or Bengali and rural speakers of Marathi
were considered to have some of the hardest sets of MTIs to 'correct'.

1969), helping to seemingly set the house of chaotic accents in order. As a result, it ended up being defined differently by various stakeholders. Anuj, a worker who had been on calls for six months, considered a neutral accent to be one in which, 'I can be myself. I just speak slowly and use my own accent. I don't have to sound artificial. The trainers tell me I have a very Indian sounding accent, but the customer can understand me, so what is the problem?' For Sagar Gharpure, a trainer involved with a government sponsored training organization, a neutral accent was one tending to American modes of pronunciation—aspirated syllables and soft middle t's. He pronounced 'd-a-u-g-h-t-e-r' as 'dawder' and rolled his r's at the end of the word. Other workers and trainers considered aspirated 'p', 'k', and 't' sounds as the only real differences between an Indian and a neutral accent. If anything, they emphasized an accent closer to what they called a 'British accent' which however, tended to be different than the ways they spoke in their offline lives.

All trainers stressed clarity, communicability, and the possibility of conducting a successful sales call or customer service conversation, as the results expected of a neutral accent. Some even abandoned attempts at removing the dreaded MTI. Anna, a young worker who was holding down her second job spoke about her training period as stress-free and very easy to handle. 'They never trained us on US or UK at all. They trained us on general talking, neutral accent basically. We don't have any MTI training or don't sound US, UK anything. Very clear, very slow', she said. Managers, who were far more concerned with the ability to recruit and retain workers, also found the emphasis on accent frustrating. Sujay Shukla, a human resource manager, ranted:

> The first and foremost thing we learnt was, you don't need an accent knowledge. In US, there are more than eighty dialects. There is Spanish, there is French, French Canadian, Mexican kind of English. Maybe in the UK there is the northerners, the southerners, the Londoners. There are different kinds of languages.
>
> Within these people, there are the Indians, the Asians, the Chinese, the Sindhis, the Gujaratis, the Malayalees, different different types of English. There are people who are from the Eastern Europe side working in UK. They have a different language. How do people communicate

there? They easily understand right? Do I need to stress everytime that I have a UK or US accent? Not required.

Sujay Shukla had reinterpreted the linguistic milieu of the UK to correspond with that of India. He emphasized the diversity of language within the UK in order to back his argument that one did not need any sort of specifically British accent, because such an entity was neither singular nor was anything of the sort existent within the UK.

I argue that the deployment of the neutral accent in this instance helped construct the utterance in two ways—it attempted to dislocate it from its surrounding geography and its culturally enunciated failings, while also disavowing the blatant hierarchies embedded in demands to speak in American or British accents. However, the claims of such neutrality stood easily foiled. Despite celebratory claims to the effect that accents, neutral or otherwise, were merely additive and could be transposed onto existing English language skills in four to six weeks, the actual results were far less palatable to trainers, managers, and most importantly to clients and customers abroad. The plethora of genres influencing the utterance, which in itself was only defined as 'customer service' in a 'neutral accent', resulted in multiple accents and modes of speech creating the possibility of an 'agentive moment' (Daniel 1997: 191) that emphasized the continued absence of an American, British, or neutral accent. By this, I mean that while there seemed no clear indication of dissent or resistance in attaining a different language identity, the very presence of different influences in the face of a hegemonic linguistic regime, and the persistence of locally learnt organic English accents, can be read as a form of agency arising from the conjunction of a set of circumstances and dissident histories. This agentive moment, I argue, is what gave rise to the very advocacy of a neutral accent, one that in its own presence and heterogeneity, helped destabilize the neutrality of corporate demands for an American or a British accent.

## Speak English

When I started working at the call centre, I was initially struck by the discomfort a number of trainees felt with the English language.

Most trainers attempted to dispel workers' insecurities apropos language by exhorting them to speak in English all the time and by insisting that it was ultimately only a matter of practice. Many workers disregarded such insistence and behaved mostly like truant children, smirking and willing to speak in English only when trainers were spotted in the vicinity. But an equal number took these demands seriously and attempted earnestly to practise their English.

Workers I met during fieldwork, were from varied socioeconomic backgrounds. While some had moved from nearby towns for work, others were in the city in order to simultaneously pursue undergraduate education. Their familiarity with English ranged from complete fluency and ease of use, to tentative halting, and awkward phrasing. Besides issues of pronunciation, a large number of workers had difficulty speaking fluently and constructing thoughts in English. They often shared their sense of frustration in trying to render complex thoughts in a language in which they only possessed a fragmented fluency. Their vocabularies were limited, and their understanding of sentence construction rusty from limited conversational practice.

However, they were desirous of attaining fluency in English. For many of the agents in the call centre, English was not their first language. Only a very small percentage of urban middle-class men and women could claim English as their first language. Often workers' families were some of the most well-off in the provincial and rural areas that they called their 'native place'. Their parents were engineers, doctors, and educators and had tried hard to instil in their children the will for upward mobility, or at the least, the maintenance of middle-class-ness. One of the crucial characteristics of such mobility was the ability to be fluent in English. Andrew, one of my respondents, shared how his brother and he would be made to write essays in English every day as a way to improve their English:

> What happened is, I was studying, I had come from a place where language training is minimum. So whatever I learnt was from my elder brother, and my mom and dad. Because Dad used to make us read magazines and we used to read Mandrake comics and Superman comics and that was the only source and some English movies, good English movies.

That was the only source we can copy the accent, or learn English from. And, my mom and dad, at home also, they used to push me. *Chalo aise likho* [Write like this]. Write an essay on this thing. And even if there were lot of mistakes, they would say, good good. Good work. So, this thing helped a lot. But again, during the college time, we never used to speak in English. Whatever was there, it was an internal thing again.

In many ways, I could relate to this experience of the province. I grew up in what might be called a mofussil town. Part of the national landscape of industrializing townships, Rasayani, so named because it was home to a plethora of chemical industries (chemical translates as 'rasayan' in Hindi), was home to a dozen factories and its populations. My family and I were part of the 'colonies' that housed the managerial, white-collar population of the town. The colonies were the elite and preserved their status by way of language, consumption, mannerisms, and habits. I grew up speaking English and greeting my parents' friends in English and speaking English at home as much as my native Tamil.

The ability to speak fluently and confidently in English has always been a prominent means of attaining cultural capital in the Indian middle-class milieu. It is part of a set of knowledge skills that allows people to either enhance or maintain their social situation. Using a certain mode of speech in English brings them symbolic capital through prestige as well as material rewards (Bourdieu and Thompson 1991). Control over the English language is read as a sign of education, which is a sign of investment in class mobility (Urciuoli 1996). However, as Urciuoli argues, people only develop their sense of what codes mean in specific relations and contexts. While middle-class-ness configured this understanding of language hierarchy, call centre work emphasized this on a different register.

Since the 1990s, there has been an increasing recognition that no matter the disparagement of English language usage in populist politics, it is nevertheless the language of not only cosmopolitanism, but also opportunity (LaDousa 2008). Investments in the Indian service industry channeled this history into effective transnational profits. Many service sectors such as retail, airline, hospitality, and outsourcing further contributed to this increasing demand for English-speaking workers. As a result, language training and the need for linguistic competence announced themselves boldly across urban spaces (Figure 4.1). During the time that I was in Pune, from 2006 through 2007, I saw advertisements on billboards, classified ads for private language lessons, and workshops by self-proclaimed experts, all attempting to mediate access to the English language. One of them read, 'Learn English; Develop Personality; Gain Success'.

Language politics in India have historically reacted badly to upsurges in the promotion of English language usage, and similar scenes were played out in Pune. In January 2006, the Shiv Sena, a right-wing political party prominent in the city, stormed Senapati Bapat road, one of the main thoroughfares in Pune, and stoned a Domino's pizza outlet and Piramyd's, a retail chain and upmarket mall respectively. The activists were protesting against the English signage, according to the police. No people were reported to be hurt in this act of vandalism. The Sena activists had also threatened to attack a McDonald's outlet on Junglee Maharaj or J.M. road, but the presence of the police prevented it. Sena activist, Ajay Shinde, stated that shopkeepers had been urged to change the signage on the name boards from English to Marathi over the previous week. While some of them had obliged, others were being conveyed the message 'in Sena's language', he said (*Times of India*, Pune Edition, 8 January 2006). While many read this as a continuation of the Shiv Sena's agenda of whipping up frenzy against the enemy within, there were other equally 'compelling' reasons for the critique of English language hegemony. Rajeswari Sunder Rajan summarizes elegantly, the underlying and motivating forces that propel critiques as including the following:

> ... the increase in India's economic and military status; the consequent tokenism of such post-colonial affiliations such as the Commonwealth; the formation of significant third world alliances such as the Non-Aligned Movement (NAM) and the South Asian Association for Regional Co-operation (SAARC); global support for the anti-apartheid movement; third world vigilance against economic exploitation and neo-colonization by multinational corporations and international funding agencies; and significantly, the anti-English propaganda of certain national political parties in response to internal divisive tendencies within the country. (1992: 13)

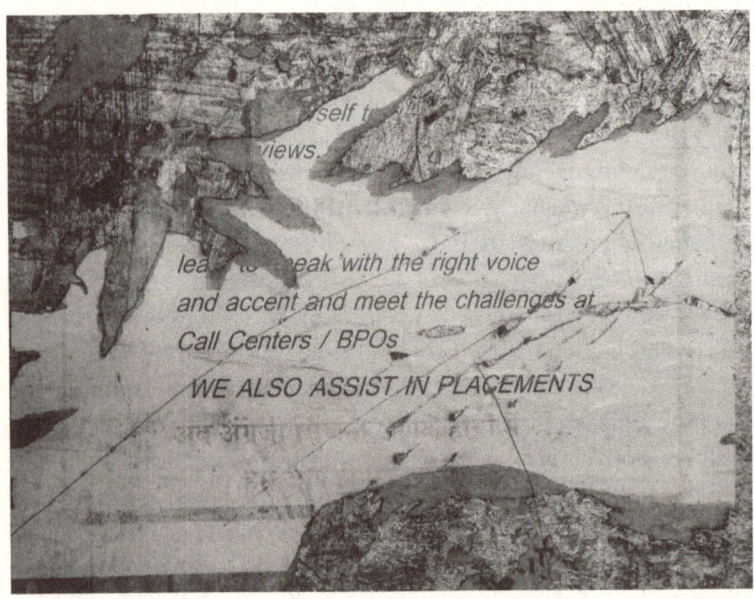

**Figure 4.1** Learning to Speak
*Source*: Author.

The state, however, was not merely represented by right-wing ideologies and also voiced its language politics through other means. In 2007, I volunteered to work for a leading government-affiliated civic body in Pune. Since I had already spent some months training at the call centre, I was asked if I could conduct workshops for older government employees in Pune. The workshops were meant to talk about language, as well as presentation and management skills. I never ended up training for these workshops, but I did see banners for communication programs week after week as I rode by the imposing gates to the institute's campus. This institution, the 'only government-recognized call centre training institute' in Pune, also worked with young men and women with very little knowledge of English in order that 'our people' were not to be 'left behind'. According to Anil Deo, a trainer at the institute, their objective was to 'groom up the Marathi people so we can groom them in the coming corporate world'. When I asked him if teaching people English was not counter intuitive to the linguistic integrity of the nation, he responded:

> What the government is doing is okay from the perspective that when you go outside you need certain things. Government knows that it is an international language. If they went to develop their state, they need language.

In this case, the inside and outside were re-defined in the need to deal with both global influx of work and changing standards of professionalization. Such attempts and discourse can be seen as helping the nation-state preserve integrity and identity even while coupling such a mandate with the corporate call for globalization and economic liberalization.[7] English was therefore, variously and

---

[7] The paradoxical politics of the need to be fluent in English have been widely documented by scholars in South Asian Studies. For the a historical analysis of the politics of language education in Maharashtra, see Veronique Bénéï (2005). For a case study of how multiple language markets subvert the Indian government's language policies, see Chaise LaDousa (2008).

Also see Chaise LaDousa (2007) for an analysis of the ways in which language ideology can be seen to construct particular notions of the Indian state.

continually defined as the language of progress and mobility, one that the nation could not afford to ignore (Bénéï 2005; LaDousa 2008, 2007).

### Sneaky Subjects and Forked Tongues

During the time I worked as a communications trainer, I encountered various levels of fatigue among my fellow trainers. My colleagues often lamented the fact that it was getting more and more difficult to train workers. Their current batches of trainee workers, they said, had to be taught everything right from constructing a sentence to appropriate word usage. Accent, they thought, continued to be an elusive goal in the face of these other 'basic' language impediments. In these accounts, language and accent were constructed in a clear chronology of training modules. Sentence construction, grammar, and appropriate word usage were considered the primary building blocks. Tone featured after such language competence, and accent functioned as a finishing touch. In the day-to-day workings of the training process, I often found trainers rebuking workers thus, 'Accent maarne se kuch naheen hoga, pehle bolna seekh [It's no use getting the accent, learn how to speak first]'.

Given the increasing demand for workers, high levels of attrition, and the consequent search for new labour populations in provincial India, the call centre had increasingly been recruiting young workers with a regional language education, in the hope that they could be trained to communicate in English. The assumption was that workers could develop the minimal language skills required to deal with a defined set of customer service scenarios, or possibilities. Thereafter, experience on the job was expected to provide enough repetitive instances that the workers could then effectively communicate within a limited range of business situations. Language in case of call centre work was thus sought to be unmoored from both its status as knowledge as well as its entanglement with middle- or upper-middle-class upbringing.

All trainers had between two to six weeks to turn a language problem into communicative success, and were therefore instructed to follow a 'problem-solution' approach. We enumerated bits and parts of sentences, enunciation, and tone. We taught workers noun and verb forms, intoned long and short vowels, and attempted to prevent them interchanging 'v' and 'w' sounds. 'Bite your v's and kiss your w's', we implored. Language training became a process of repetition and memorization. When after a month, I observed and listened in on agents taking calls, there seemed to have been palpable change. Agents repeated sentences suggested by the trainers. Words were confidently mispronounced. Their grammatical structures were garbled, but there were no stuttering pauses. Agents spoke assertively and their sentences flowed. Language disabilities had metamorphosed into smart communication. The lessons they had learnt well were on presentation, tone, and confidence—in other words, a complete repertoire of 'soft skills'. They were indeed, talking the talk. Many of them had what Sheetal, an agent with a year of experience working in a call centre, called 'convincing power'. She elaborated thus:

> They know what they want to say in their head, but because they are not fluent in speaking English, they don't speak English at home. So they can't put it into words. So sometimes you have to actually help them formulate it in words. I've seen people have those problems. Because I speak English at home.
>
> They had trouble but they would actually manage to convince a person to talk to them for 45 minutes. Which was amazing. Because they couldn't actually speak well. But they had good convincing power. So, they managed to do it. They would actually hire many people who didn't speak all that well, because of their need for people.

'Convincing power' or the ability to speak charismatically and persuasively came to be understood as one of the ways by which to disguise and overcome lack of fluency in English. As a result, training programs in the call centre tried to ensure minimal fluency and familiarity with the language, while emphasizing confidence and the ability to be assertive. While I do not argue that this delinked English from its status connotations, I do seek to bring attention to how its aesthetic force was both strengthened and supplemented by a selfhood confident of getting by in the world.

This training in becoming 'confident' catered to many workers entering the call centre with their own agendas. Workers were young students, often just out of high school or completing their undergraduate education with little idea of Weberian corporate discipline. When instructed to speak in English all the time, few complied. As Ravi stated, '*Kitni der Angrezi main bakne ka? Kantal aa jaata hai* [How long can I jabber in English? I get bored after a while]'. However, such resistance was neither uniform nor openly rebellious. Workers were clearly aware of the performance parameters and the minimal language skills they needed to exhibit, in order to keep their job. While possessing limited ability to communicate in English, they worked hard at both English language and their presentation skills in order to be perceived as competent, not only in the call centre, but in future careers, interviews for graduate school, and other urban service industries.

Many trainees in the classes I conducted were very open about their having joined the organization in order to gain lessons on professionalism. They had entered the call centre in a bid to obtain the requisite skills for becoming a professional, English-speaking, transnational worker. Language skills and 'personality training' as imparted in the call centre could travel to other service industries such as retail, hotel management, and airline services. Workers often joined the call centre only to resign immediately after undergoing communications training, and being certified as competent speakers. As Rohan, a former call centre worker shared his experiences, he said,

> My language has improved a lot thanks to you. Since childhood I was studying in an English school, but all Gujaratis around me. Now I try and converse a lot in English. I have been successful at all my interviews since leaving.

For Rohan, the call centre stint had been akin to a language training workshop rather than a professional workspace. It had functioned as a refresher course to address what he considered gaps in his education.

## Who Will Train the Trainer?

My introduction to the emotional terrain of the call centre was primarily through my experiences as a voice and accent trainer.

This possibility was enabled by a serendipitous combination of professional networks, middle-class background, and life in US academia. I discovered that my colleagues in the call centre, similarly had varied linguistic and educational backgrounds. Some, like myself had been hired on account of life experiences in the US and the UK, others were former agents who had moved up the organizational ladder and still others, were former English school-teachers. The content of training manuals were often configured by a small sub-set of senior trainers, some of whom had experiences in language teaching, in consultation with senior management. As a result, not all trainers were uniformly conversant with language teaching as a set of rules. A trainer, who had been promoted from her role as an agent, once complained tearfully about having been terrorized by the rookie workers, '*Bahut badmaash hain, they ask me about grammar. Ab mujhe kya pata ki subject aur object kya hota hai?* [They are upto no good, they ask me about grammar. Now what do I know what subject and object are?]'.

Workers however, also often idolized trainers. Their attachments to trainers ranged from hero-worshipping them, to ridiculing others, as also to developing romantic or sexual feelings towards male and female trainers alike. Uniformly many workers spoke openly of their admiration and respect for those who had taught them to 'speak right', as one shared. They remembered trainers' names, and spoke about them as people who had instilled a sense of 'proper' speech and self-esteem. Trainers functioned as workers' touchstones, sounding boards, objects of attachment, mentors, and/or ideal speakers. Mimicking them worked to attend to the requirements of voice and accent training, as well as to pandering to trainers' egos and their subjective notions of the 'right' accent and tone.

One morning, I walked into the training session to see ten of the agents sniggering and whispering in conspiratorial tones. I began running them through sentence formations and customer service phrases. One of the students interjected with a question and asked as to the correct pronunciation of the proper noun, Virginia—an exercise we had run through *ad nauseam* the previous week. As was my wont, I cocked an eyebrow to indicate my disapproval and surprise at the question. Suddenly, I found myself staring at ten other faces similarly cocking an eyebrow before they all burst into laughter. I couldn't help but grin at this mimicry of gesture, one I had used to great effect earlier and which clearly did not serve its purpose anymore.

Trainers affected various means to teach agents. These ranged from humiliation, shaming, and authoritarian and stentorian tones, to cajoling, friendship, camaraderie, and sometimes, sexual innuendo and romantic flirting. In some ways, trainers' methods formed what Brenda Weber has called 'affective domination'—a combination of 'shame and love-power' (Weber 2007: 81). Chakrabarty (2002) states that the gate by which one enters modernity (citizenship or nationality) always has a *durwan* (guard) posted outside, himself only partially admitted to the rites of equality; his job is thus to be mean, to bully, and to exclude. Trainers, I argue, served such a function by playing out some scene of idealized language and comportment, a space that they themselves only partially comprehended, but felt themselves deserving of, thanks to either class position, travel abroad, and/or other signs of a middle- and upper-middle-class upbringing. Also, in comparison to young agents, trainers considered themselves better purveyors of style, speech, and professionalism. While possessing varying and inconsistently competent levels of language skills, they did not hesitate to make fun of specific workers in their absence, mimicking inflected pronunciations, or language usage. During evaluation sessions where a set of trainers passed judgement on workers' performances over the phone, the trainer leading the process would often have to intervene and request other trainers to have more respect for the feelings of workers.

Makeovers serve as a near-perfect analogy to this process except that in the case of call centres, training was not a part of public culture, but rather served as an important rite of passage within the organization. Humiliation seemed to be part of what one must endure in order to effect transformation and at some point, there was a shift from shaming to love-power, which signalled the endpoint of this process. Many workers expressed their admiration, respect, and gratitude to trainers, once they had quit the call centre, claiming that it was these specific trainers who had eased them into call centre work. James shared his experiences about training and his trainers in unabashed admiration:

> And then, the voice and accent training, it lasted for two weeks. And I had a trainer from Canada. His name was Nick Cramer. And one of them was Amit Thatte. They make you work. They were too good. First they used to be really tough on me. Then they said, James you did good. I felt so good.

Similarly, many other agents remembered former trainers by name and even stayed in touch after leaving the call centre. I retained my cell phone number after quitting the call centre and would often receive phone calls from former workers up to two years after I had quit work.

## Limits of the Hybrid and the Fluid

While I have posited language as fluid and increasingly modular in the instance of the call centre, it reached its limits soon enough. For example, when I attended a call centre interview with an aspiring worker who had ten years of experience in the hotel management industry, he was asked to talk about himself. He responded in halting English and was promptly sent away. Evaluations of expertise were clearly contingent upon questions of demand and supply, and notions of flexibility. The worker in this instance was no doubt judged as too old and hence lacking the flexibility to be trained in English language skills.

It was difficult to observe the failure to perform. It was difficult to fail. This was especially true of young students and trainees who were yet to attain the cynicism and expertise of work. During training sessions, they cried, raged, stood speechless, and often just glared as trainers, managers, colleagues, and American clients pointed out their inability to be a good speaking subject. Workers tried hard to deliver correct speech in the face of various pressures. The job itself was at stake. For many, this avenue functioned as the first test of their ability to be professional workers and earning members of the family. Further, memories of school and college evaluations were never far behind. As Saira, a young high-school graduate said, 'It looks so bad. I fought so much to come work here; I can't fail'.

Even as worker intake into the call centre industry rose at exponential rates, the limits to this arrangement were sometimes starkly and poignantly exposed. At Systematix, trainers and the applicants they interviewed over the phone, would only be located a few floors apart. Evaluation or calibration sessions often ended with trainers sneaking off to the interview location to see who it was that had performed badly or spoken in regionally accented language and slang. Trainers often reacted, to what they considered was ludicrous English language speech, by high-five-ing each other and passing comments like heckling back-benchers in a high school class. Anaita, who was the training manager, would be forced to adopt a stern tone in warning them to hold their laughter. In one such session that I was a part of, we interviewed a man who identified himself as Ramoji. He answered the phone and did not say anything except hello. When asked as to who was speaking, he said, 'Myself Ramoji'. It was clear to the person asking the questions, in this case Anaita, that the man could not understand anything being said. Subsequent questions, even when spoken slowly, elicited no response except sounds of acknowledgement. To every question, Ramoji would reply '*haan* [yes]', 'ok', and 'yes'. Finally, in frustration, Anaita asked him to end the call and usher in the next person. He did so and the room erupted into laughter.

A colleague called Jeevan declared, '*Pata naheen kahaan kahaan se aa jate hain, sourcing paagal ho gaya hai kya?* [Where all do they come from? Has sourcing lost its mind?]'. The others speculated that he must have entered the organization along with the other hopefuls for 'walk-in' interviews. Reema said, '*Isko laga hoga ki mereko bhi call centre mein kaam karne ka hai? Full khede-gaon*[8] *type lagta hai* [He must have thought that even I want to work in a call centre, seems like a complete villager]'. Anaita re-dialled for the next interview candidate, only to find Ramoji back on the line. He apparently had hung up and stayed there, not understanding Anaita's instructions. She then spoke to him in Hindi but he

[8] The meaning of *khede-gaon* is a little more specific than just *gaon* which is a village. *Khede-gaon* indicates an emphasis on village-ness or lack of knowledge of the city and its ways.

continued to stay online. Finally, someone in the room told him in Marathi to bring the next candidate in. Ramoji went offline. In this instance, one can see the limits of 'opportunity', 'personality development', and 'success'. While many learnt to speak English, present themselves well, and overcome fear, first-time work jitters and recalcitrant tongues, Ramoji had to be sent back.

\* \* \*

The business of the transnational call centre depended largely on workers' abilities to communicate in the English language. Media accounts and business journals have all focused on the advantage that a large, urban, middle-class, and English-speaking population proved in the creation of the voice-based Indian outsourcing economy. Two areas, however, remained ambiguous in this supposition. One was the understanding of the Indian middle class in itself an inadequately defined broad population, possessing varied levels of cultural capital (Fernandes 2006), and the changes it has experienced to its internal make-up over the first decade of the twenty-first century. The second important predicament had to do with the tenability of attempts to harness and commodify the cultural capital of this class into a homogenous, linguistic, and vocal offering.

There are three aspects to the question of language training that this chapter has examined. One, what are the facets of language that were sought to be co-opted in the service of the call centre? Two, how was language commoditized by breaking it up into its component parts? Also, how did this presuppose the emotional labour of a speaking subject that could inject language with certainty, conviction, and care? Lastly, what questions of both historical and contemporary subjectivity can one find inherent to this moment of speech and the process of training the worker to speak? In the service of a serviceable language, the call centre industry attempted to flatten regional difference and varied histories of English language education into a professional and efficient process of language deployment. While embedded in the belief, that the colonized in this instance are not 'passive actors of a Western script' (Sharpe 1995), this chapter is however not about resistance. I have sought to dislocate agency from the speaking subject onto the processes of language standardization. By sketching how flexibility incorporated itself furtively into the techniques, definitions, and indeed, understanding of how English works in this milieu, this chapter has sought to examine how the day-to-day work of the call centre was rendered effective. Whether through 'mimicry' or by re-inscribing flexibility onto the very processes that would render subjects flexible, one can begin to identify agency and possibility. In the final analysis, I argue this to be not merely the deployment of culture towards managing a workforce, but also the cultural manifestation and inscription of flexibility.

The 'failures' and subsequent modifications of language training reveal how the road to a hegemonic flexibility is tenuous, and often deviates in ways unforeseen by discourse tending to either pro- or anti-globalization stances. Rather than understanding the inability of agents to reproduce accent and 'neutral' English as resistance to neo-colonial globalization, I concentrate on the aspirations that animated workers' efforts, and the impact of such training on questions of subjectivity and flexibility in the service economy that I chronicle.

Posters, advertisements, advertorials, and telesales spots attested to a continuing, and in some ways accelerated concern, with the ability to communicate in English. If one were to believe this evidence, then it wouldn't be difficult to suggest that English had become the *lingua franca* of an India seeking to become global. In such a world, it is perhaps possible to see apocalyptic visions of a teeming million learning how to make the subject agree with the verb, use articles at appropriate places, and speak English 'correctly'. However, I contend that understanding everyday communication around the call centre is an important window to the globalization of English, towards understanding linguistic hegemony as a contradictory process. More importantly, I argue that they re-define over the longer term, the realm of the normative in language, communication, and forms of linguistic identity.

At the same time, what are also important are the ways in which flexible capital schools new labour populations. While borrowing from a past that created English-speaking populations, new service economies nevertheless allowed for an increasing cache of labour forces by relaxing the norms of the linguistic aesthete and reconfiguring ways of attaining communicative efficiency and corporate subjectivity. I argue that by noticing the changing boundaries of 'good' English, we can chart a path to understanding how globalization re-configures commodities and selves. I argue that in case of the call centre, the politics of English had been rearticulated in conversation with the opportunities made possible by globalization. To what extent then does this also expose the messy nature of globalization that seeks to create a universally recognizable, communicable worker and yet often ends up with a particular local/global subject—impure, mixed up, and crafty?

In concluding, I offer an anecdote. As I was leaving India to return to graduate school in Austin, Texas, I visited a new privatized bank in my hometown Rasayani, a semi-urban industrial estate in western India. I needed to transfer my salary account, which had been created when I started working at the call centre. In chatting with the bank officer Akash, who was helping me with procedures, we discovered that we had attended the same high school and had common friends. I updated him on my whereabouts in the US, we chatted about people we knew in common, and caught up on our life paths. While glancing at my paperwork, he noticed that I had worked with a call centre for a few months. So now, Akash had two bits of information to help map my educational competence. One, I was working on a doctoral degree in the social sciences in the US and two, I had worked in the BPO industry. He remarked, 'Oh you worked at a call centre, that is why your English is too good'.

# 5

## THE AFFECTIVE CORPORATION

### Regimes of Affective Labour

Many scholars of globalization are in agreement that capitalist modernity is without a doubt, intimate. In other words, capitalist modernity works from within the intimate lives of its subjects. However, notions of its effects on such lives continue to follow either one of two familiar streams of rhetoric within globalization narratives of the twenty-first century. On the one hand, those living in the 'polished, expensive, globally networked cities of the West' (Elliott and Lemert 2006: 2) seem to be beset by a loss of emotional connection, a condition of contagion as widespread as the movement of goods, capital, and people. Even as mobilities of capital create possibilities of connection, human relations are said to be primarily individualistic, and ravaged by an increasing distance from *communitas*. Coming to modernity and its attendant forms of life, communication, and labour seems to bring with it a necessary alienation. Consider, for example, Sherry Turkle's work on social communication and virtual worlds. Building upon her studies of children and identity in digital worlds, Turkle, in her recent book, *Reclaiming Conversation* (2015) investigates the ways in which technology mediates communication, thereby doing away with constraints of time and space, while simultaneously rendering its users devoid of empathy and connection. Similar to her thesis are numerous academic and popular treatises on the increasing distance we seem to inhabit between the mechanics of our lives and our ability to be invested in them. While Turkle's *bête noire* is this 'robotic moment', others have been concerned with the ways in which new forms of technology and connection help put work at the heart of daily concerns, at the expense of other possibilities of intimacy and engagement, to the extent that one of the monopolizing registers for feeling love or attachment becomes work (Gregg 2011).

An adjacent view, on the other hand, holds that globalization itself builds upon and is received through forms of intimacy, and that indeed, practices of consumerism, production, and work stem not from the homogenization of the world but through and within the intimate feelings of participating subjects (Ilouz 1997b; Rutherford 2016; Wilson 2004). Globalization in this alternate conception encompasses both a constitutive intimacy as well as a set of culturally, but also intimately specific ways in which subjects respond to large-scale processes of economic and political change. The editors of a volume titled *Love and Globalization*, for example, are interested in how 'love is a highly productive tool for social analysis, revealing some of the most basic ways that human societies organize social life, meaning, and intimate experience, as well as how individuals enact, resist, or transform social discourses of love within specific cultural and historical contexts' (Padilla et al. 2007: ix). Yet others show, how forms of intimacy we understand under labels such as love, have been formed under, and are always already part of the neoliberal complex of late capitalism (Ilouz 1997a). Perhaps, useful in these deliberations might be an understanding of capitalism as a modality of often conflicting but co-existing feelings. Ara Wilson in her ethnography on the sexed and gendered market economies of Bangkok, for example, shows the many logics that capitalism co-exists with, and re-invents. In her understanding, the 'realization of intimate lives through capitalist venues both reproduces and transforms aspects of identity, social relationships and cultural meanings' (Wilson 2004: 193).

The call centre industry, and indeed, India's foray into the service economies of post-Fordist capitalism have been theorized as creating regimes of affective labour (Mankekar and Gupta 2016). These regimes can be seen as instantiations of what Aihwa Ong, among others, understands to be the gendered labour politics of postmodernity, wherein labour forces are produced and maintained through social regulations, regimes of bodily discipline, and culturally located formations of kinship and gender (Ong 1991). Affective labour, in this formulation, is considered a particular and important enunciation of immaterial labour, or 'labor that produces an immaterial good, such as a service, knowledge, or communication' (Hardt 1999: 94). If immaterial labour is the umbrella concept that produces among other things, affects, its primary goal is towards the production of social relationships, in the absence of which it will not produce economic value (Lazzarato 1996). Hardt builds upon postmodern formations of kin work and care labour in his understanding of immaterial labour, and theorizes affective labour as being 'at the very pinnacle of the hierarchy of laboring forms' (Hardt 1999: 90).

In her seminal work on airline stewardesses, Arlie Hochschild defines this in a narrower fashion as emotional labour, or the kind of labour, which 'requires one to induce or suppress feeling in order to sustain the outward countenance that produces the proper state of mind in others—in this case, the sense of being cared for in a convivial and safe place' (Hochschild 1983: 7). Hochschild's concerns in this work follow Marxist understandings of the commodity and have to do with how the performance of such a service can produce alienation from self. Theorists of affective labour, on the contrary, are not concerned with authenticity and self, as much as they are concerned with the ways in which such work practices 'produce collective subjectivities, produce sociality, and ultimately produce society itself' (Hardt 1999: 89). Recent enunciations of such labouring practices involve themselves with socio-political, and indeed deeply economic arrangements, that organize what can and cannot be felt in order to secure for subjects a good life. They goad us towards imagining, 'how the world might look, feel, or sound if experienced by an actor situated in a particular place and time' (Rutherford 2016: 286).

In this chapter, I examine social formations and their relation to modernizing markets, and ask: What kind of collective subjectivities are produced by labouring practices? By what means are they corralled into the performance norms of new service economies, thereby rendering the production of human connection central to the practice of work? Are human relations the casualties that fall prey to the bulldozing effects of capitalizing markets? Or are they the agentive forces instrumental in disrupting capitalist regimes? I trace formations of affect and intimacy in the call centre corporation, and investigate questions of community and relatedness in a bid to engage with these questions. Within various accounts of bureaucracy, Fordist and Taylorist regimes of work and time, and commoditization of body and emotion, I examine the practices and experiences of the call centre community by seeking to understand them as affective, and immaterial labour. I locate these experiences as transient, yet familiar, even as I read them through vocabularies of family, community, empathy, and love in order to trace their resilience and location. While scholars of affective labour seem to be in agreement that labour regimes co-opt emotional lives, what is unclear is whether this signals a new form of life or merely the rapacious nature of a capital formation that swallows life in its wake. More often than not, life lies, somewhere in between. Recent work on economies of surrogacy by a number of excellent feminist scholars, for example, has demonstrated how moves to ban the industry in India have been opposed by participating surrogates, many of who respond to the possibility by demanding better regulatory practices acknowledging their labour as well as relationship to the commissioning parents and child they bear—the process therefore lying 'somewhere between contractual labour and motherly altruism (Pande 2010: 978). Other scholars have also shown how they pose their labour as an act of virtue, and a morally reciprocal relationship between surrogates and the commissioning parents (Majumdar 2014).

Drawing upon these theoretical and ethnographic possibilities, I organize this chapter around the question of the labour required to produce affects, as well as alternate locations for affective experiences in the call centre. In the first part of this chapter, I detail processes geared towards producing positive affects in the customer. I examine the question of voice, its training, and its relation to identity and self. In the second half of the chapter, I look at the intentional as well as accidental production of the call centre as a set of 'affective atmospheres' (Anderson 2009). For Anderson, these atmospheres are ambiguous, floating 'between presence and absence, between subject and object/subject and between the definite and indefinite', abetting the experience of affect 'beyond, around, and alongside the formation of subjectivity', and allowing us therefore to think of atmospheres as being able to 'interrupt, perturb and haunt fixed persons, places or things' (Anderson 2009: 78). I am interested, therefore, in such atmospheres as produced as well as felt, and therefore possessing the possibility to interrupt. If the business of the call centre was to produce affects, then I also ask as to the ways in which such deployment produced affected subjects, both through the process and the place of work, and if there might be a way to imagine such subjects in their multiple inhabitations.

## Customer Servicing Selves

What forms the mechanics of the labour required to produce affects in customers? In the call centre, labour was rooted in the concept of customer service as important to producing customer satisfaction and hopefully, an ongoing relationship. The primary affective work practice of the call centre was, therefore, the production and maintenance of a customer relationship, which involved attending to and resolving transnational queries and concerns over a five to ten minute phone call; in other words, with very little time to develop one. The worker was however, only one of the many modalities of producing such a relationship.

Customer satisfaction in new service economies, a seemingly sophisticated improvement on traditional marketing concepts, revolves around what a classic marketing text has defined as, a 'person's feeling of pleasure or disappointment which resulted from comparing a product's perceived performance or outcome against his/her expectations' (Kotler and Keller 2006: 144). The terms to note here are 'feelings' and 'perceived'. In other words, the corporation needs to be able to influence both feelings and perceptions surrounding its product or service. As follows from these business discourses, customer service demands that any and all points of engagement need to be marked by the corporation. From the point of time that the customer comes in contact with anything that the organization can claim as its own—a billboard, a television advertisement, an employee—the looming clock starts ticking. The seller's store frontage, an article in a journal, a newspaper report, sales personnel, their terms of speech and tone of voice, all become part of the 'customer experience'.[1] The corporation in such a framework stands defined not as one physical entity, but as a vast network of nodes of contact, wherein contact is defined loosely as the affective production of the sense of contact. The call centre worker was also such a point of contact, and had therefore to be taught to actively embody and produce 'positive' affects.

To be a good call centre professional, the worker needed to not only read but also adroitly deploy the emptiness of the language of customer service. She had to be trained to use pleasantries, allay fears, restore confidence, and ensure that the hundred odd customers that called in every night were assured not only a useful, but also a pleasant conversation. Small talk, politeness, and concern therefore became part of the work that the agent performed. In the new regimes of service economies, the emphasis can be seen to have shifted to 'customer experience' as a bundle of affects.

Workers took pride in their ability to solve situations, and allay customers, and understood the modification of voice, tone, and language as routes to not only the manipulation of the customer, but indeed, the world. Their successful performance of the job was intimately related to their sense of self as competent, and this allowed for diligence and discipline in their adoption of

[1] The rise of the Public Relations or PR industry can be seen to be the other side of the coin, in that, it arose primarily to defend corporate interests against critical analyses, and to promote consumption in the early twentieth century. Edward Bernays, often considered the founder of PR, authored several influential books during this time, outlining the application of the social sciences towards the engineering of consent. A counter to this, is of course, Edward Herman and Noam Chomsky's seminal work *Manufacturing Consent* (1988), which rued this 'propaganda model of communication' in its deleterious effects and consequences.

these processes. Often, notwithstanding the hostility, impatience, or non-co-operation of the customer at the other end of the line, the worker had to produce positive affects, and indeed a favourable outcome to the conversation. This single-minded ability to perform the requirements of customer service, while remaining calm in the face of abuse, was articulated by Deepak, a customer service agent who had been on the job for three years:

> The last time I was having a word with a US client, he asked me one question. He said, Deepak, tell me, how often do you get frustrated? This was a casual talk that we were having. We were having some personal talk about the process. I said, every second. He said, how come you control all this? I said, Sir, there is a saying in English, you can't stop the bird from flying across your head, but you can always stop them from building a nest in your hair. He started laughing.

Dilip, another agent of long standing tenure, when speaking with a worker called Anand on the latter's first day of taking calls similarly cautioned him, 'You shouldn't get nervous. The customer then takes advantage of the situation. Stay calm and be cool. Speak confidently'. The need to stay unruffled demanded a management and performance of self. One is reminded of James Scott's theorization of resistance and agency, wherein he argues that training in verbal facilities 'enables vulnerable groups not only to control their anger but to conduct what amounts to a veiled discourse of dignity and self-assertion within the public transcript' (Scott 1990: 137). My understanding of labour in the call centre acknowledges workers to be similarly vulnerable to bad feedback and abuse from customers, but argues that their labour practices are a socialization into the ways in which self, voice, and comportment could produce desirable affects in the world. The logical understanding in this argument is that workers open themselves to abuse and derision, suffering it in the hope that they learn how to inure themselves to call centre work's abusive effects, while simultaneously manipulating customers' bad feelings into positive and indeed lucrative affects. Such a process, as might be obvious, is never fully accomplished, but is more importantly fundamentally paradoxical. On the one hand, the worker aspires to immunity and invulnerability, while on the other, seeks to makes connection and conversation. How then, does one think of individual autonomy and identity in this scenario, without concluding that affective labour produces automatons whose very feelings are subject to the vagaries of late capitalism? Is there any possibility of imagining agents that possess agency?

## Self Knowledge

*Governance through enterprise construes the individual as an entrepreneur of his own life, who relates to others as competitors and his own being as a form of human capital. In this organized self-relation, individual autonomy is not an obstacle or limit to social control but one of its central technologies.*

—Lois McNay, 'Self as Enterprise: Dilemmas of Control and Resistance in Foucault's *The Birth of Biopolitics*' (2009: 63)

Bourdieu and Giddens are often considered the foundational theorists of agency, even as they build on the arguments of Marx, Weber, and Durkheim on the relationship of the individual to society. Giddens' *Theory of Structuration* (1984), discusses the ways in which people's actions, are both constrained and enabled, by the very social structures that they go on to either reinforce or reconfigure. This is perhaps but an extension of Bourdieu's notion of the *habitus* as a generative process that defines a range of practices and representations as actions possible within this milieu, which then reproduce or reconfigure the *habitus* (Bourdieu 1977, 1990). However, neither Giddens nor Bourdieu are able to adequately examine how social reproduction at some point engenders social transformation (Sewell 1992). Further, neither structuration theory, nor the *habitus*, open up space to think about the rapid dissolution and reconfiguration of norms within globalized landscapes (Appadurai 1996). Bourdieu argues, that the ways in which agents see and shape the world is also part of the same world that creates these individuals (Bourdieu 1977). The concept of identity in this approach is one in which there is no pre-social identity. In Stuart Hall's understanding, for example, identities are made visible by being performatively sutured into subject positions made available through larger cultural codes (Hall 1996). In this process, they also render themselves unstable, divided and haunted by the outside, or in other words, by the values and affiliations that have been temporarily closed off through the process of identification.

Addressing one half of this equation is Erving Goffman's work on the interaction order. For Goffman, the self occupies no social space (MacIntyre 1985: 32), and so his precise emphasis is on everyday routines, which he understands in terms of a performance or drama (Goffman 1969), and as a game (Goffman 1961). In each set of routines, interaction is co-operative, organized, ordered, and rule-governed. However, such interaction occurs in a world of negotiation and transaction, which interactional routines themselves enable and create, and therefore, this is a universe in which implicit and explicit rules are resources rather than determinants of behaviour. Collectively, Goffman imagines this as an interaction order (1983), or the face-to-face domain of dealings between embodied individuals. The interaction order and 'social structure' are implicated in each other, in a relationship of 'loose coupling' (Goffman 1983: 11) where each is entailed in the other, but neither determines the other.

Bourdieu's notion of 'habitus' (1977: 72–95; 1990: 52, 65) is also suggestive of such an order, although in his account, the individual is much more the locus and product of a field of social relations. Habitus is a corpus of dispositions, embodied in the individual, and generative of practices in ongoing and improvisatory interactions with social fields. Bourdieu emphasizes the improvisational quality of interaction, namely the range of behaviours made possible by the 'habitus' within which the individual attempts to gain cultural capital. In Bourdieu, such activity is realized in *le sense pratique* (feel for the game, a pre-reflexive and embodied practical knowledge). This, according to him, is a mode of knowledge not fully knowledgeable about its own principles, but constituted by reasonable behaviour (Bourdieu and Passeron 1990: 109).

Identity then features in many accounts as the socializing concept of the self—the affiliations and larger formations that simultaneously offer and deny it the possibility of self-sameness. In this body of work, the self is always posed in relation to an outside or a cultural sphere. In the Cartesian *cogito*, the self is subject, in the dual sense of being subjected to the conditions of the world, and simultaneously, being the agent of knowing and doing in that world. But the Western notion of self, or the *cogito* that knows and is known, has also been soundly critiqued for being autonomous, egocentric, and non-cognizant of non-western selves.

In the instance of call centre workers, I therefore turn to Foucault's analysis of practices of the self, wherein desiring individuals subject self and soul to all manner of transformation, and indeed believe in the possibilities of such, in pursuit of a set of transcendental goals (1988). Although Foucault's account is a historical analysis of the relationship between thought and practice in Western society, I argue that call centre workers, among others, might well be the consummate subjects of his larger project, that of the ways and the conditions under which the self constitutes itself as a subject.

Let us also consider the possibilities of figuration as a process that might help explicate notions of selfhood, subjectivity, and identity in relation to call centre workers as embodied individuals, social subjects, and collective formations. Figuration, as opposed to representation, has a self-conscious relationship to epistemological structures. It offers a partial and situated knowledge, and tends towards continually shifting subject positions. Figures are more powerful than stereotypes and fuller than representations. As John Hartigan points out, figures 'call attention to the way people come to consider their identities in relation to potent images that circulate within a culture' (Hartigan 2005: 16). To Hartigan, the value of figures is in their analytical deployment to explicate how the representational dynamics of collective identities are 'neither "real" nor "unreal" in an empirical sense' (Hartigan 2005: 18). There are two parts to this use of figuration in relation to my project. First being the subjects that 'inhabit' these figures—a site replete with questions of agency, mobility, and consciousness. Who are call centre workers and where do they come from? How and why do they make themselves available to the call centre economy? Some of these questions have been addressed in Chapter 2. The second part of such deployment relates to questions of culture, history, and power immanent to the desires of such subjects in relation to a set of 'potent images'. How did globalization produce itself as aspiration and future? Wherein do we locate the *telos* of late capitalism in developing economies? What do call centre workers desire even as they invest in the process of everyday work?

Individual selves configure themselves, I argue, by alternatively succumbing, buying into, participating, negotiating, and refusing stereotypes in various situations of constraint and empowerment. Identities, in that sense, are interpreted. Or to use, Stuart Hall's concept of identity, 'sutured' (1996). 'Identity', in these various literatures is therefore rendered, described, and deployed as a relational, fragmented, shifting, invented, negotiated, processual, and contingent concept. After all, the term identity, as Rogers Brubaker and Frederick Cooper note, contains a multiplicity of analytical and theoretical density,

> It is used to highlight non-instrumental modes of action; to designate same-ness across persons or sameness over time; to capture allegedly core, foundational aspects of selfhood; to deny that such core, foundational aspects exist; to highlight the processual, interactive development of solidarity and collective self-understanding; and to stress the fragmented quality of the contemporary experience of 'self', a self unstably patched together through shards of discourse and contingently 'activated' in differing contexts. (Brubaker and Cooper 2000: 8).

The advantage to deploying the notion of figuration in relation to identity is that it involves a measure of active agency, an escape from Foucault's technologies of domination, which produce an always already enslaved subject. It might be possible to argue that this is a description of the ways in which people actually live, in which case one might well read this as a reminder for the anthropologist.

In light of the above discussions, I therefore suggest that it is far more pertinent to ask what agents do, and examine the ways in which such doing brings about effects/affects in the world, than to ask what it means. In other words, rather than a search for the cognitive content or interiority of an identity, albeit fluid, I ask about the daily conditions of identity formation. The question of identity in relation to affective labour, I therefore argue, is not of one that examines the actions of free agents in the world, or even of previously innocent agents who are then reconfigured into subjects of late capitalism. It is instead, the relentless examination of processes of promissory transformation that workers perform, herald, celebrate, lament, rationalize, and inhabit. It is a close look at bodies in the world as they go about their business. And in the call centre, what might such bodily business entail?

## Voices in Bodies

Discussions on affective labour in the call centre have focused on the question of customer service at the point of its delivery, and its singular orientation towards affects such as care, nurturance, appeasement, resolution, happiness, satisfaction, joy, connection, empathy, and intimacy. Part of this mandate involved, as detailed in the previous chapters, the modification of workers' worlds-views, temporal schedules, and language practices. In continuation of the previous chapter wherein I discussed the deployment of language and accent, I now turn to the management of voice, tone, and comportment.

The disembodied labour of call centre work was primarily dependent upon the deployment of voice, which was the only access the customer had to the worker's body and labour. The voice in this instance was considered the outward manifestation of the agent's true feeling, and the only sign of the body at the end of the telephone line. The voice stood in for the physical presence of the service agent as well as the agent's sense of willingness to be there and help the customer. The onus on the voice was immense and the possibilities for interpretation equally varied. Lest it run amok, there were prescribed for its conduct, not only, language, bodily discipline, and aesthetically specific tonality, but also, a clear and assertive sense of possibility. Agents, for example, often expressed the belief that one could manage a customer by merely maintaining an unflappable softness and clarity in voice, thereby indicating assertion. In their experience, shakiness automatically elicited abuse and remonstration. Even if the content of communication was to be inappropriate, unpleasant, or not to the liking of the customer, the voice could be employed to smooth ire and manage affect.

Voice quality in most cases referred to the technology that mediated calls. However, it was also a term that was employed in relation to agents' voices. For example, workers with shrill voices were asked to lower their pitch to sound better. Voice was identified in terms of its ability to be assertive not aggressive, soft not harsh, polite not rude, competent not tentative, and pleasant not shrill. Alternating between masculine and feminine elements, it was meant at producing maternal assurance and paternal surety. Trainers ran through musical exercises in class so workers could exhibit better control over the tone of voice, speed of delivery, and clarity of text. Both language and voice needed to come together to exhibit the true feelings of the body that could not be seen or read. The materiality of voice was important in its ability to convey the prescribed and performed 'true self' of the agent, ever willing to make the customer happy. The agent needed to therefore learn to enter into productive relations with the voice.

One of the primary concerns of workers had to do with the maintenance of such a voice. All were asked to drink water at regular intervals of time, and refrain from consuming sodas and cold water, or juices during their nightly shifts. Agents were advised to adopt lower pitches than those of their regular voices in order to convey surety and authority, as well as preserve voice. Many demonstrated for me their call centre voices as opposed to how they sounded outside the call centre. When I asked if this was something they thought to be untrue to their real selves, most scoffed it away as merely a mode of performance, and indeed laughed at my seeming need for eliciting answers full of drama and conflict. When I pursued the question and argued that such performance could be seen as tantamount to falsity, one of them, Sapna, a 20 year old worker, responded thus,

> I mean, what exactly is a true voice, anyway? My voice sounds different when I wake up, so different when I am speaking to my boyfriend. I think it's all okay. I mean, this is the whole point, right? We sound different in different situations. To me, it's a learning. I once spoke to a

very angry customer and didn't know what to do. He kept shouting. So then I had an idea. When I want something from my father, I speak slowly and softly; I did the same thing. Immediately, he went calm.

In *A Voice and Nothing More* (2006), Mladen Dolar argues that the voice not only connects but also stands between body and language, and noise and meaningful articulation. I am reminded by Sapna's words, of his narrative set piece, wherein the aggressive exhortations of an Italian commander to his soldiers to attack the enemy lie unheeded because the beauty of his voice stands in direct opposition to the cruelty of the actions he wishes them to undertake. Dolar calls this, at one level, a failed interpellation (2006: 3), but at another, a reconstitution of the hearing community from one of the soldiers in a battle, to one of those who can appreciate an aesthetic and beautiful voice. The work of the voice in the call centre was towards a similar reconstitution of customers from irate and angry communities, disappointed with the world of goods and services, to those who could recognize transnational empathy and support, and regain trust not only in the corporation, but indeed in the power of capitalism to fulfil needs and desires.

While it is obvious that the voice needed to be managed since it was the only part of self that was available to the customer, the body itself was also called to transformation through a very clear articulation of the need to manage posture, comportment, and facial gestures. While training workers, managers constantly iterated that the voice was contained within the body and that they were all part of a complete person. Only when consistent in its component parts, would the self be able to communicate itself as truly willing to the task at hand. The calls to maintain smiles and an erect posture were therefore considered necessary routes to a pro-active attitude. Some organizations had mirrors at individual computer stations so that agents could observe their faces while speaking on the phone. An online advertisement for such a 'PC Mirror' reads, 'Increase sales and customer satisfaction by upto 16 per cent',[2] and explains, 'By checking your image before and during a conversation, you can help

---

[2] Available at http://www.pcmirror.com/.

ensure the success of your sale'. Another website titled 'Call centre coach' elaborates:

> The PC Mirror PAT system helps you maintain your:
>
> Posture – While speaking on the phone good posture is very important. It will help your employees maintain their energy, lower stress on their neck, back and wrists and help them keep a positive attitude.
>
> Attitude – The proper attitude is the foundation to phone success. Using PC Mirror to ensure, that you 'Smile while you dial' greatly helps since 'people can hear when you smile'. It will help you maintain and quickly regain your composure, when necessary.
>
> Tonality – 85 per cent of communication over the telephone is interpreted by the tonality and attitude of the speaker's voice. The proper tonality is like a solid handshake. It facilitates sales and happy customers—the absolute key to any successful business.

Systematix, the call centre that I conducted fieldwork at, had no such structure of self-monitoring. However, my friend Ganesh who worked with a large software and services multinational, informed me that his organization's office did have mirrors at individual workstations.

> Q: So do you know what mirrors supposedly do?
> A: Well apparently if you are physically smiling when you answer the phone you come across as being smiley on the phone.
>
> Q: I thought so. Can I also ask you what you think of that? The mirrors?
> A: I think that it makes sense.
>
> Q: How so?
> A: Well it reminds people to be happy/smiley. Sometimes I'm on the phone, pacing up and down in my drawing room and find myself scowling and realize that I'm being too intense [Ganesh has floor length mirrors in his drawing room] and I immediately ease up.

Ganesh, however, had never worked at a call centre. When I shared this story about the mirrors with another colleague at Systematix, we both expressed incredulity and had a good laugh. My colleague Nitin added that this would only encourage self-love, instead of love towards the customer. While Systematix didn't encourage what

Nitin considered to be mere preening, there were other forms of monitoring in place. Trainers would eavesdrop on rookie workers' voice calls—a process called barging—and remark, '*Khaana naheen khaya kya?* [Haven't you eaten today?]', '*Abey koi mar gaya kya?* [Has someone died today?]', or '*Hans na mere yaar* [Smile a little my friend]'. In a training session, the manager lectured workers on the merits of good cheer:

> Treat every call like it is your first call. For you, it might be the hundredth one. For the customer, it is the first. People can hear your attitude in your voice. If you smile, they know you are happy to be there. We need to provide service, but we need to do it happily. That's how we can understand productivity. You know how Bhutan measures its GDP? Not in Gross Domestic Product but Gross Domestic Happiness. We need to think like that.

At the back of the room where I was seated, a worker piped up, 'My jaws hurt from being too happy'.

My fieldwork in the call centre, uncannily brought to mind the young trainee from Arlie Hochschild's narrative, who diligently writes on her notepad, 'Important to smile. Don't forget smile' (1983: 4). Training processes at Systematix included similar notes for 'feel-good' communication. The inclusion of standard phrases like 'I'm happy to help', 'Have I managed to solve your problem today?', and 'I am very sorry about the problems you have been having', were drilled into the agent to the extent that every possible situation required a solicitous remark, thereby signalling corresponding modes of empathy. Agents often remarked on the ubiquity of the p's and q's. Even as these did not necessarily produce a concomitant empathy or understanding in the agent, the production of such signs was essential to the performance of call centre work. Some workers remarked to me that these spilled over into their regular communication where they would respond in similar ways to family and friends. Many found such repetitive use of polite terminology stodgy and stifling. What they did absorb in the process despite their resistance, however, was an understanding of such speech, tone, and voice as essential to the production of affect in the customer.

## Business-Friendliness

Within the lore that happy agents produced happy customers were
also embedded notions of Indian workers as possessing far more of
a capacity for empathy than their cold and emotionally inept North
American counterparts. Workers believed that they were better at
being able to make connections with customers and were hence,
able to provide superior levels of service. Many agents expressed
their ability to be good customer service personnel in this language
of human connection. Zeenat Ghalebaani, for example, shared her
experiences at work and told me about enjoying conversations over
phone calls because she tried to be friendly with customers.

> Talk to the customer. Ask them, how has your day been today. Believe
> me, Americans love to talk … make them feel comfortable, speak well.
> Some of them are really lonely. If you just say, how has your day been
> today?

Others similarly expressed this belief in universal humanity, and
how 'they are just like us'. At the same time, 'they' were also different, as was 'American society'. Repeatedly, workers spoke about
older men and women calling from the US simply because they
were lonely. From their stories, workers had formed an image of
America as a heartless country, comfortable with letting its older
populations suffer solitude and helplessness. That they would gain
succor from conversations with young men and women across the
oceans, as opposed to their own families and friends, was a concept
that seemed to highlight to these Indians, the profligacy of American
culture. They assured me, when relating stories of such calls, that
they always tried to offer older callers enough time and attention.
There was in their stories a clear emphasis on their own culturally
learnt empathy. In this self-orientalizing move was also embedded
the feeling of a different kind of power and indeed a sense of supe-
riority over the countries they served. These narratives bear striking
familiarity with scholarship on feminized and gendered work,
and the ways in which earlier regimes simultaneously extolled and
exploited the dexterity of 'nimble-fingered workers' in the free
trade zones of the global South (Elson and Pearson 1981). However,
in performing a reversal—an occidentalism if you will—workers

were also staging humaneness, albeit in its inefficiency as well as unprofitability, as agency as well as 'true' customer service. This humaneness, however, had to be alternatively tempered and managed, lest it be read as excessive familiarity, untoward curiosity, and an indiscreet sociality.

Distance was a keyword. The ways in which distance and nearness were maintained or transgressed delineated the differences between a professional, a professional human being, and a humane professional. Zeenat, for example, favoured friendliness, but also stated that one needed to be 'business-friendly'. As a result, in her training sessions, she emphasized the need to not be overly curious or concerned about customers' personal lives and life circumstances. 'Don't say that you are sorry if a customer tells you that he or she is divorced', she would say, 'for all you know, it was a happy divorce'. Agents would smirk and giggle at this pronouncement. The exact nature of such a specific category as 'business-friendly' within the varied spectrum of relationships that can be described as friendly, evaded definition. Conditions of gender, race, class, and context underlined and mediated forms of speech, innocent and otherwise, to produce friendliness between the agent and customer. However, in the varied hierarchies that were both denied and affirmed in the daily activities of the call centre were embedded the cues for managing distance. Consequently, one who was insensitive to the performative dimension of call centre speech was likely to end up being the sociopath of this symbolic universe. Periodically, such sociopathic behaviour in the form of uncontained friendliness had to be defused, in order for this symbolic order to be upheld. Business friendliness was however, I argue, a realm of constant speculation, and a field fraught with many symbolic breaks, brought about by inappropriate behaviour. What happened in these instances of inappropriate behaviour, was not the inability to read, but a misreading or perhaps even an excessive reading.

In the first week of January 2009, an *Indo-Asian News Service* article titled, 'Indian Call Centre Employee Punished for Harassing British Woman' was picked up and broadcast by a number of online news portals. British Telecom (BT) had received a complaint from one of its customers stating that she had been receiving creepy

messages from an employee at BT's call centre. Having previously
called the customer centre in order to have an engineer sent to install
a telephone at her house, she had subsequently been contacted by the
agent who wanted to know where she lived and what she was doing
for the day. The agent's name was reported as Hemant. However,
the woman's identity was not disclosed in the article. Hemant
had subsequently sent her a number of text messages on her phone,
she had reported, some of which were included in the article:

> Hello, Hemant this side with whom you spoke two hours ago regard-
> ing ur BT order. U must be thinking dat why I called u up second time
> without any reason of the call but to be honest I got attracted towards
> u and ur wonderful voice. Can I be ur friend?
>
> As precious as u r to me, as precious only few can ever be, I know all
> friends r hard to choose but u r someone I never want to lose. Take care xxx.

The woman's boyfriend called Hemant and informed him that
he was being reported to the police, at which point the messages
stopped. The woman also reported that, 'The messages were inappropriate and very creepy. I felt as if I was being stalked. I was left
feeling scared and violated and I am worried he is still able to access
information of female customers' (*Indo-Asian News Service* 2009).

The messages were indeed inappropriate in many ways. They
brought to the fore questions of privacy, race, professionalism, gender, and grammar all in one text. One wonders as to what manner
of desire might have fuelled this transoceanic burst of sentiment.
Did Hemant, in his cubicle, attending to one British caller after
another find a moment of connection in the caller's 'wonderful
voice'? Did he see this as a way to bring nearer one of the many
callers who were to him not even a face, but only a voice? Did she
speak kindly to him and chat in a manner that assured him that she
was ready and waiting for him to make a move? Had he been egged
on by colleagues who saw him flirting on the phone with a caller?
Was it merely a dare? Did he fill the emptiness of 'customer service'
with content of his own and break the symbolic understanding of
call centre communication?

The language used by the agent is instructive. As an undergraduate student in Pune, I remember girls mocking boys who would

approach them sometimes sheepishly, and sometimes in manly fervour to ask the question, 'Will you make friendship with me?' Friendship was, of course, the euphemism for flirting, dating, and maybe a relationship. In the gender-charged environment of my teenage years in Pune in the 1990s, friendship was sometimes, as far as the language of a beating heart could go. The call for friendship was often the signalling of a possible future courtship. Of course, the subtext to the mocking that such a question faced was that women always considered the badly phrased and ungrammatical question to be a class marker. One who deigned to ask a question such as this would most likely be of the lower middle class or gauche middle class. The question revealed as much about intent as about lack of felicity in the English language. Refusals to 'friendship', however, often had unforeseen repercussions as in the case of the British woman who felt 'stalked'. Partly inspired by storylines of popular Hindi films, friendship between members of the opposite sex were, and continue to be, a source of tension, and a platform for speculation, especially in co-gendered environments.[3] The biggest modern hits of Hindi cinema like *Maine Pyar Kiya* [I Have Loved], (Barjatya 1989) for example, have continued to perpetuate the hegemonic sentiment of heterosexuality through oft-quoted dialogues such as, '*Ek ladka aur ladki kabhi dost naheen hote* [A girl and a boy are never friends]'.

Following David Novak's assertion that, 'contemporary subjects live much of their lives through media' (2010: 41–2) and 're-appropriate' such media content for goals of their own, it is not difficult to see the episode of stalking reported in newspapers as an affective spillover that remediated the rules of courtship learned from other quarters to deploy them over a transnational telephone call. This form of engagement was, perhaps, how Hemant imagined his membership in a global society. Remediation in Novak's understanding is the 'repurposing of media for new contexts of

---

[3] Popular media and scholarship have commented on the use of 'stalking' as a narrative device to convey true love. The films of Bollywood as well as the plotlines of the romantic comedy in Hollywood have been discussed in these analyses. See for example, Lippman (2015) and Nirpal Dhaliwal (2015).

use' (2010: 41)—in other words, a creative act of dubbing, 'not simply to copy, but to grasp the thing you behold; to name it as your own' (2010: 54). Readers of Barthes might find such remediation merely a renaming of older rules for love, and the attempt at a culturally scripted lover's discourse (Barthes 1978). In any case, by repurposing his own subjectivity through the script of a persistent and persisting lover, Hemant had exceeded his affective role at the call centre.

Once, I had a stalker. Much as one is warned about the vicissitudes of fieldwork, it is not until the event of a crisis that such possibilities manifest themselves as real. During my rookie days, in the first month of work at the call centre, I observed in many ways how workers' relationships with their trainers were marked by varying levels of trust, intimacy, wariness, expectation, and desire. Observations on trainers' appearances, demeanor, and authoritarianism or lack thereof were calibrated on a daily basis by male and female workers alike. Female workers wanted to know as to where I bought my clothes, and male workers would attempt to talk to me about my social life. Even as I calculated that a certain level of informality would ease my association with agents while at the same time erase the gendered tensions of the encounter, little did I know that these gestures on my part were themselves likely to be interpreted within other scripts.

Ranjit was a new trainee at Systematix. He had been recruited as part of the team for a large airline company. While most popular accounts have emphasized the monotony of call centre work and its relative ease, actual experiences varied between types of processes. Airline processes, for example, required workers to remember a large amount of information, such as weather reports, and airport codes and advisories while also delivering them at short notice in order to make quick decisions at the time of the sales process. Trainees in the airline sector of call centre work often experienced a high degree of frustration with the levels of expertise required to service this process.

Ranjit was a reluctant trainee. He would almost always walk into the training sessions in a daze. His eyes would often be bloodshot, his voice low, and his face sallow. As a rookie trainer I would empathize, wondering if the demands of work were proving too much for Ranjit to handle. I similarly empathized with a number of other trainees and would often help them through performance assessments and training sessions. Ranjit and I would chat. He began to confide in me and shared that a recent relationship failure had left him depressed, and often anxious. I surmised from his physical appearance that he was suffering some form of substance abuse—his eyes were sunken in, and his stories often sounded disconnected. I offered support as and when possible and tried to help him get through training modules. Ranjit began to have even more difficulty once training moved to a nightly schedule. Senior trainers once caught him snoozing outside the room during an ongoing class, and threatened to boot him out of the company. After repeated warnings it became obvious that Ranjit was not going to be able to continue, and at this point, he left without notice.

Meanwhile I had also resigned from the call centre. I maintained my networks among various workers, and often chatted with them via text messages or on the phone. While it was common practice for workers to have access to trainers' contact details, including their cell phone numbers, I had tried to restrict the number of people who could get in touch with me. Ranjit was one of the few who had access to my contact details. I had shared my phone number during a particularly difficult training stint, when his performance was being repeatedly questioned and he was under a lot of stress, and had offered to help him with any questions he may have on upcoming tests. While he did not seek my help at that time, he began sending me text messages once he left the company. His attempts at communication started off in a relatively unassuming manner. Messages ranged from, 'How are you today?' to SMS poetics such as, 'A Friendship is Sweet when it's NEW, It's Sweeter when it's TRUE, But It's Sweetest when the friend is like U'. Soon enough, they moved on to messages of a more intimate nature, often asking me out or letting me know that he wanted to meet with me. When I did not respond, Ranjit's messages turned belligerent and resentful. He indicated that he had thought that I was interested in him and that I was 'different'. He would call me at odd hours and often from unfamiliar phone numbers. His melodramatics stretched to having his female colleagues, who were also known to me, call up and ask to meet for coffee. In the face of my continued recalcitrance, and in a final instance of narrative excess, a friend of his called to let me know that Ranjit had suffered a road accident, and a subsequent brain stroke, and had therefore had to be moved out of the city. All of the above I later confirmed to be untrue when I came to know that he had been communicating with other trainers to secure a job at the same time as the alleged accident. I never heard from him after this last message. Much like Hemant, Ranjit's misreading produced an affective excess that went nowhere.

Stories of affective labour locate the performance of emotion only in the instance of producing service. I argue that in the Indian call centre, this affective or immaterial labour was not just a function of customer service or the demeanor that needed to be maintained when dealing with customers over the phone, but could additionally be located in the ways workers formed emotional relations and attachments with their managers, customers, and colleagues in the corporation. Even as such behaviour was neither 'business-friendly' nor transculturally kosher, it was nevertheless a sign of the kinds of attachment, which I argue, index a form of labour even as they do not stay within its bounds. In other words, possibilities of flirtation and other forms of intimacy were produced in the wake of, and sometimes, in resistance to the work of the call centre. Even if such attachment was sometimes in excess, I argue that one needs to pay attention to its existence in order to understand immaterial labour as related not only to a series of acts but also to a set of atmospheres. If we must attend to the collective affects that call centre workers belabor under, then we must also ask as to how these are felt. An atmosphere becomes a useful way to understand the spatial charge of the call centre, because, in Ben Anderson's words, ' ... the concept of atmosphere is good to think with because it holds a series of opposites—presence and absence, materiality and ideality, definite and indefinite, singularity and generality—in a relation of tension' (Anderson 2009: 80). It is in such a tense milieu that the call centre worker functions in a state of burgeoning excess. Such an excess is, of course, difficult to sustain and workers lasted at the call centre from anywhere between two to six months before moving on to other prospects. Often, they took breaks and returned to call centre work at some other organization. Questions of attrition in the call centre often do not take into account horizontal movement between call centres. I argue that understanding these forms of attachment are crucial to an analysis of worker mobility, and attrition, even as organizations scrambled to manage such loss in other ways.

### Un-Official Affects

Even as the production of affects in customers was identified as the primary immaterial labour of the call centre, a series of other affective performances and acts also contributed to maintaining the cohesiveness of the organization and its labour pool. One of the primary problems facing the Indian call centre industry was a high rate of attrition, explained by many as a factor of the low entry barriers and high horizontal mobility within the industry, as well as the mismatch between the promises of an easy job, and the actual demands of the profession (Krishnamurthy 2004). At Systematix, the call centre where I worked, official figures ranged from 30 to 70 per cent depending on the kind of process being served. One of the problems identified by company personnel, besides the monotonous nature of work, and the often abusive environment when on calls, was the inability of the call centre to foster a sense of belonging given the varied levels of hierarchy between the clients, workers, and customers at the end of the telephone line. Even as workers represented multinational corporations, their outsider status as members of a transnational outsourcing industry rendered difficult the process of being seen as legitimate members of the client's company and culture.

In this section, I look at the work involved in trying to create a call centre community within the organization. I am concerned here specifically with examining how such a corporate community can be understood in terms of its social relationships even as the space of the call centre is primarily a space of work, and if such relationships can be seen in contrast and cohort with other forms of

virtual connection or lack thereof between workers and customers.
I draw continuity here between the forging of transnational relationships between agents and callers, and the production of sociality
in the immediate environs of the call centre. In my understanding,
the forms of work involved in creating this community must also be
analyzed in order to read the call centre corporation as an affective
labour complex.

During my time at Systematix, I observed many of such forms
of immaterial labour in relationships between workers, managers,
colleagues, and clients. The status of such labour seemed to defy
an easy understanding of work as opposed to leisure, or public
as opposed to private, or truth as opposed to affectation. Others
have theorized these new forms of spatial and temporal continuity between work and personal lives, or the so-called public
and private in late capitalism. Gilles Deleuze, for example,
understands such a formation to be symptomatic of 'societies of
control', where 'one is never finished with anything—the corporation, the educational system, the armed services being metastable
states coexisting in one and the same modulation, like a universal
system of deformation' (1992: 5), and in which the 'the man of
control is undulatory, in orbit, in a continuous network' (1992: 6).
This continuous network at the call centre entangled in its web
workers, managers, and clients as they worked, partied, lived, and
loved together.

Very few accounts have explored the affective intensity of such
community formation. Placing corporate community narratives at
the heart of theorizations of affective labour, I argue, might help
explain the ways in which the former defy easy divisions of agency
and structure. In my understanding, such relations were neither
intentionally fostered by the corporation, nor were they completely
unrelated to the work of the call centre. They were in excess, even
as they fell within the purview of labour practices at the call centre.
They were both personal and professional, and exactly the kind of
defiance of corporate rules that one might consider to be agentive.
Yet, as I go on to argue, these community formations also allowed
for the preservation and indeed retention of workers within the
industry, if not within a specific corporation.

*We Are Family*

*And so argues Durkheim ... to be a member of a kinship group, it is sufficient to have something of the totemic being, of the sacred quality that serves as the group's collective emblem.*

—Emile Durkheim 1898, (quoted in Schneider 1984: 100)

The Indian call centre I investigated was a peculiar space in its vulnerability to sentimentality and emotion. Workers were young and often adolescents when they began to work in the industry. Most fell within the age group of 17–20 years, and were often simultaneously pursuing a college education. In the city of Pune, many lived on their own since they were students from out of town. The work regimes of the call centre foreclosed the space of college to them as they were unable to work through the night and study during the day. Many ended up registering for distance education courses, or in other instances, continued to be on the rolls of colleges but hardly ever attended classes. Similarly, a lack of societal connections within the city, given their migrant status, rendered the corporation and the call centre community their primary network. The call centre becomes their space of not only work, but also sociality. It was also simultaneously their first experience of emotional and professional adulthood, even as they were incorporated, I argue, into an alternate system of kinship.

Over the many months that I conducted research in and around the call centre, I repeatedly encountered a distinct formation of community, relatedness, and cultural connection. Managers had intimate relations with employees, and vice-versa. Workers were as aware of their colleagues' personal lives, love affairs, family problems, and bodily maladies as they were of their work schedules and responsibilities. The call centre fostered intimacy of a particularly intense order. The space and time of the call centre in a sense, invited an excavation of personal lives in an ostensibly professional atmosphere.

How do we explain this? What analysis do we bring to this transnational corporation as harboring a form of intimacy that is neither encouraged nor allowed in most 'professional' spaces? Are we seeing a reconfiguration of the classic categories of anthropological kinship that understood corporate functions as extending from existing kin groups (Befu and Plotnicov 1962)? What, in this account, is the corporate family?

I argue that the call centre industry in India was facilitated by forms of intimacy, as much as accounts of rational, bureaucratic efficiency. These forms of intimacy approximated the language of kinship, even as one can argue for this to be a culturally and intimately mediated enunciation of flexible capital. I argue that if the corporation, and specifically the call centre that I reference, were to be understood as a social system, then the study of relatedness also forms part of its affective atmospheres, and can illuminate specific strategies for mediating tension, responsibilities and reciprocities. In this section, I refer specifically to the socio-cultural aspects of relationships in the organization that had no biological basis, but mimicked the reciprocities commonly understood within the framework of kinship. I trace such kinship on two registers, paternalism and patriarchy.

By kinship, I refer not to a literal investigation of either blood relations or even fictive kinship, but instead, to the employment of the terms, or the language of kinship. I explore how relations between workers, managers, and the corporation were mediated through language and practices that invoked filial relations. Unpacking this community can show how forms of relatedness facilitated certain forms of production, by creating for workers a sense of connection that served as an anchor in a corporation that was unable to foster and maintain official structures of belonging. Here, I do not want to make a separation between forms of community in the corporation, and the corporation's intentional modes of work. As many have reminded us, corporations are intensely social forms, and 'shape human experience not only in spectacular and disastrous ways but also in mundane, everyday, ambivalent, and positive ways' (Welker et al. 2011: S3). In this research, therefore, is the need to look at corporate forms themselves as producing cultural logics that may or may not produce continuity with familiar modes of belonging, such as kinship, even as it continues to commit to 'an understanding of the formation of subjects in and through corporations' (Welker et al. 2011: S6).

### How I Became a Father

*To be powerful, men imagine themselves as the mothers of other men.*

—Janet Carsten, Introduction in *Cultures of Relatedness* (2000: 19)

'They call my wife all the time too', Rohan said. We were chatting at a coffee shop and being continually interrupted by calls from his team members. Rohan's job designation was that of a team leader, and he had the responsibility of managing ten agents at a large call centre corporation. I wondered where this conversation was leading to as it did not make sense to me that his subordinates would need to communicate with his wife. 'She advises them', he continued, 'and talks to them about boyfriend, girlfriend, family problems. When they can't find me, they call her'. These kinds of relationships, he informed me, were rather common and he further suggested that this was one of the reasons why the call centre had such an emotionally charged atmosphere. When asked how and why he had developed such close relationships with his subordinates, he attempted to explain both the vagaries and the compulsions of being a call centre manager.

> Now all these guys are really young, right? So everyday, they have new issues. They don't live at home. Or when they do, they don't see their parents in the day, because they are sleeping. So what happens? They come to me. Their work life is their life. So everyday, I have to deal with a new problem. My girlfriend broke up, my boyfriend broke up, I've started my period. I'm pregnant and need leave for an abortion. What can I say? I've become an expert at dealing with these things now.

Rohan's account, while a testimonial to his own ability to develop paternalistic relations with his employees was, however, not singular. Many mid-level and senior employees shared the multiple and daily ways in which workers were dependent upon them for emotional support and advice. Some even felt it their duty to be there for them in times of need. The relationship and its necessities however, were usually couched in the language of efficiency, and inevitability. Rohan, for example, continued to explain, attempting to show how this was also part of his job.

> Unless they are happy, they won't work. So I have to make sure I tell people, go out and cry for an hour, I will give you a break. But after

crying, come back and work for two hours. It might seem heartless but they understand and respect me more if I do that.

In order to maintain a state of good cheer among this highly mobile and very young worker population—managers, trainers, and team leaders had to also continually coax agents into a 'feel good' state. Consequently, agents that performed well and maintained a good call volume and reviews, were often pampered by their trainers and managers, who were willing to wait on them hand and foot, in order to motivate them and maintain their call momentum. They would bring them water at their workstations, let them have breaks at unorthodox times, and offer them a higher level of leeway than other workers. In the process, the relationships formed between workers, managers, and trainers, began to reproduce other familiar structures of connection.

To return to our ethnographic epiphany, Rohan's account was a story of tough love, and of the father who could provide love and discipline in equal measure. The narrative is familiar and can be replicated across sites of work and performance. The figure of the father features chronically on other axes of loss, absence, and reinvention. In Ashim Ahluwalia's surrealistic and inventive feature *John and Jane* (2005), for example, the nightscape of the call centre is populated by the strange young call centre workers of a global age. The theme of absent fathers, whose sons must then seek adulthood by participating in contractual work and the narrative of progress, runs like an invisible thread through this documentary, shot partly like a science-fictional representation of a call centre world.

With the changing demographic of call centre workers, from middle- to lower-middle-class, many workers supported their families primarily through their jobs at the call centre. Others found in call centre work a way to support themselves and become financially independent because their middle-class parents were unable to provide for their education and upkeep in a rapidly globalizing, and therefore consumptive and expensive milieu. Men and women, thus found in call centre work their ticket to adulthood, whether as independent individuals or as primary bread earners. While it is perhaps a reductive explanation to relocate the absent father figures onto managers, it is still instructive to this research analysis that paternalism was performed at a site which featured as a rite of passage for young men and women seeking to become global and professional workers. It is also necessary, I argue, to interrogate such paternalism and ask as to what kind of ideal types of men and women it considers adequate, to the task of protection, support, and love.

### How to Be a Good Daughter

'*Yeh hamaari bacchi hai* [She is our child]', Amit declared. He was chatting with his colleague, and they were both gossiping about an American client who had asked me if I would show him around town and help him buy some art. The child that they referred to in this instance, was me. At this time, I was working as a language trainer assigned to Amit's team to coach workers, as well as liaison between the American client firm and the Indian team. Bryan Mitchell, a representative of the client organization had been stationed in the Pune office for a month, and he and I had gotten to be friends at work. Bryan would visit the floor often and we would chat in between my training sessions. This, of course, did not go unnoticed and was fodder for the gossip mills. While gossip about liaisons was a regular occurrence in the call centre, American clients were particularly noticeable, and hence any account of a romantic relationship was enough to spark widespread speculation. Questions of gendering and race were, of course, implicit in such gossip.

Bryan was interested in buying art and I offered to introduce him to a friend of mine who was an art curator. When Amit heard about this, he let loose a barrage of invectives, which sounded strangely familiar in their clichéd quality. 'She is our child', he declared. 'Tell him not to come anywhere close to her!' He then asked me if Bryan was being a bother, to which I responded that I was perfectly comfortable with him, which of course, went unheeded. For a few days after this incident, Amit kept up the tirade. He would shadow me at work, and approach and intercede whenever he noticed Bryan in the vicinity. He even threatened to bar Bryan from the floor where I worked. Time and again, I heard about how I was their child. At this time, I was in my late twenties. Amit was in his mid-thirties.

Simultaneously, I heard from other colleagues about my boss reacting to Amit's reportage on the incident. My immediate superior, Suman, was the head of the training division and had been the one keen to hire me at the call centre. She was a woman in her mid-thirties, who had once described to me her role to be that of 'leading her flock'. An immensely efficient and successful woman, Suman was known to run a tight ship. On hearing about the possible dalliance between one of her subordinates and the American client, she had apparently wondered as to how this would go down with the corporation. Her primary concern, I gathered, was about how appropriate it was to be romantically involved with a client. In her understanding, it transgressed the basic confidentiality requirements of the corporation. While I amusedly wondered as to what kind of romantic confidences she was afraid of, and how she had assumed a single narrative to be the truth of the situation, I was also struck by the consonance in the stances that Suman and Amit displayed, albeit for different reasons.

The concerns of Suman and Amit are not new to corporate spaces. The term 'workplace romance' even has its own Wikipedia entry, which states, as to how such a phenomenon might interrupt productivity and affect morale. Even the venerable anthropologist Margaret Mead, for example, asked for a taboo against organizational incest, one 'that says clearly and unequivocally, "You don't make passes at or sleep with the people you work with"' (Mead 1978: 31). Mead typifies, perhaps, the section of feminist critique of workplace romances that is concerned with the protection of women in a patriarchal and male-dominated workplace culture, where all forms of relationality are doomed to be underwritten by power hierarchies, even as other feminist positions theorize women's sexuality at the workplace as being a site of liberation and possibility (Williams et al. 1999). The emphasis on such taboo, in contemporary times, however, seems to be clearly US-centric (Zelizer 2009), and many have rightly remarked, how this is seemingly a move towards protecting an increasing number of women in workplaces from sexual harassment, while in fact, being a cautionary move in order to shield corporations against litigation (Boyd 2010). In India, laws against sexual harassment at workplaces have only come up in recent times, with the passing of The Sexual Harassment of Women at Workplace (Prevention, Prohibition and Redressal) Act in 2013. Feminist legal scholar, Ratna Kapur, has however argued that, 'sexual harassment law and policy as developing in India is compromising women's sexual and equality rights, reinforcing a conservative sexual morality and encouraging a punitive response to what is deemed to be sexually unacceptable conduct' (2001).

If Suman and Amit were to be seen to represent both themselves and the corporation, together they typified for me, the need to protect the figure I personified, from the foreign client. In one account, I was a vulnerable woman and in the other, a vulnerable woman worker. In both accounts, I had been appropriated into the structure of both filial and corporate patriarchy. In all cases, my virtue and knowledge needed to be confined to the inside.[4] In the previous chapters, I have shown how debates on the viability of call centres were played out around questions of promiscuity, sexuality, and crime. In the current account, I offer kinship relations as a way of also understanding how managers themselves interpret their relations with workers in terms of the codes of family. My gendered location in the corporation was produced not just through the rules of corporate engagement, but also through the codes of patriarchal kinship.

Kinship works in this instance to unpack bureaucratic and rational means of ordering workers in the organization. The daily life of the call centre moved between the languages of work, discipline, family, love, and belonging. I therefore ask—what happens in dealing

---

[4] Other scholars have noted similar dynamics in the ways that corporate managers develop relations with female workers. Linda Green's account of maquilas in Guatemala, for example, shows how factory managers and workers interact in a manner that reproduces and reinscribes 'household patriarchal relations' (2008: 115). In this research, what is additionally instructive is the way in which female workers become sites for resolving and maintaining the separation between the national and the global.

with the appearance of the terms of kinship and its attendant connotations in the absence of the biological basis for these relations?
My ethnography indicates that one of the key ways to imagine and
articulate connections with your colleagues was through the idioms
of kinship. In keeping with studies of what Janet Carsten has called
the 'new kinship' (2000), this analysis is also configured around
gender, as much as the family. Through events configured paternalistic and patriarchal, I argue that structures of connection akin
to fictive kinship often underline, permeate, and indeed reinforce
hierarchically defined structures of corporate authority.

However, in one set of interpretations, family and the language
and performance of kin relations might serve as a fault-line. I am
tempted to take this label of the corporate family seriously, as one
that is not just a form of corporate interaction but also a reminder
of certain forms of loss and absence. I argue that the corporate family in my analysis is a form of protection, a guarantee against the
fragility of this space and time, and an anchor, albeit temporary. The
codes and language of kinship formed a bulwark against the work
of flexible capital that demanded of workers, reinvention on an
everyday scale. Even in a milieu as flexible, mobile, and travelling as
the call centre, workers and managers performed the codes of family as a way to undercut corporate life, even as these codes furthered
the very agenda of flexible capital.

To this extent, kinship in the call centre serves as both, symptom
and caution. Even as it is a symptom of forms of loss and nostalgia
for belonging, continuity, and love, it is nevertheless also a way
to make workers work. What is therefore produced may well be
characterized as the corporate takeover of a vulnerable population that believes in the narrative of progress, while also seeking
other forms of connection and reason for being in the world.
However, it is worth asking whether this can produce an adequate
critique of corporate forms as always vulnerable in themselves, to
the unstable and unpredictable effects of these kinship relations,
and whether such vulnerabilities show up in the relaxation of
rules, the hesitation to reprimand, and the contravention of hierarchies. Let me end this permanent dialectical and flip-floppy conversation by thinking through Zizek, who in the opening chapter of

*The Sublime Object of Ideology* (1989), titled 'How Did Marx Invent the Symptom' argues that:

> The 'normal' state of capitalism is the permanent revolutionizing of its own conditions of existence: from the very beginning capitalism 'putrefies', it is branded by a crippling contradiction, discord, by an immanent want of balance: this is exactly why it changes, develops incessantly—incessant development is the only way for it to resolve again and again, come to terms with, its own fundamental, constitutive, imbalance, 'contradiction'. (1989: 53)

### In the Aftermath of Affects

Across the registers of intimacy, community, love, and kinship that this chapter has sought to delineate, its primary engagements lie with affect. Affect, in contemporary anthropology, has what one might call a 'shimmery' career. When spoken of in the context of people and their worlds, it seems to want to capture something that will not succumb to capture. Consider, for example, the explanation offered by Gregory Seigworth and Melissa Gregg in their introduction to *The Affect Theory Reader*:

> Affect, at its most anthropomorphic, is the name we give to those forces—visceral forces beneath, alongside, or generally other than conscious knowing, vital forces insisting beyond emotion—that can serve to drive us toward movement, toward thought and extension, that can likewise suspend us (as if in neutral) across a barely registering accretion of force-relations, or that can even leave us overwhelmed by the world's apparent intractability. Indeed, affect is persistent proof of a body's never less than ongoing immersion in and among the world's obstinacies and rhythms, its refusals as much as its invitations. (2010: 1)

Such an understanding is cognizant of, and pays obeisance to social forces, while refusing to think of the body as anything but an equal and agentive participant in this world of sociality. If we take seriously their insistence on affect as 'forces of encounter' and as a marker of the body's 'belonging to a world of encounters' (Seigworth and Gregg 2010: 2), then we must also step back from our insistence on worlds as fully formed, and of structures of kinship, love, and intimacy, as pre-ordained, and therefore easily apprehensible. The modality of affect, that I have hoped to corral in this chapter, relates to the ways in which the everyday produces encounters that exceed structures we understand to be given, and to my hopes that, 'persistent, repetitive practices of power can simultaneously provide a body (or, better, collectivized bodies) with predicaments and potentials for realizing a world that subsists within and exceeds the horizons and boundaries of the norm' (Seigworth and Gregg 2010: 7). At the same time, such an approach is also keenly aware that these bodies are not individual actors, 'possessing self-derived agency and solely private emotions within a scene or environment' (Seigworth and Gregg 2010: 8). Keeping in mind Brian Massumi's assertion, which defines affect in terms of bodily responses as autonomic responses, which are in excess of conscious states of perception, and points to a 'visceral perception' preceding perception (Massumi 2002), I have attempted to show how actors inhabited these moments of realization via, and yet exceeding and deviating from familiar routes and vocabularies, some of which I have identified as love, kinship, and intimacy. My primary interest persists in understanding the nature of working life in the call centre. Can it be separated from non-work life? What status does it take on and how do we understand its centrality to the workers' sense of the world? To address this, I take inspiration from Deleuze when he says:

> We are in a generalized crisis in relation to all the environments of enclosure—prison, hospital, factory, school, family … the corporation has replaced the factory, and the corporation is a spirit, a gas. (1992: 3–4)

This chapter is an attempt to capture the fleeting yet permanently sporadic events of intensity and fervour around the Indian call centre. I do not argue a straightforward relationship wherein emotional or affective labour is appropriated to the cause of flexible capital. Instead, I ask how intimacy itself becomes the realm of professional life. I argue that the 'felt' nature of call centre life is a collection of a set of atmospheres; a range of feelings that both accidentally and intentionally evoke the specificity of urban, Indian, call centre lives. We return therefore in this last chapter to Stewart's poesis of everyday feeling, of 'ordinary affects', that 'pick up density and texture as they move through bodies, dreams, dramas and social worldings of all kinds' (Stewart 2007: 3). In other places, she writes:

> All the world is a bloom space now. A promissory note. An allure and a threat that shows up in ordinary sensibilities of not knowing what compels, not being able to sit still, being exhausted, being left behind or being ahead of the curve, being in history, being in a predicament, being ready for something-anything-to happen, or orienting yourself to the sole goal of making sure that nothing (more) will happen. (Stewart 2010: 340.)

In this 'bloom space', aesthetics and public intimacy are intertwined in new ways as part of what Lazzarato calls 'worlds', 'spaces formed by capitalism whose aim is not to create subjects (as happened in the older disciplinary regimens) so much as the world within which the subject exists' (Lazzarato 2004, quoted in Thrift 2010: 295).

Lastly, I offer what Shaka McGlotten has theorized as the always already virtual propensity of intimacy, in that 'intimacy is supported by a range of discourses and practices, but as an experience it is composed largely of feelings, feeling more or less connected, as if one belongs or doesn't' (McGlotten 2013: 9). I locate the affective labour of the Indian call centre economy in these efforts that call centre workers made, towards self, and others, in order to belong, both to the corporation and to the world. In the process, they forged relations, produced encounters, and set off conflict.

# 6

## AFTERWORD

*If, on the contrary, power is strong this is because, as we are beginning to realise, it produces effects at the level of desire—and also at the level of knowledge. Far from preventing knowledge, power produces it.*

—Michel Foucault (Foucault and Gordon 1980: 59)

### A Call Centre Story

The call centre I speak of is a creature of the imagination. Pieced together from narratives, interviews, sound bites, and ephemera that traversed my apartment at all times of the day and night, my call centre is an entity inhabited by fictional denizens and paper cut-outs. I have named it, described it, energized it, and made known the unseen machinations of various powers. There is another call centre though, one that is implicated in this exercise and yet escapes its narrative because it declares that it doesn't warrant one. This call centre is forever banal. It is populated by people who stave sleep at one in the morning, wait for their cabs, sleep through the ride, enter the office, and swipe identity cards to walk into their workspaces; they talk, they file, they report. They mull over small victories and bigger disappointments, wrapping themselves up in the minutiae of the night or even perhaps day, to gather it into a larger story and a smaller week.

This book seeks to explain the forms of entanglement that characterize a mode of work and a way of life. These forms increasingly defined the worker's engagement with life. There are forms of stickiness and attachment that fuel such engagement and entanglement. Money, power, professionalism, skill, hope, talent, beauty, possibility, opportunity, modernity—such are the multivalent descriptors of stickiness. How then does one pull such explanations into a singular frame?

In this research, I have noted how flexibility as a necessary caveat for upward mobility came to be inscribed onto a new and expanding class of young, labouring subjects in urban India. Multinational call centres creatively co-opted and reanimated existing, historical markers of middle-class-ness in India in order to (*a*) stage language, comportment, and 'professional' and 'proper' codes of conduct as valuable to relations of production, and (*b*) channel larger amounts of workers into an aspirational middle-class category, one composed through economic mobility as well as new forms of 'professional' and social etiquette.

In examining the nightly life of young workers, I am concerned with the changing class composition of the call centre. The processes specific to the call centre such as nightly work and accent training become in my manuscript a way to examine the borders and anxiety-led internal contradictions of the historically mythical and discursively over-determined Indian middle class (Beteille 2001; Mazzarella 2005; Varma 1998). The Indian middle class has come to prominence in the first half of the twentieth century on two different counts: one, its economic upsurge, and two, its sudden and publicly vocal political presence. The politics of the middle class, as many have demonstrated, are not new (Beteille 2001; Deshpande 2003; Fernandes 2006; Mazzarella 2005). The divisive character of this section of the population has been the legacy of colonial rule, as well as postcolonial state-led policies of development that favoured and incorporated an existing middle-class into structures of socio-economic and bureaucratic power. However, over the 1990s, this class has also increasingly pushed for economic reform as an antidote to the failures of the Indian state. The resultant increasing pace of development has delivered a paradoxical reward. Even as the Indian middle class now enjoys the consumerist lifestyle afforded by free market ideology, it must work

harder to define its own cultural boundaries that are being rapidly
subsumed by socio-economically equal new middle classes. This
book is an ethnographic exploration of the material and symbolic
processes that underlie this controversial middle class expansion
and locates call centres within this socio-political milieu. Through
a nightly exploration of the painful, tenuous, and often frustrat-
ingly difficult practices that young call centre workers must follow
in order to come to middle-classness, I seek to animate not only
the slow and difficult progress of such 'successful' socio-economic
mobility, but also the tenacity of the cultural barriers it must
address. Through an exploration of the ways in which workers were
pulled into the call centre and the ways in which they sought to stay
or leave, I explore the desiring subjects of the middle-class promise.

Varied anthropological literatures have analyzed emergent
transnational spaces of work (Smart and Smart 2003) in their
'supralocal/local linkages' (Low 1996: 387), and described concurrent transformations as flexible and dialectical. This project
is critically informed by an examination of such contingent,
hierarchical, and gendered dialogue. I see the call centre worker
as straddling an important space that simultaneously contests and
informs the normalized 'scapes' (Appadurai 2001, 1996) of the
global economy. In this project, the call centre is a symptom of the
ongoing effort to render life normal in the face of constant change.
Despite my nostalgia and reservations, the call centre and its work
practices are normative, in that, knowledge, regimes, discourses,
and everyday life together conspired to make it ordinary. I use
ordinary in Kathleen Stewart's sense of 'a shifting assemblage of
practices and practical knowledges, a scene of both liveness and
exhaustion, a dream of escape or of the simple life' (Stewart 2007: 1).
The call centre life is a thing that has happened, and keeps
happening. However, I contend that such a notion of happening
occurs within the desires and aspirations for a certain kind of life,
and is alternatively caught up in and released from the tempo of
such desire. By this, I refer to the active engagement of workers
and subjects in structures of desire and desiring, and their capricious belief in a future that they actively seek to construct.
I argue that people, and in this case, workers find themselves

compelled to expend effort towards normality and possibility. Such an effort—I term 'flexibility'. Workers' abilities to make sense of constant change, while my own inability to reconcile with all that I saw and felt, were all caused by variedly desirous engagements with flexibility.

## Scales and Units

This research examines the machinations of multinational corporations as they incorporate large number of labour forces worldwide into transnational work. I engage with questions such as: What complex negotiations underlie the ostensible success of new service economies in India? What are its cultural and political determinants and ramifications? On what grounds are the claims of state, capital, and culture being contested or reified, and what do such negotiations mean for service workers and their aspirations to mobility within the landscape of urban India? Through these lenses, I provide a thick description of the history, construction, maintenance and disruption of the call centre corporation as a site, as also the ways in which this particular story of late capitalism was stabilized.

The call centre work population in Pune was, across all differences of positionality and subjectivity, a collective. It was a unitary entity, in that, both discourse and workers' daily practices inexorably ordered this collective around the call centre. I have attempted to chart the life of such a differentially composed entity by exploring various scales and units of call centre life. This book charts the movements of the call centre industry and shows how corporations corralled the Indian middle-class population into the life and orientation of such a working collective—in other words, how they created the collective. It outlines an alternate chronology of business development by way of the call centre's constituent labour population and their movements in and out of the organization. Further, it argues that the ways in which this set of workers was coaxed into call centre work speaks of a mode of labour formation peculiar to the outsourcing industry and its commitment to flexibility at all levels of operation. It also shows how such a commitment remained incomplete and paradoxical, thereby leading to frequent human resource crises. Such crises consequently demanded frenzied and chronic attempts at more efficient forms of recruitment, training, and retention, a process that Steven Epstein terms 'recruitmentology' (Epstein 2007), and identifies as common to other industries, such as the medical research sector in the US. This in turn, both expanded and confounded the boundaries of the Indian middle class. I have also focused on a nightly view of call centre work, and on the life of this collective, while emphasizing its incomprehensibility to the non-call-centre world. I examine the spatial and temporal separation of this population from its surrounding urban space and critique such separation as partial, and hence, provocative. While transnationality was ostensibly brought into being through such separation, its lived experience continued to be local and national, and the friction between the two came to light through various instances of sleeplessness, drug usage, fatigue, violence, censure, and crime.

This book also examines call centre life through units of language and speech, and the disciplinary apparatuses that attempted to streamline voice, accent, and body in the service of work, and theorizes call centre speech as one that had effects on the ways in which workers' viewed themselves and sought to construct their presence in the world. Lastly, I examine call centre work as a form of affective labour and outline the various intimate atmospheres through which such labour can be examined and critiqued. Together, the chapters argue that a certain form of service work ordered workers' lives by demanding 'flexible' life practices. I argue that this flexibility of nightly labour was a mode of collective enunciation— by state, corporation, urban space, bodily effort, and discourse—that upheld call centre work. Even as it drew upon existing markers of Indian middle-class-ness, it brought about simultaneous changes in its boundaries and markers, and produced a call centre world.

## Working

*1–800–Worlds* produces a simultaneously nostalgic and future-oriented analysis of the urban Indian service economy. My own subject position is lodged in the increasingly service-oriented bent of the 'new' India, while my memories of childhood are inundated with the hierarchies and the social lives of an older industrial economy. My sepia-tinted photographs bear testimony to company picnics and beautiful bourgeois women in long plaited hair. In the pictures, there are men who stand in corners and talk about the factory, and there are children who are taught to say the right things to the married women, in order of their husband's rank in the industrial hierarchy. The managing director married his secretary and left a sea of whispers in his wake. The operations manager played badminton in his tight white shorts and sprinted across the court, to the other side, to fetch the shuttle for his partner, the managing director. Everybody was marked into a grid of mutually intelligible names, places, animals, and things.

Call centres are part of a different economy. And yet, capitalism continues to order lives. Life seems distributed equally—one part habit, one part delirium. Arjun listens to calls all day long, but can also go to flying school with the money that he has not yet put away, studying for entrance exams in the time that he has not yet invested. Abusive customers bother Ratna at night, but in the day she haunts the streets of the Tulsi *baug* market for the right glassware to display in her new apartment—an apartment she owns at the age of 27.

Even as agents worked, they were taught to understand the world in very particular ways. The world was mediated through work. As opposed to college and student life, the work environment was 'real'. One learnt what the real world looked like from within the premises of the corporation. This was the incubator for grown-up skills. A call centre worker learnt how to balance home and life. She learnt how to respect authority, but question it when necessary. Unless, of course, her promotion were to depend on how well she catered to her superior's ego. She formed relationships, developed an understanding of things that matter, and added items to the cubicle where she worked in order to make it her own. Sometimes she melted into the background and eavesdropped to stay informed about movements of people, money, and reputations. At others, she spoke loudly, making her voice heard and her opinions known. At all times, she was made aware of the need for worldliness. Workers managed time and navigated space, and committed to working eight hours a day in order to take home a salary. They entered into a contractual regime. Work became the anchor around which the other parts of their lives were ordered. Work became their mode of definition, of life, and of self. In interviews over many months, I found across all respondents an eagerness, willingness and indeed, compulsion to explicate who they were. Typical reactions peppering our conversations ranged from, 'The way that I am … ', 'I have always been …' to 'I became … '. Some often spoke of themselves in the third person. Participants actively constituted themselves through a continuous and ongoing verbalization of their self-decipherment in relation to work. For all purposes, the space of work was also the space of self. Many found it difficult to leave.

## Co-Optation, Inhabitation, and an Uneasy Love

*Call centre is like … falling in love with the wrong person basically. Initially, it's all good. You want to leave it, but you can't leave it. Because you don't know what to do after that.*

—Kunal Barot, 25 year old customer
service executive

Interviewing Kunal Barot, one weekend in my studio apartment, I burst into laughter as he explained his inability to leave the call centre. Three years prior to this Saturday afternoon of March 2007, Kunal and I had chatted about his then newly embarked upon career in a well-known call centre in Pune. He had seemed very enthusiastic at that point and had argued vociferously against his friend Reema—also a call centre worker—who had insisted that the work was mind-numbing and life-sapping. He had agreed that the work was repetitive; he had yet found it exciting and had seemed quite happy with the lifestyle it afforded him. Three years later, in the ethnographic present of this written piece, he was bemoaning the ways in which his world had shrunk into that of the call centre. It had taken him three years to leave.

Kunal's was not an isolated tale. While entering the call centre was, for many workers, in equal parts accidental, intentional, and casual, leaving was never as easy. By leaving, I refer not just specifically to a call centre—the industry, or this form of work. I also refer to comportment, orientation, and a way of inhabiting the world—a world. The nightly routine of coming to work, speaking in an accent, chatting with colleagues, flirting with co-workers and trainers, standing in line while complaining about overcooked, over or under-salted, and oil-laden cafeteria food, anticipating the next high pressure call, and battling yet another shift in the life of the call centre world became embedded in the worker's body as a series of habits difficult to abandon.

The end of my own stint at the call centre was traumatic. I tried to resign a number of times—a total of four to be precise. I finally mustered the courage to do so when I was promoted and could no longer treat the work as a temporary prospect. The prospect of leaving was however, frightening. My days yawned wide and I did not know how I would ever get back to the life of a researcher. My social circles would diminish, I feared, and I would not have my time organized or weekend accounted for—life as I knew it, would become uncertain and time, a liability.

The organization, in turn, did its best to stop me from leaving. My superiors offered various incentives, including the freedom to work from home, a change of city if I should so prefer, and many months of leave. I was given motivational speeches, protective sermons, and caring and beseeching counter offers. A manager also offered me a job with a rival company that he knew people at, should I be so interested.[1]

At various points, I doubted my decision to leave. I wondered if I had done the best I could in terms of research work. Alternatively I considered staying on and working, since I enjoyed the job and was good at it. In an uncanny fashion, I constantly questioned my decision to be an anthropologist and researcher, and couldn't help wondering if I had committed a grave mistake by thinking

---

[1] Poaching was rampant in the call centre industry. Skills could migrate horizontally across corporations and experienced workers were always in demand since they did not have to be re-trained.

of abandoning an ascending and profitable corporate career where I was clearly 'wanted' and had a clear and measured understanding of my worth. I imagined this to be a serendipitous second chance. This had become my life-world and it had become difficult for me to 'utter certain truths' and to cross the 'the normative and onto-logical boundaries of that world' (Mazzarella 2003: 33). I had been 'gradually, progressively, really, and materially constituted through a multiplicity of organisms, forces, energies, materials, desires, thoughts, etc.' (Foucault and Gordon 1980: 97).

I argue that working in a call centre led to forms of attachment. These were forms of attaching to work, to co-workers, to the milieu, and to money and its purchasing power. These attach-ments brought young workers closer to 'the satisfying *something* that you cannot generate on your own but sense in the wake of a person, a way of life, an object, project, concept, or scene' (Berlant 2011: 2). Berlant argues that such optimistic attachment invites a return to the mise en scène of fantasy, in the hope that in that moment, the objective will be achieved, the truth will come forth, and that which you deserve will make itself manifest; a good life so to speak. Fantasy in her analysis is a repository of ideal futures, how people will become something, and she asks as to what happens when those fantasies start to fray, and lose traction. I locate this project a little adjacent to, and a little before, that question. My ethnography is situated within the processes through which such optimism was produced, and how it sought traction. Berlant is interested in 'the ordinary as a zone of convergence of many histories, where people manage the incoherence of lives that proceed in the face of threats to the good life they imagine' (2011: 10). I view flexibility as one of the techniques of such man-agement, and the call centre as one of the sites that both inspired and cohered such a technique.

The act of work, others' and mine, lay in the daily performance of a series of acts. I argue that the Indian call centre and its trans-national work regimes sought to create a particular orientation to the world. How then do we understand workers as 'working' in the call centre? What might be the nature of such a work life? Can it be analyzed separately from non-work life? What status does it take on and how do we understand its centrality to the workers' sense of everyday/night life? Is this, in Lauren Berlant's terms, a form of 'cruel optimism' (Berlant 2011)? Is the act of working in a call centre ultimately detrimental to the fantasy of some kind of good life, a life in the service of which Kunal had begun working in the call centre in the first place?

### The End of the Line

In 2008, even as I was wrapping up fieldwork for this project, BPO work had begun moving to greener locales. By the time I arrived at a working manuscript in 2014–15, I was receiving frantic missives from a number of friends and colleagues to tell me that the end was nigh. The call centre industry was moving from India to the Philippines (*The Economist*, 16 February 2016) and around 2015, news reports began to appear with headlines declaring the latter to be the new call-centre capital of the world. Business articles announced that the Philippines was the next 'hot' destination for outsourced call centre work, and a much better one than India at that, given how Filipinos' experiences under American colonialism had rendered their accent 'American' at best, and 'neutral' at worst.

The website of a Filipino call centre called 'Taking You Forward', analyses in an article entitled 'Call Centre: Philippines Overtakes India as World's No. 1', the five reasons for this victory (Quinto 2014). These include, 'Culture Compatibility (Filipinos have the exceptional ability to adapt easily to different cultures ... After the US ruled the country for several decades, Filipinos embraced American culture instead of rejecting it.)'; 'Neutral Accent (Indians can speak English fluently but their noticeable native accent remains problematic.)'; 'Strong Government Support'; and 'Hospitality and Devotion to Work (Filipino hospitality, which is famous all over the world, and the Filipinos' devotion to hard work attract foreign companies to do business in the Philippines.)'.

All of this sounded remarkably familiar; uncanny even. If we follow the Freudian understanding of the 'uncanny' as 'that class of terrifying which leads back to something, long known to us, once very familiar' (Freud 1999: 219), then we might have to recast this tale as one of capitalist tragedy in the first instance, and farce in the second. However, Freud adds that not everything that is known and familiar is terrifying, unless something new is added to it (Freud 1999: 220). The desires of the Filipino economy then, might follow a very different narrative than the Indian call centre economy, even as it seems to have been founded upon a similar set of premises. And now that we can see the prospects of the call centre industry to have moved on from India, what significance then is this long-short tale?

## The Force of Desire and the Fraying of the Good Life

The desires of the call centre economy, I argue, were intricately tied up with the complex that Information Technology constituted in post-1990s urban India. Information technology became one of the key points of hope and attention even as education, advertising, and technological and financial investments together fostered a new, flexible, workforce and its concurrent labour regime. This is a familiar story etched across a million trade journals, newspaper articles, leftist critiques, right-wing celebrations, and centrist caution. However, much like in Susan Harding's tale of figures, discourses, language, and the public force of fundamentalist Protestants in America (Harding 2000), the future hopes of India's new service economies had to be conjured. The middle class was constitutive of this project, and flexibility became desirable not as the quality of an existing middle class, but as a quality that would mediate the path to becoming so. Herein lay its force, and perhaps its anxiety. I argue that the call centre marked the borders of middle-class anxiety over the loss of those discursive boundaries that hitherto guarded and privileged those that were rightfully middle class. Even as the lower middle class and the middle class threatened to collapse into a ubiquitous economically able category, older forms of middle-classness, and the forms of comportment and mannerisms they referenced continued to police the borders between these ambiguous categories. Such policing then lent both validity and force to the desire to become 'rightfully' middle class, a desire that was of course Sisyphean and erosive, and in its final intent, elusive.

I argue that the desires that workers sought to fulfil, through becoming ever more flexible, extracted a price and corroded the body. I posit that the danger in practicing such 'flexibility', is the ability to purely operational thinking—what Richard Sennett calls 'mental superficiality' (Sennett 2006: 131). In other words, flexibility also erodes worlds as much as it makes possible other worlds, which must then promptly face erosion. If one is forever part of a fragmented mobile milieu, then as Sennett asks, 'What values and practices can hold people together? (Sennett 2006: 3) I have tried to illustrate the daily practices of flexibility to avoid naming these values. I have attempted to demonstrate how arduous and tenuous the process of being flexible is, and the ways in which the ease of a flexible life appears alternatively possible and impossible. Flexibility apparently does not lead to a radical post-modern assemblage of selves (Deleuze and Guattari 1987). It is surprisingly recalcitrant and extremely creaky.

Someone somewhere has perfected a routine. He has figured out sleep. He has conquered light. He has transcended time. He has trained the body. He eats often, he eats in small quantities, he pretends night is day and day night, he drinks water, he sits up straight, he sleeps eight hours no matter when he goes to bed, he speaks softly, and he shows us the way. Someone somewhere is a good worker. Someone somewhere is a good subject.

Someone somewhere else wants it to stop. She suffers blood clots and health problems. She does not eat well and suffers heartburn. Her neighbours make snide comments about her work hours to her mother-in-law, and she does not get to spend enough time with her child. She feels listless and bored. She has been passed over for promotions because she cannot spend more than eight hours at the call centre. She will someday be a good worker, a good subject.

The will to flexibility is viscous—it adheres to the body. At the same time, this tendency, I argue, also wears away at the subject, slowly. Much like in the case of young gymnasts, flexing the body extracts a cost. You win some, you lose some. But then, when you are young, everything is possible. You are pliable. And you can be made to work. I remember as a child being very pleased when people would trust me with important work—grocery shopping, delivering

messages, and answering the phone. I think of the eagerness to flexibility as the eagerness of youth, its belief in its invulnerability, and
its chutzpah.

Fifty years after this project, I imagine, I will ask what happened.
The fantasy of the good post-call-centre life has frayed, and seems
to have been replaced by another that mimics it. But in the
ethnographic present of circa 2007, in response to my doomsday
conspiracies, one of my respondents Smriti growled, 'This is a rat
race, not a morning walk'. So we learn the meaning of competition and opportunity differently, through words such as first mover
advantage and early adopters. This perhaps is the meaning of
globalization, not the world opening out, but the world descending
on us and applying pressure, till we lose all sleep staying awake in
the hopes of making it. But we do not live our daily lives this way.
Tension does not suffuse every waking moment. We make possible
other worlds. Or we believe in this one. We become flexible.


**Postscript**

Friday, 4 May 2007

Suman Singh,
Location Head, Training, Pune

Dear Suman,
I regret to inform you that I will be unable to continue work with
Systematix due to significant personal reasons. It has been a pleasure working on your team and I hope to be in touch and associate
with the organization in the near future. Thanks also for your consideration and generous support of all my work and participation.

Best Regards,
Mathangi Krishnamurthy

# REFERENCES

Abraham, Itty. 1998. *The Making of the Indian Atomic Bomb: Science, Secrecy and the Postcolonial State*. London: Zed Books.

Abu-Lughod, L. 1993. *Writing Women's Worlds: Bedouin Stories*. Berkeley: University of California Press.

———. 2000. *Veiled Sentiments: Honor and Poetry in a Bedouin Society*. Berkeley: University of California Press.

Acker, Joan. 1990. 'Hierarchies, Jobs, Bodies: A Theory of Gendered Organizations'. *Gender & Society* 4: 139–58.

Ahluwalia, Ashim. 2005. *John & Jane*. India: Future East Film.

Ali, Shaad. 2002. *Saathiya*. India: Kaleidoscope Entertainment Pvt. Ltd.

Althusser, Louis and Etienne Balibar. 1977. *Reading 'Capital'*. 2nd edition. London: NLB.

Anderson, Ben. 2009. 'Affective Atmospheres'. *Emotion, Space and Society* 2: 77–81.

Aneesh, A. 2006. *Virtual Migration: The Programming of Globalization*. Durham: Duke University Press.

———. 2015. *Neutral Accent: How Language, Labour, and Life Become Global*. Durham and London: Duke University Press.

Appadurai, Arjun. 1996. *Modernity at Large: Cultural Dimensions of Globalization*. Minneapolis, Minnesota: University of Minnesota Press.

———. 2001. 'Grassroots Globalization and the Research Imagination'. *Public Culture, Winter 2000* 12(1): 1–19.

Babu, P. Remesh. 2004. 'Cyber Coolies in BPO: Insecurities and Vulnerabilities of Non-Standard Work'. *Economic and Political Weekly* 39(5): 492–97.

Bajaj, J.L. (ed.). 2001. *The Indian State in Transition*. New Delhi: National Council of Applied Economic Research.

Bakhtin, M.M., Michael Holquist, and Caryl Emerson. 1986. *Speech Genres and Other Late Essays*. Austin: University of Texas Press.

Barjatya, Sooraj R. 1989. *Maine Pyar Kiya*. India: Rajshri Productions.

Barthes, Roland. 1978. *A Lover's Discourse: Fragments*. New York: Hill and Wang.

Basi, J.K. Tina. 2009. *Women, Identity and India's Call Centre Industry*. Abingdon, UK; USA & Canada: Routledge.

Baudrillard, Jean. 1993. *The Transparency of Evil: Essays on Extreme Phenomena*. London, New York: Verso.

Bauman, Zygmunt. 1998. 'On Postmodern Uses of Sex'. *Theory, Culture & Society* 15(3–4): 19–33.

Befu, H. and Leonard Plotnicov. 1962. 'Types of Corporate Unilineal Descent Groups'. *American Anthropologist* (64): 313–327. doi:10.1525/aa.1962.64.2.02a00070.

Bénéï, Véronique. 2005. 'Of Languages, Passions and Interests: Education, Regionalism and Globalization in Maharashtra, 1800–2000'. In *Globalizing India: Perspectives from Below*, Jackie Assayag and Chris Fuller (eds), pp. 141–64. London: Anthem.

Benessaieh, Afef. 2003. 'Seven Theses on Global Society: A Review Essay'. *Cultural Dynamics* 15(1):103–26.

Benjamin, Walter, Hannah Arendt, and Harry Zohn. 1968. *Illuminations*. New York: Harcourt, Brace & World.

Berlant, Lauren. 2008. 'Thinking About Feeling Historical'. *Emotion and Society* 1(1): 4–9.

———. 2011. *Cruel Optimism*. Durham and London: Duke University Press.

Beteille, Andre. 2001. 'The Indian Middle Class'. *The Hindu*, 5 February. Available at http://www.thehindu.com/2001/02/05/stories/05052523.htm. (last accessed on 20 May 2010).

Bhabha, Homi K. 1994. *The Location of Culture*. London; New York: Routledge.

Bidwai, Praful and Achin Vanaik. 2000. *New Nukes: India, Pakistan and Global Nuclear Disarmament*. New York: Olive Branch Press.

Blim, Michael. 2000. 'Capitalisms in Late Modernity'. *Annual Review of Anthropology* 29: 25–38.

Bourdieu, Pierre. 1977. *Outline of a Theory of Practice*. Cambridge; New York: Cambridge University Press.

Bourdieu, Pierre. 1984. *Distinction: A Social Critique of the Judgement of Taste*. Translated by R. Nice. London: Routledge.

———. 1990. *The Logic of Practice*. Stanford: Stanford University Press.

Bourdieu, Pierre, Richard K. Harker, Cheleen Mahar, and Chris Wilkes. 1990. *An Introduction to the Work of Pierre Bourdieu: The Practice of Theory*. New York: St. Martin's Press.

Bourdieu, Pierre and Jean Claude Passeron. 1990. *Reproduction in Education, Society, and Culture*. London; Newbury Park, California: Sage in association with Theory, Culture & Society, Department of Administrative and Social Studies, Teesside Polytechnic.

Bourdieu, Pierre and John B. Thompson. 1991. *Language and Symbolic Power*. Cambridge, Massachusetts: Harvard University Press.

Boyd, C. 2010. 'The Debate over the Prohibition of Romance in the Workplace'. *Journal of Business Ethics* 97: 325–38. doi 10.1007/s10551-010-0512-3.

Brenner, Neil. 2004. *New State Spaces: Urban Governance and the Rescaling of Statehood*. Oxford; New York: Oxford University Press.

Brettell, Caroline. 2003. *Anthropology and Migration: Essays on Transnationalism, Ethnicity, and Identity*. Walnut Creek, California: Altamira Press.

Brubaker, R. and F. Cooper. 2000. 'Beyond "Identity"'. *Theory and Society* 29(1): 1–47.

Brutt-Griffler, J. 2002. *World English: A Study of Its Development*. Clevedon, England: Multilingual Matters Press.

Bryant, Nick. 2006. 'Magazine targets the "Indian lad"'. *BBC News Delhi*, 27 January. Available at http://news.bbc.co.uk/2/hi/south_asia/4633216. stm (last accessed on 28 January 2008).

Byres, Terence J. 1998. *The Indian Economy: Major Debates Since Independence*. Delhi and New York: Oxford University Press.

Carpentier, James and Pierre Cazamian. 1977. *Night Work: Its Effects on the Health and Welfare of the Worker*. Geneva: International Labour Office.

Carsten, J. 2000. 'Introduction'. In *Cultures of Relatedness: New Approaches to the Study of Kinship*, Janet Carsten (ed.), pp. 1–36. Cambridge; New York: Cambridge University Press.

Castells, Manuel. 1996. *The Rise of the Network Society*. Cambridge, Mass.: Blackwell Publishers.

Certeau, Michel de. 1984. *The Practice of Everyday Life*. Berkeley: University of California Press.

Chakrabarty, Dipesh. 2002. *Habitations of Modernity: Essays in the Wake of Subaltern Studies.* Chicago: University of Chicago Press.

Chakravartty, Paula. 2004. 'Telecom, National Development and the Indian State: A Postcolonial Critique'. *Media, Culture and Society* 26(2): 227–49.

Chandrasekhar, C.P. and Jayati Ghosh. 2002. *The Market That Failed: A Decade of Neoliberal Economic Reforms in India.* New Delhi: LeftWord.

Chatterjee, Partha. 1990. 'The Nationalist Resolution of the Women's Question'. In *Recasting Women: Essays in Indian Colonial History*, K. Sangari and S. Vaid (eds), pp. 233–53. New Brunswick, NJ: Rutgers University Press.

Chen, Nancy N. and Trinh T. Minh-ha. 1992. '"Speaking Nearby:" A Conversation with Trinh T. Minh-ha'. *Visual Anthropology* 8(1): 82–91.

Chengappa, Raj. 2000. *Weapons of Peace: The Secret Story of India's Quest to be a Nuclear Power.* New Delhi: HarperCollins Publishers.

Comaroff, Jean and John Comaroff. 2006. 'Reflections on Youth, from the Past to the Postcolony'. In *Frontiers of Capital: Ethnographic Reflections on the New Economy*, G. Downey and M.S. Fisher (eds), pp. 267–81. Durham: Duke University Press.

Corbridge, Stuart and John Harris. 2000. *Reinventing India: Liberalization, Hindu Nationalism and Popular Democracy.* Cambridge, UK; Malden, MA: Polity Press; Blackwell.

Cowie, Claire. 2007. 'The Accents of Outsourcing: The Meanings of "Neutral" in the Indian Call Centre Industry'. *World Englishes* 26(3): 316–30.

Cukor, George. 1964. *My Fair Lady.* USA: Warner Bros. Pictures.

D'Monte, Leslie. 2010. 'Industry, Government Join Hands Against Mumbai Cyber Crime'. *Business Standard*, 24 May.

Daniel, E. Valentine. 1997. *Chapters in an Anthropography of Violence.* India: Oxford University Press.

De, Rajneesh, Stanley Glancy, and R.P. Srikanth. 2002. 'BPO is new pie-in-sky for India Inc.' Available at: http://www.expresscomputer-online.com/20020218/focus1.shtml (last accessed on December 9 2009).

Dean, Mitchell. 1999. *Governmentality: Power and Rule in Modern Society.* London: SAGE.

Debord, Guy. 1970. *Society of the Spectacle.* Detroit: Black & Red.

Deleuze, Gilles. 1992. 'Postscript on the Societies of Control'. *October* 59 (Winter 1992): 3–7.

Deleuze, Gilles and Félix Guattari. 1987. *A Thousand Plateaus: Capitalism and Schizophrenia*. Minneapolis: University of Minnesota Press.

Dement, William C. and Christopher Vaughan. 1999. *The Promise of Sleep: A Pioneer in Sleep Medicine Explores the Vital Connection Between Health, Happiness, and a Good Night's Sleep*. New York: Delacorte Press.

Deshpande, S. 2003. *Contemporary India: A Sociological View.* New Delhi: Viking.

Dhaliwal, Nirpal. 2015. 'Does Bollywood Normalize Stalking?' *The Guardian*, 29 January. Available at https://www.theguardian.com/film/filmblog/2015/jan/29/does-bollywood-normalise-stalking (last accessed on 25 February 25).

Diddee, Jaymala, Samita Gupta, and Sandesh Bhandare. 2000. *Pune: Queen of the Deccan*. Pune: Elephant Design Pvt. Ltd.

Dirks, Nicholas B., Geoff Eley, and Sherry B. Ortner. 1994. *Culture/Power/History: A Reader in Contemporary Social Theory*. Princeton, NJ: Princeton University Press.

Dolar, Mladen. 2006. *A Voice and Nothing More*. Cambridge, MA; London: MIT Press.

Donner, Henrik and G.D. Neve. 2011. 'Introduction'. In *Being Middle-Class in India: A Way of Life*, Henrike Donner (ed.), pp. 1–22. NY; USA and Canada: Routledge.

Douglas, Mary. 1963. *The Lele of the Kasai*. London: Published for the International African Institute by the Oxford University Press.

Du Gay, Paul. 1996. *Consumption and Identity at Work*. London; Thousand Oaks, Calif.: SAGE Publications.

———. 1997. 'Introduction'. In *Production of Culture/Cultures of Production*, Paul du Gay (ed.), pp. 1–10. London; Thousand Oaks, California; Sage in association with the Open University.

Durkheim, Émile. 1898. 'Kohler, Professor J., Zur Urgeschichte der Ehe. Totemismus, Gruppenehe, Mutterrecht'. *L'Année sociologique* 1: 306–19. Review.

Dwyer, Rachel. 2000. *All You Want Is Money, All You Need Is Love*. London: Cassell.

Elliott, Anthony and Charles C. Lemert. 2006. *The New Individualism: The Emotional Costs of Globalization*. London; New York: Routledge.

Elson, Diane and Ruth Pearson. 1981. 'Nimble Fingers Make Cheap Workers: An Analysis of Women's Employment in Third World Export Manufacturing'. *Feminist Review* 7 (Spring): 87–107.

Epstein, Steven. 2007. *Inclusion: The Politics of Difference in Medical Research*. Chicago: University of Chicago Press.

Fernandes, Leela. 2000. 'Nationalizing "The Global": Media Images, Cultural Politics and the Middle Class in India'. *Media, Culture and Society* 22: 611–28.

———. 2006. *India's New Middle Class: Democratic Politics in an Era of Economic Reform*. Minneapolis: University of Minnesota Press.

Fernandez-Kelly, Maria. P. 1983. *For We Are Sold, I and My People: Women and Industry in Mexico's Frontier*. Albany, NY: SUNY Press.

Foley, Douglas E. 1990. *Learning Capitalist Culture: Deep in the Heart of Tejas*. Philadelphia: University of Pennsylvania Press.

Foucault, Michel. 1985. *The History of Sexuality, Vol. II: The Use of Pleasure*, Robert Hurley (translated). New York: Pantheon.

———. 1988. 'Technologies of the self'. In *Technologies of the Self: A Seminar with Michel Foucault'*, Luther H. Martin, Huck Gutman, and Patrick H. Hutton (eds). Amherst: University of Massachusetts Press.

Foucault, Michel and Colin Gordon. 1980. *Power/Knowledge: Selected Interviews and other Writings, 1972–1977*. New York, NY: Pantheon Books.

Freeman, Carla. 2000. *High Tech and High Heels in the Global Economy: Women, Work and Pink-Collar Identities in the Caribbean*. Durham, NC: Duke University Press.

———. 2014. *Entrepreneurial Selves: Neoliberal Respectability and the Making of a Caribbean Middle Class*. Durham, NC: Duke University Press.

Freud, S. 1999. 'The "Uncanny"'. In *The Standard Edition of the Complete Psychological Works of Sigmund Freud, Volume XVII (1917–1919): An Infantile Neurosis and Other Works*, pp. 217–56. London: Vintage.

Friedman, Thomas L. 2007. *The World Is Flat: A Brief History of the Twenty-First Century*. New York: Farrar, Straus and Giroux.

Fukuyama, Francis. 2002. *The End of History and the Last Man*. New York: Perennial.

George, S. 2000. '"Dirty Nurses" and "Men Who Play": Gender and Class in Transnational Migration'. In *Global Ethnography: Forces, Connections and Imaginations in a Post-Modern World*, M. Burawoy (ed.), pp. 144–74. Berkeley: University of California Press.

Giddens, A. 1984. *The Constitution of Society: Outline of the Theory of Structuration*. Cambridge: Polity Press.

Gill, Lesley. 2000. *Teetering on the Rim: Global Restructuring, Daily Life, and the Armed Retreat of the Bolivian State*. New York: Columbia University Press.

Goffman, E. 1961. *Encounters: Two Studies in the Sociology of Interaction.* Indianapolis, IN: Bobbs Merrill.

———. 1969. *The Presentation of Self in Everyday Life.* London: Allen Lane.

———. 1983. 'The Interaction Order'. *American Sociological Review* 48: 1–17.

Goldring, L. 2001. 'The Gender and Geography of Citizenship in Mexico-U.S. Transnational Spaces'. *Identities* (7): 501–37.

Green, L. 2008. 'Notes on Mayan Youth and Rural Industrialization in Guatemala'. In *The Anthropology of Globalization: A Reader*, Jonathan Xavier Inda and Renato Rosaldo (eds), pp. 101–120. Malden, Oxford, and Victoria: Blackwell Publishing.

Gregg, Melissa. 2011. *Work's Intimacy.* Cambridge and Malden: Polity.

Grewal, Inderpal. 1996. *Home and Harem: Nation, Gender, Empire, and the Cultures of Travel.* Durham: Duke University Press.

Gupta, Akhil. 2009. 'Traveling Theory in the Corporate World: Management Jargon in a Call Centre in India'. Paper presented at the 'Annual Meeting of the American Anthropological Association', Philadelphia, 2–6 December.

Gupta, Akhil and James Ferguson. 1997. 'Discipline and Practice: "The Field" as Site, Method and Location in Anthropology'. In *Anthropological Locations: Boundaries and Grounds of a Field Science*, Akhil Gupta and James Ferguson (eds), pp. 1–46. Berkeley: University of California Press.

Hacking, Ian. 1990. *The Taming of Chance.* Cambridge, England; New York: Cambridge University Press.

Hall, Stuart. 1996. 'Introduction: Who Needs "Identity"?'. In *Questions of Cultural Identity*, Stuart Hall and Paul du Gay (eds), pp. 1–17. London: SAGE Publications.

Hansen, Thomas Blom and Finn Stepputat. 2005. *Sovereign Bodies: Citizens, Migrants, and States in the Postcolonial World.* Princeton, NJ: Princeton University Press.

Harding, Susan Friend. 2000. *The Book of Jerry Falwell: Fundamentalist Language and Politics.* Princeton, NJ: Princeton University Press.

Hardt, Michael. 1999. 'Affective Labor'. *Boundary* 26(2): 89–100.

Hardt, Michael and Antonio Negri. 2000. *Empire.* Mass.: Harvard University Press.

Harriss-White, Barbara. 2003. *India Working: Essays on Society and Economy.* Cambridge; New York: Cambridge University Press.

Hart, Keith. 2000. 'Reflections on a Visit to New York'. *Anthropology Today* 16(4): 1–3.

Hartigan, J. 2005. *Odd Tribes: Toward a Cultural Analysis of White People*. Durham, Duke University Press.

Harvey, David. 1990a. 'Between Space and Time: Reflections on the Geographical Imagination'. *Annals of the Association of American Geographers* 80(3): 418–34.

———. 1990b. *The Condition of Postmodernity: An Enquiry into the Origins of Cultural Change*. Cambridge; MA, Oxford; UK: Blackwell.

———. 2000. *Spaces of Hope*. Edinburgh: Edinburgh University Press.

Hebdige, D. 1988. 'Object as image: The Italian Scooter Cycle'. In *Hiding in the Light*, D. Hebdige (ed.), pp. 77–115. London: Routledge.

Herman, Edward S. and Noam Chomsky. 1988. *Manufacturing Consent: The Political Economy of the Mass Media*. New York: Pantheon Books.

Ho, Karen. 2009. *Liquidated: An Ethnography of Wall Street*. Durham: Duke University Press.

Hochschild, Arlie Russell. 1983. *The Managed Heart: Commercialization of Human Feeling*. Berkeley: University of California Press.

Ilouz, Eva. 1997a. *Consuming the Romantic Utopia: Love and the Cultural Contradictions of Capitalism*. Berkeley and Los Angeles: University of California Press.

———. 1997b. *Cold Intimacies: The Making of Emotional Capitalism*. Cambridge and Malden: Polity.

Inamdar, Nadeem. 2007. 'Safety Rules Stand Widely Ignored'. *Express India*, 5 November.

*Indo-Asian News Service*. 2009. 'Indian Call Centre Employee Punished for Harassing British Woman'. 10 January. Available at: http://www.gloccal.com/news/68-call-centre/174-indian-call-centre-employee-punished-for-harassing-british-woman.html; http://indiatoday.intoday.in/story/Indian+call+centre+employee+punished+for+harassing+Britis h+woman/1/24949.html (last accessed on 20 February 2010).

Ishiguro, Kazuo. 1986. *An Artist of the Floating World*. London; Boston: Faber and Faber.

Jeffrey, Craig. 2010. *Timepass: Youth, Class, and the Politics of Waiting in India*. Stanford, CA: Stanford University Press.

Joshi, Sandeep. 2007. 'Two held for BPO Employee's Murder'. *The Hindu*, 4 November. Available at: http://www.thehindu.com/todays-paper/two-held-for-bpo-employees-murder/article1942613.ece (last accessed on 20 April 2012).

Joshi, Satyajit. 2007. 'Wipro Staffer Raped, Killed'. *Hindustan Times*, 4 November. Available at: http://www.hindustantimes.com/india/

wipro-staffer-raped-killed/story-UVFHUKSHJ5q1MYqoweZeCL.html (last accessed on 10 August 2011).

K., Kalpana. 2017. *Women, Micro-Finance and the State in Neo-liberal India.* London. New York: Routledge.

Kandiyoti, D. 1991. 'Identity and its Discontents: Women and the Nation'. *Millennium: Journal of International Studies* (20): 429–443.

Kanter, Rosabeth Moss. 1977. *Men and Women of the Corporation.* New York: Basic Books.

Kapur, Ratna. 2001. 'Sexcapades and the Law: Evaluating the Sexual Harassment Guidelines'. *Seminar Magazine: Towards Equality—A Symposium on Women, Feminism, and Women's Movements* 40: 40–53.

————. 2002. 'A Love Song to Our Mongrel Selves: Hybridity, Sexuality, and the Law'. *Social and Legal Studies* 8(3): 353–68.

Karim, Lamia. 2011. *Microfinance and Its Discontents: Women in Debt in Bangladesh.* Minneapolis: University of Minnesota Press.

King, Robert D. 1997. *Nehru and the Language Politics of India.* Delhi; New York: Oxford University Press.

Kolker, Andrew, Louis Alvarez, Trey Wilson, and Centre for New American Media. 1986. *American Tongues.* New York, NY: New Day Films.

Kondo, Dorinne K. 1990. *Crafting Selves: Power, Gender, and Discourses of Identity in a Japanese Workplace.* Chicago: University of Chicago Press.

Kothari, Rajni. 1991. 'State and Statelessness in Our Time'. *Economic and Political Weekly* 11/12: 553–8.

Kotler, P and K. Keller. 2006. *Marketing Management* (12th ed.). NJ: Prentice-Hall.

Krishnamurthy, Mathangi. 2004. 'Rebels or Resources: A Study of Identity Management in Indian Call Centres'. *Anthropology of Work Review* 25(3–4): 9–18.

————. 2011. 'Furtive Tongues: Language Politics in the Indian Call Center'. In *Chutnefying English: The Cultural Politics of Hinglish*, Rupert Snell and Rita Kothari (eds), pp. 82–97. India: Penguin.

LaDousa, Chaise. 2007. 'Of Nation and State: Language, School, and the Reproduction of Disparity in a North Indian City'. *Anthropological Quarterly* 80(4): 925–59.

————. 2008. 'Disparate Markets: Language, Nation and Education in North India'. *American Ethnologist* 32(3): 460–78.

Lazzarato, Maurizio. 1996. 'Immaterial Labour'. Translated by P. Colilli and E. Emery. In *Radical Thought in Italy: A Potential Politics*, M. Hardt and P. Virno (eds), pp. 133–47. Minneapolis and London: University of Minnesota Press.

———. 2004. 'From Capital-Labour to Capital-Life'. *Ephemera* 4: 187–208.

Lippman, Julia R. 2015. 'I Did It Because I Never Stopped Loving You: The Effects of Media Portrayals of Persistent Pursuit on Beliefs about Stalking'. *Communications Research*. doi:10.1177/0093650215570653.

Low, Setha. 1996. 'The Anthropology of Cities: Imagining and Theorizing the City'. *Annual Review of Anthropology* 25: 383–409.

Lugo, Alejandro. 2008. *Fragmented Lives, Assembled Parts: Culture, Capitalism, and Conquest at the U.S.-Mexico Border*. Austin: University of Texas Press.

Lukose, Ritty. 2009. *Liberalization's Children: Gender, Youth and Consumer Citizenship in Globalizing India*. Durham, NC: Duke University Press.

Macaulay, Thomas Babington and G.M. Young. 1967. *Macaulay, Prose and Poetry*. Cambridge, Massachusetts: Harvard University Press.

MacIntyre, A. 1985. *After Virtue: A Study in Moral Theory*. London: Duckworth.

MacLeod, Jay. 1995. *Ain't No Makin' It: Aspirations and Attainment in a Low-Income Neighborhood*. Boulder, Colo.: Westview Press.

Majumdar, Aninidita. 2014. 'Nurturing an Alien Pregnancy: Surrogate Mothers, Intended Parents and Disembodied Relationships'. *Indian Journal of Gender Studies* 21(2): 199–224.

Malinowski, Bronislaw. 1961. *Argonauts of the Western Pacific: An Account of Native Enterprise and Adventure in the Archipelagoes of Melanisian New Guinea*. New York: Dutton.

Mandle, Jay. 2000. 'The Student Anti-Sweatshop Movement: Limits and Potential'. *Annals of the American Academy of Political and Social Science* 570 (Dimensions of Globalization): 92–103.

Mankekar, Purnima. 1999. *Screening Culture, Viewing Politics: An Ethnography of Television, Womanhood, and Nation in Postcolonial India*. Durham: Duke University Press.

Mankekar, Purnima and Akhil Gupta. 2016. 'Intimate Encounters: Affective Labor in Call Centers'. *Positions: East Asia Cultures Critique* 24(1): 17–43.

Marcus, George E. 1998. 'Introduction'. In *Corporate Futures: The Diffusion of the Culturally Sensitive Corporate Form*, G.E. Marcus (ed.), pp. 1–14. Chicago and London: The University of Chicago Press.

Marcus, George E. and Dick Cushman. 1982. 'Ethnographies as Texts'. *Annual Review of Anthropology* 11: 25–69.

Martin, Emily. 1994. *Flexible Bodies: Tracking Immunity in American Culture from the Days of Polio to the Age of AIDS*. Boston: Beacon Press.

Massey, Doreen B. 1984. *Spatial Divisions of Labour: Social Structures and the Geography of Production*. London: Macmillan.

Massumi, Brian. 2002. *Parables for the Virtual: Movement, Affect, Sensation*. Durham, NC: Duke University Press.

Mauss, Marcel. 1990. *The Gift: The Form and Reason for Exchange in Archaic Societies*. London; New York: Routledge.

Mazzarella, William. 2003. *Shoveling Smoke: Advertising and Globalization in Contemporary India*. Durham, NC: Duke University Press.

———. 2005. 'Middle Class'. In *Keywords in South Asian Studies*, R. Dwyer (ed.). Available at http://www.soas.ac.uk/csasfiles/keywords/Mazzarella-middleclass.pdf (last accessed on 7 June 2013).

McDowell, Linda and Joanne P. Sharp. 1997. *Space, Gender, Knowledge: Feminist Readings*. London; New York: Arnold; co-published in the US by J. Wiley.

McGlotten, Shaka. 2013. *Virtual Intimacies: Media, Affect, and Queer Sociality*. Albany: State University of New York Press.

McNay, Lois. 2009. 'Self as Enterprise: Dilemmas of Control and Resistance in Foucault's *The Birth of Biopolitics*': *Theory, Culture & Society* 26(6): 55–77.

Mead, Margaret. 1978. 'A Proposal: We Need Taboos on Sex at Work'. *Redbook* (April): 31–8.

Melbin, Murray. 1987. *Night as Frontier: Colonizing the World after Dark*. New York; London: Free Press.

Miller, Toby. 2008. *Makeover Nation: The United States of Reinvention*. Columbus: The Ohio State University Press.

Mills, Mary Beth. 1999. *Thai Women in the Global Labour Force: Consuming Desires, Contested Selves*. New Brunswick, N.J.: Rutgers University Press.

———. 2003. 'Gender and Inequality in the Global Labor Force'. *Annual Review of Anthropology* (32): 41–62.

Mirchandani, Kiran. 2004. 'Practices of Global Capital: Gaps, Cracks and Ironics in Transnational Call Centres in India'. *Global Networks: A Journal of Transnational Affairs* 4(4): 355–74.

———. 2012. *Phone Clones: Authenticity Work in the Transnational Service Economy*. Ithaca, NY: Cornell University Press.

Miyoshi, Masao. 1993. 'A Borderless World? From Colonialism to Transnationalism and the Decline of the Nation-State'. *Critical Inquiry* 19(4): 726–51.

Mookerji, Madhumita. 2004. 'Buy, Buy '03: Consumer Spend Jumps 16%'. *The Economic Times*, 9 August.

Nadeem, Shehzad. 2011. *Dead Ringers: How Outsourcing is Changing the Way Indians Understand Themselves*. Princeton, NJ: Princeton University Press.

Nandy, Ashis. 1988. 'Introduction: Science as a Reason of State'. In *Science, Hegemony and Violence: A Requiem for Modernity*, Ashis Nandy (ed.). Tokyo, Japan: United National University. Available at: http://archive.unu.edu/unupress/unupbooks/uu05se/uu05se00.htm (last accessed on 30 August 2016).

Narayan, K. 1993. 'How "Native" Is A Native Anthropologist'. *American Anthropologist*, New Series, 95(3): 671–86.

NASSCOM. 2008. *Indian ITES-BPO Industry—Fact Sheet*. New Delhi: National Association of Software and Service Companies.

NASSCOM-McKinsey & Company. 2009. *Perspective 2020: Transform Business, Transform India*. New Delhi: Magnum Custom Publishing.

Newfield, Christopher. 1998. 'Corporate Culture Wars'. In *Corporate Futures: The Diffusion of the Culturally Sensitive Corporate Form*, G.E. Marcus (ed.), pp. 15–22. Chicago and London: The University of Chicago Press.

Nonini, D. M. 1997. 'Shifting Identities, Positioned Imaginaries: Transnational Traversals and Reversals by Malaysian Chinese'. In *Ungrounded Empires: The Cultural Politics of Modern Chinese Transnationalism*, A. Ong and D.M. Nonini (eds), pp. 203–27. London/New York: Routledge.

Novak, David. 2010. 'Cosmopolitanism, Remediation, and the Ghost World of Bollywood'. *Cultural Anthropology* 25(1): 40–72.

Office of the Registrar General and Census Commissioner, India. 2001. Census Data Online–2001. Available at http://censusindia.gov.in/2011-common/censusdataonline.html. (last accessed on 12 January 2016).

Ong, Aihwa. 1991. 'The Gender and Labour Politics of Postmodernity'. *Annual Review of Anthropology* 20: 279–309.

———. 1999. *Flexible Citizenship: The Cultural Logics of Transnationality*. Durham, NC: Duke University Press.

Osella, F. and C. Osella. 2000. 'Migration, Money and Masculinity in Kerala'. *Journal of the Royal Anthropological Institute* (NS) 6: 117–33.

Padilla, Mark B., Jennifer B. Hirsch, Miguel Munoz-Laboy, Robert E. Sember, and Richard G. Parker. 2007. 'Introduction: Love and Globalization: Cross-Cultural Reflections on an Intimate Intersection'. In *Love and Globalization: Transformation of Intimacy in the Contemporary World*, Mark B. Padilla, Jennifer S. Hirsch, Miguel Munoz-Laboy, Robert E. Sember, and Richard G. Parkers (eds), pp. ix–xxx. Nashville: Vanderbilt University Press.

Palmer, Bryan D. 2000. *Cultures of Darkness: Night Travels in the Histories of Transgression*. New York: Monthly Review Press.

Pande, Amrita. 2010. 'Commercial Surrogacy in India: Manufacturing a Perfect Mother-Worker'. *Signs: Journal of Women in Culture and Society* 35(4): 969–92.

Parameswaran, Radhika. 2002. 'Reading Fictions of Romance: Gender, Sexuality, and Nationalism in Postcolonial India'. *Journal of Communication* 52(4): 832–51.

Patel, Reena. 2010. *Working the Night Shift: Women in India's Call Centre Industry*. Stanford, Calif.: Stanford University Press.

Pateman, Carole. 1986. 'Introduction: The Theoretical Subversiveness of Feminism'. In *Feminist Challenges: Social and Political Theory*, Carole Pateman and Elizabeth Gross (eds), pp. 1–10. Sydney: Allen & Unwin.

Pennycook, Alastair. 1998. *English and the Discourses of Colonialism*. London; New York: Routledge.

Pitroda, S. 1993. 'Development, Democracy and the Village Telephone'. *Harvard Business Review* 71(6): 66–76.

Poster, Winifred. 2007a. 'Saying "Good Morning" in the Middle of the Night: The Reversal of Work Time in Globalized ICT Service Work'. *Research in the Sociology of Work* 17: 55–112.

———. 2007b. 'Who's On the Line? Indian Call Centre Agents Pose as Americans for U.S.-Outsourced Firms'. *Industrial Relations* 46(2): 271–304.

Prakash, Gyan. 1999. *Another Reason: Science and the Imagination of Modern India*. Princeton, NJ: Princeton University Press.

Puri, Jyoti. 1999. *Woman, Body, Desire in Post-Colonial India: Narratives of Gender and Sexuality*. New York: Routledge.

Quinto, Leovina. 2014. 'Call Center: Philippines Overtakes India as World's No. 1'. 15 December. Available at http://www.takingyouforward.com/blog/sme/call-centre-philippines-overtakes-india-as-worlds-no-1/ (last accessed on 15 January 2017).

Radhakrishnan, Smitha. 2011. *Appropriately Indian: Gender and Culture in a New Transnational Class*. Durham, NC: Duke University Press.

Rajagopal, Arvind. 1999. 'Thinking About The New Indian Middle Class: Gender, Advertising and Politics in an Age of Globalization'. In *Signposts: Gender Issues in Post-Independence India*, Rajeswari Sunder Rajan (ed.), pp. 57–100. New Delhi: Kali for Women Press.

———. 2001. *Politics after Television: Religious Nationalism and the Reshaping of the Indian Public*. Cambridge; New York: Cambridge University Press.

Ramanathan, Vaidehi. 2005. *The English-Vernacular Divide: Postcolonial Language Politics and Practice*. Clevedon; Buffalo: Multilingual Matters.

Rudnyckyj, Daromir. 2011. *Spiritual Economies: Islam, Globalization, and the Afterlife of Development*. Ithaca: Cornell University Press.

Rutherford, Danilyn. 2016. 'Affect Theory and the Empirical'. *Annual Review of Anthropology* 45: 285–300.

Safa, Helen. I. 1995. *The Myth of the Male Breadwinner: Women and Industrialization in the Caribbean*. Boulder, CO: Westview Press.

Sassen, Saskia. 1996. *Losing Control?: Sovereignty in an Age of Globalization*. New York: Columbia University Press.

———. 2001. *The Global City: New York, London, Tokyo*. Princeton, N.J.; Oxford: Princeton University Press.

Schneider, D.M. 1984. *A Critique of the Study of Kinship*. Ann Arbor: University of Michigan Press.

Scott, James C. 1990. *Domination and the Arts of Resistance: Hidden Transcripts*. New Haven: Yale University Press.

Seigworth, Gregory J. and Melissa Gregg. 2010. 'Introduction'. In *The Affect Theory Reader*, Melissa Gregg and Gregory J. Seigworth (eds), pp. 1–25. Durham, NC: Duke University Press.

Sennett, Richard. 1998. *The Corrosion of Character: The Personal Consequences of Work in the New Capitalism*. New York: W.W. Norton.

———. 2006. *The Culture of the New Capitalism*. New Haven: Yale University Press.

Sewell, William H. 1992. 'A Theory of Structure: Duality, Agency and Transformation'. *The American Journal of Sociology* 98(1): 1–29.

Sharman, Russell Leigh and Cheryl Harris Sharman. 2008. *Nightshift. NYC*. Berkeley: University of California Press.

Sharpe, Jenny. 1995. 'Figures of Colonial Resistance'. In *The Post-Colonial Studies Reader*, G.G. Bill Ashcroft and Helen Tiffin (eds), pp. 99–103. London; New York: Routledge.

Sheth, D.L. 1990. 'No English Please, We're Indian'. *The Illustrated Weekly of India*, 19 August, pp. 34–37.

Singh, P. and A. Pandey. 2004. 'Women in Call Centres'. *Economic and Political Weekly* 40(7): 684–8.

Sklair, Leslie. 2001. *The Transnational Capitalist Class*. Oxford; Malden, Massachusetts: Blackwell.

Smart, Alan and Josephine Smart. 2003. 'Urbanization and the Global Perspective'. *Annual Review of Anthropology* 32: 263–85.

Sonntag, Selma. 2000. 'Ideology and Policy in the Politics of the English Language in North India'. In *Ideology, Politics and Language Policies: Focus on English*, T. Ricento (ed.), pp. 133–49. Amsterdam; Philadelphia: John Benjamins Publishing Company.

Soorkar, Sanjay. 2004. *Saatchya Aat Gharat*. India: Everest Entertainment.

Srivastava, Sanjay. 2007. *Passionate Modernity: Sexuality, Class, and Consumption in India*. New Delhi: Routledge.

Steger, Brigitte and Lodewijk Brunt. 2003. 'Introduction: Into the Night and the World of Sleep'. In *Night-Time and Sleep in Asia and the West: Exploring the Dark Side of Life*, Brigitte Steger and Lodewijk Brunt (eds), pp. 1–23. London; New York: Routledge.

Stewart, Kathleen. 2007. *Ordinary Affects*. Durham, NC: Duke University Press.

———. 2010. 'Afterword: Worlding Refrains'. In *The Affect Theory Reader*, Melissa Gregg and Gregory J. Seigworth (eds), pp. 339–53. Durham, NC: Duke University Press.

Stoller, Robert J. 1975. *Perversion: The Erotic Form of Hatred*. New York: Pantheon Books.

Sunder Rajan, Kaushik. 2006. *Biocapital: The Constitution of Postgenomic Life*. Durham: Duke University Press.

Sunder Rajan, Rajeswari. 1992. 'Fixing English: Nation, Language, Subject'. In *The Lie of the Land: English Literary Studies in India*, R. Sunder Rajan (ed.), pp. 7–28. Oxford; New York: Oxford University Press.

Taussig, Michael T. 1999. *Defacement: Public Secrecy and the Labour of the Negative*. Stanford, California: Stanford University Press.

*The Economist*. 2016. 'The End of the Line'. 16 February. Available at http://www.economist.com/news/international/21690041-call-centres-have-created-millions-good-jobs-emerging-world-technology-threatens (last accessed on 15 January 2017).

*The Hindu*. 2006. 'Association Wants to Create Special Education Zone'. 28 December. Available at http://www.thehindu.com/todays-paper/tp-national/tp-tamilnadu/association-wants-to-create-special-education-zone/article3040063.ece. (last accessed on 18 January 2012).

Thompson, E.P. 1967. 'Time, Work, Discipline and Industrial Capitalism'. *Past and Present* 38: 56–97.

Thrift, Nigel. 2000. 'Performing Cultures in the New Economy'. *Annals of the Association of American Geographers* 90(4): 674–92.

*Times of India* (Pune Edition). 2006. 'Sena Declares War on English Name Boards'. 8 January. Available at http://timesofi ndia.indiatimes. com/articleshow/1363376.cms. (last accessed on 10 November 2008).

———. 2010. 'Understanding the Material Practices of Glamour'. In *The Affect Theory Reader*, Melissa Gregg and Gregory J. Seigworth (eds), pp. 289–308. Durham, NC: Duke University Press.

Trawick, Margaret. 1990. *Notes On Love in a Tamil Family*. Berkeley: University of California Press.

Tsing, Anna Lowenhaupt. 2005. *Friction: An Ethnography of Global Connection*. Princeton, NJ: Princeton University Press.

Turkle, Sherry. 2015. *Reclaiming Conversation: The Power of Talk in a Digital Age*. New York: Penguin Press.

Upadhya, Carol and A.R. Vasavi. 2006. *Work, Culture, and Sociality in the Indian IT Industry: A Sociological Study*. Bangalore: NIAS and IDPAD.

———. 2008. *In an Outpost of the Global Economy: Work and Workers in India's Information Technology Industry*. Delhi; London: Routledge.

Urban, Gran and Kyung-Nan Koh. 2013. 'Ethnographic Research on Modern Business Corporations'. *Annual Review of Anthropology* (42): 139–58.

Urciuoli, Bonnie. 1996. *Exposing Prejudice: Puerto Rican Experiences of Language, Race, and Class*. Boulder, Colorado: Westview Press.

van der Veer, Peter. 2005. 'Virtual India: Indian IT Labour and the Nation-State'. In *Sovereign Bodies: Citizens, Migrants and States in the Postcolonial World*, Thomas Blom Hansen and Finn Stepputat (eds), pp. 276–90. Princeton: Princeton University Press.

van Wessel, Margit. 2004. 'Talking About Consumption: How an Indian Middle Class Dissociates from Middle-Class Life'. *Cultural Dynamics* 16(1): 93–116.

Varma, Pavan K. 1998. *The Great Indian Middle Class*. New Delhi; New York, NY, USA: Viking.

Venn, Couze and Tiziana Terranova. 2009. 'Introduction: Thinking After Michael Foucault'. *Theory, Culture & Society* 26(6): 1–11.

Virilio, Paul. 2000. 'The Kosovo War Took Place in Orbital Space: Paul Virilio in Conversation with John Armitage', Patrice Riemens (translated). *C Theory 89*. Available at: http://www.ctheory.com/article/a089.html (last accessed on 9 December 2009).

Visweswaran, Kamala. 1994. *Fictions of Feminist Ethnography*. Minneapolis: University of Minnesota Press.

Weber, Brenda. 2007. 'Makeover as Takeover: Scenes of Affective Domination on Makeover TV'. *Configurations* 15(1): 77–99.

Weber, Max, Edward Albert Shils, and Henry A. Finch. 1969. *Max Weber on the Methodology of the Social Sciences*. Glencoe, Illinois: Free Press.

Welker, Marina, Damani J. Partridge, and Rebecca Hardin. 2011. 'Corporate Lives: New Perspectives on the Social Life of the Corporate Form—An Introduction to Supplement 3'. *Current Anthropology* (52): S3(Supplement to April 2011): S3–S16.

Wenthe, William. 2007. '"The World" Is Too Much With Us'. *The Yale Review* 95(2): 116–30.

Williams, Christine L., Patti A. Giuffre, and Kirsten Dellinger. 1999. 'Sexuality in the Workplace: Organizational Control, Sexual Harassment, and the Pursuit of Pleasure'. *Annual Review of Sociology* (25): 73–93.

Wilson, Ara. 2004. *The Intimate Economies of Bangkok: Tomboys, Tycoons, and Avon Ladies in the Global City*. Berkeley: University of California Press.

Wolf, D.L. 1992. *Factory Daughters: Gender, Household Dynamics, and Rural Industrialization in Java*. Berkeley: University of California Press.

Wolf-Meyer, Matthew J. 2006. 'Precipitating Pharmakologies: Making "Normal" Sleep'. Paper read at the 'Annual Meeting of the American Anthropological Association', San Jose, California, 15–19 November.

———. 2012. *The Slumbering Masses: Sleep, Medicine, and Modern American Life*. Minneapolis: University of Minnesota Press.

Xiang, Biao. 2007. *Global 'Body Shopping': An Indian Labour System in the Information Technology Industry*. Princeton, NJ; Oxford: Princeton University Press.

Zelizer, V.A. 2009. 'Intimacy in Economic Organizations'. *Research in the Sociology of Work* (18): 23–55.

Žižek, Slavoj. 1989. *The Sublime Object of Ideology*. London: Verso.

———. 2004. 'The Ongoing "Soft Revolution"'. *Critical Inquiry* 30 (Winter 2004): 292–323.

# INDEX

# ABOUT THE AUTHOR

**Mathangi Krishnamurthy** is assistant professor of anthropology at the Department of Humanities and Social Sciences, IIT Madras, India. She is currently pursuing a project on bodily imaginations in relation to new genetic diagnostic technologies. Her areas of interest include the anthropology of work and gender, medical anthropology, urban studies, globalization, and affective labour. She has published on questions of English language usage, the anthropology of work, and the anthropology of gender.